AF541717

Fabric Structure and Design

Fabric Structure and Design

Darshan Chaturvedi

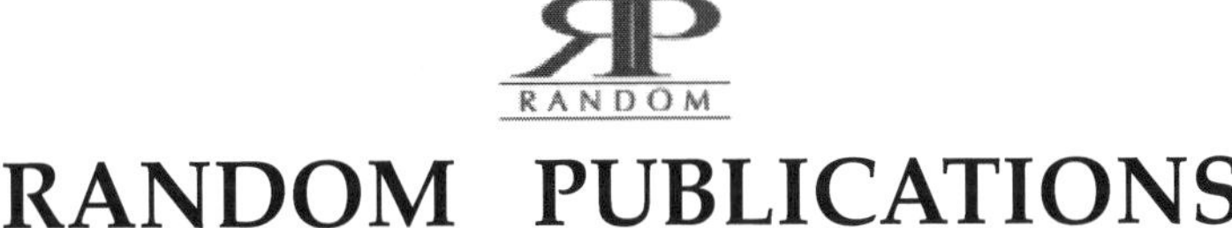

RANDOM PUBLICATIONS
NEW DELHI - 110 002 (INDIA)

Fabric Structure and Design

ISBN 978-93-51112-61-7

Published in 2014 in India by

RANDOM PUBLICATIONS

4376-A/4B, Gali Murari Lal, Ansari Road

New Delhi-110 002

Phone: +9111-43580356, 23289044

E-mail: randomexports@gmail.com; sales@randompublications.com; info@randompublications.com

Reprinted 2025

Type Setting by: Friends Media, Delhi-110089

Digitally Printed at: Replika Press Pvt. Ltd.

Preface

A laminated fabric usually is composed of a reinforcing polyester scrim pressed between two layers of unsupported PVC film. For most fabric structure uses, however, it refers to two or more layers of fabric or film joined by heat, pressure, and an adhesive to form a single ply. With an open-weave or mesh polyester scrim, the exterior vinyl films bond to themselves through the openings in the fabric. Heavier fabric scrims, however, are too tightly woven to allow the same bonding. In this case, an adhesive is used to bond the exterior films to the base fabric. A good chemical bond is critical to both prevention of delamination and development of seam strengths. The seam is created when vinyl-coated fabrics are welded together. The adhesive enables the seam to meet shear forces and load requirements for a structure at all temperatures. The adhesive prevents wicking of moisture into the scrim's fibres, which also prevents fungal growth or freezing that could affect the exterior coating's adhesion to the scrim. Adhesives are water-based to comply with EPA regulations.

Open-weave scrims generally make the fabric more economical, although this can also depend on the number and type of features that you require in the vinyl. Almost any colour and colourfastness may be incorporated into the vinyl. However, the more features added, the higher the cost of the fabric. Vinyl coated polyester is the most frequently used material for flexible fabric structures. It is made up of a polyester scrim, a bonding or adhesive agent, and exterior PVC coatings. The scrim supports the coating and provides the tensile strength, elongation, tear strength, and dimensional stability of the resulting fabric. Vinyl-coated polyester is manufactured in large panels by heat-sealing an over-lap seam with either a radio-frequency welder or a hot-air sealer. A proper seam will be able to carry the load requirements for the structure. The seam area should be stronger than the original coated fabric when testing for tensile strength. The base fabric's tensile strength is determined by the size (denier) and strength (tenacity) of the yarns and the number of yarns per linear inch or meter. The larger the yarn and the more yarns per inch, the greater the finished product's tensile strength. The adhesive agent acts as a chemical bond between the polyester fibres and the exterior coating and also prevents wicking, or fibres absorbing water, which could result in freeze-thaw damage in the fabric. The PVC coating liquid (vinyl Organisol or Plastisol) contains chemicals to achieve the desired properties of colour, water and mildew resistance, and flame retardancy. Fabric can also be manufactured that contains high levels of light transmission or can be made completely opaque. After the coating has been applied to the scrim, the fabric is put through a heating chamber that dries the liquid coating. PVC coatings are available in a range of colours, although non-standard colours can be pricey. Colours may be subject to minimum order runs that allow the coating machine to clear out traces of any previous colour. Woven fiberglass coated with PTFE (Teflon or silicone) is also a widely used base material. Glass fibres are drawn into continuous filaments, which are then bundled into yarns. The yarns are woven to form a substrate. The fiberglass carries a high ultimate tensile strength, behaves elastically, and does not suffer from significant stress relaxation or creep. The PTFE coating is chemically inert, can withstand temperatures from 100°F upwards to 450°F+. It is also immune to radiation and can be cleaned with water. Because of its energy efficiency, high melting temperature and lack of creep, fiberglass-based fabrics have been the material of choice for stadium domes and other permanent structures, particularly in the United States. However, when properly constructed, polyester structures may be equally durable.

The present book deals with all the important dimensions of this subject. It is a valuable reference source for all those concerned with this subject.

I thank all members of my team who have helped in the preparation of the book. My special thanks go to "Random Publications" who have published the book.

—Darshan Chaturvedi

Contents

1. **History** 1

- 1100–1200 in Fashion 10
- 1200–1300 in Fashion 15
- 1300–1400 in Fashion 18
- Men's Clothing 21
- Textile Manufacture During the Industrial Revolution 31
- Spinning Mule 39

2. **Fabrics from Man-made Fibers** 53

- Acetate Fabric 53
- Fabrics for Special Uses 58
- Fabrics from Natural Fibers 65
- Elements of Art 67

- Design Elements and Principles 68
- Looms and Loom Mechanisms 74
- Inkle Weaving 80

3. Traditional Looms 82

- The Simple Frame Loom 82
- Materials Needed 83
- Set Up the Loom for Weaving 86
- How to Weave on a Frame Loom 94
- The Foot-Powered Loom 99
- Free-Standing Loom Construction 102

4. Free-Standing Rug Loom 121

- Pegged Loom 121
- Jacquard Looms 128
- Dobby Looms 130

5. Woven Design Fundamentals 136

- Classification of Woven Structures 137

- Plain Weaves 139
- Warp (Weaving) 141
- Plain Weaves 143
- Twill Weaves 147
- Denim 151
- Foulard 155
- Honey Comb Weaves 155
- Huck a Back Weaves 155
- Crepe Weave 163
- Types of Crepe Fabric 163
- Scarf 165
- Headscarf 169
- Shawl 170
- Bedford Cords 177

6. Pile Fabrics 179

- Carpet Pile 179

- Carpet Types 181
- Oriental Carpets in Europe 192
- Pile Weave 197
- Warp Pile Weave 198
- Polar Fleece 198
- Extra Warp and Extra Weft Figured Fabrics 199
- Double Cloths 200
- Basic Aspects of Colours and its Effects 202
- Improvement Fastnesses and Colour Strength of Pigment Printed Textile Fabric 229

7. Welts and Piques **232**

- Pique 232
- Mock Leno Weaves 233
- Clothing Technology 235
- Tablet Weaving 236
- Heddle 239
- Indian Textiles 243

- Sari 245
- Shalwar Kameez 259
- Zari 261
- Roller Printing on Textiles 262
- Engraved Copperplate Printing 263
- Pattern 269
- Fashion Design 274

Bibliography 277

Index 279

1

Introduction

The words fabric and cloth are used in textile assembly trades (such as tailoring and dressmaking) as synonyms for *textile*. However, there are subtle differences in these terms in specialized usage. *Textile* refers to any material made of interlacing fibres. *Fabric* refers to any material made through weaving, knitting, spreading, crocheting, or bonding that may be used in production of further goods (garments, etc.). *Cloth* may be used synonymously with *fabric* but often refers to a finished piece of fabric used for a specific purpose (e.g., *table cloth*).

There are several different types of fabric from two main sources: manmade and natural. Inside natural, there are two others, plant and animal. Some examples of animal textiles are silk and wool. An example of plants is cotton.

History

The wearing of clothing is exclusively a human characteristic and is a feature of most human societies. It is not known when humans began wearing clothes. Anthropologists believe that animal skins and vegetation were adapted into coverings as protection from cold, heat and rain, especially as humans migrated to new climates; alternatively, covering may have been invented first for other purposes, such as magic, decoration, cult, or prestige, and later found to be practical as well.

Clothing and textiles have been important in human history and reflects the materials available to a civilization as well as the technologies that it has mastered. The social significance of the finished product reflects their culture. Textiles, defined as felt or spun fibers made into yarn and subsequently netted, looped, knit or woven to make fabrics, appeared in the Middle East during the late stone age. From ancient times to the present day, methods of textile production have continually evolved, and the choices of textiles available have influenced how people carried their possessions, clothed themselves, and decorated their surroundings.

Sources available for the study of the history of clothing and textiles include material remains discovered via archaeology; representation of textiles and their manufacture in art; and documents concerning the manufacture, acquisition, use, and trade of fabrics, tools, and finished garments. Scholarship of textile history, especially its earlier stages, is part of material culture studies.

Prehistoric Development

First fabric uses, likely to be felt, are thought to have been used about 100,000 years ago.

Early Adoption of Fibrous Apparel

Another genetic analysis suggests that the human body louse, which lives in clothing, may only have diverged from the head louse some 107 thousand years ago, which supports evidence that humans began wearing clothing at around this time.

These estimates pre-date the first known human exodus from Africa, although species of *Homo* (other than *Homo Sapiens*) who may have worn clothes - and shared these louse infestations - appear to have migrated earlier.

Initial Manufacture of Clothes

The development of textile and clothing manufacture in prehistory has been the subject of a number of scholarly studies since the late 20th century. These sources have helped to provide a coherent history of these prehistoric developments. Evidence suggests that human beings may have begun wearing clothing as far back as 100,000 to 500,000 years ago.

Possible sewing needles have been dated to around 40,000 years ago. The earliest definite examples of needles originate from the Solutrean culture, which existed in France from 19,000 BC to 15,000 BC. The earliest dyed flax fibers have been found in a prehistoric cave in the Republic of Georgia and date back to 36,000 BP. The earliest evidence of weaving comes from impressions of textiles and basketry and nets on little pieces of hard clay, dating from 27,000 years ago and found in Dolni Vestonice in the Czech Republic.

At a slightly later date (25,000 years) the Venus figurines were depicted with clothing. Those from western Europe were adorned with basket hats or caps, belts worn at the waist, and a strap of cloth that wrapped around the body right above the breast. Eastern European figurines wore belts, hung low on the hips and sometimes string skirts.

Archaeologists have discovered artifacts from the same period that appear to have been used in the textile arts: (5000 BC) net gauges, spindle needles and weaving sticks.

Ancient Textiles and Clothing

The first actual textile, as opposed to skins sewn together, was probably felt. Surviving examples of Nålebinding, another early textile method, date from 6500 BC. Our knowledge of ancient textiles and clothing has expanded in the recent past thanks to modern technological developments. Our knowledge of cultures varies greatly with the climatic conditions to which archeological deposits are exposed; the Middle East and the arid fringes of China have provided many very early samples in good condition, but the early development of textiles in the Indian subcontinent, sub-Saharan Africa and other moist parts of the world remains unclear. In northern Eurasia peat bogs can also preserve textiles very well.

Early woven clothing was often made of full loom widths draped, tied, or pinned in place.

Ancient Near East

The earliest known woven textiles of the Near East may be fabrics used to wrap the dead, excavated at a Neolithic site at Çatalhöyük in Anatolia, carbonized in a fire and radiocarbon dated to c. 6000 BC. Evidence exists of flax cultivation from c. 8000 BC in the Near East, but the breeding of sheep with a wooly fleece rather than hair occurs much later, c. 3000 BC.

Ancient India

The inhabitants of the Indus Valley Civilization used cotton for clothing as early as the 5th millennium BC – 4th millennium BC.

According to The Columbia Encyclopedia, Sixth Edition:

"Cotton has been spun, woven, and dyed since prehistoric times. It clothed the people of ancient India, Egypt, and China. Hundreds of years before the Christian era cotton textiles were woven in India with matchless skill, and their use spread to the Mediterranean countries. In the 1st cent. Arab traders brought fine Muslin and Calico to Italy and Spain. The Moors introduced the cultivation of cotton into Spain in the 9th cent. Fustians and dimities were woven there and in the 14th cent. in Venice and Milan, at first with a linen warp. Little cotton cloth was imported to England before the 15th cent., although small amounts were obtained chiefly for candlewicks. By the 17th cent. the East India Company was bringing rare fabrics from India. Native Americans skillfully spun and wove cotton into fine garments and dyed tapestries. Cotton fabrics found in Peruvian tombs are said to belong to a pre-Inca culture. In color and texture the ancient Peruvian and Mexican textiles resemble those found in Egyptian tombs."

Ancient Egypt

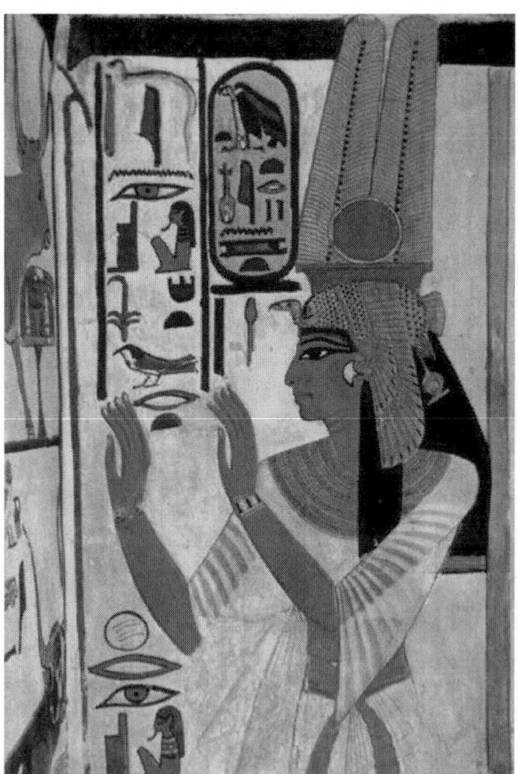

Figure: *Queen Nefertari in a sheer, pleated linen garment, Egypt, c. 1298–1235 BC*

Evidence exists for production of linen cloth in Ancient Egypt in the Neolithic period, c. 5500 BC. Cultivation of domesticated wild flax, probably an import from the Levant, is documented as early as c. 6000

BC Other bast fibers including rush, reed, palm, and papyrus were used alone or with linen to make rope and other textiles. Evidence for wool production in Egypt is scanty at this period.

Spinning techniques included the drop spindle, hand-to-hand spinning, and rolling on the thigh; yarn was also spliced. A horizontal ground loom was used prior to the New Kingdom, when a vertical two-beam loom was introduced, probably from Asia. Linen bandages were used in the burial custom of mummification, and art depicts Egyptian men wearing linen kilts and women in narrow dresses with various forms of shirts and jackets, often of sheer pleated fabric.

Ancient China

The earliest evidence of silk production in China was found at the sites of Yangshao culture in Xia, Shanxi, where a cocoon of bombyx mori, the domesticated silkworm, cut in half by a sharp knife is dated to between 5000 and 3000 BC. Fragments of primitive looms are also seen from the sites of Hemudu culture in Yuyao, Zhejiang, dated to about 4000 BC. Scraps of silk were found in a Liangzhu culture site at Qianshanyang in Huzhou, Zhejiang, dating back to 2700 BC. Other fragments have been recovered from royal tombs in the Shang Dynasty (c. 1600 – c. 1046 BC).

Under the Shang Dynasty, Han Chinese clothing or Hanfu consisted of a *yi*, a narrow-cuffed, knee-length tunic tied with a sash, and a narrow, ankle-length skirt, called *shang*, worn with a *bixi*, a length of fabric that reached the knees. Clothing of the elite was made of silk in vivid primary colours.

Ancient Japan

The earliest evidence of weaving in Japan is associated with the Jômon period. This culture is defined by pottery decorated with cord patterns. In a shell mound in the Miyagi Prefecture, dating back about 5,500, some cloth fragments were discovered made from bark fibers. Hemp fibers were also discovered in the Torihama shell midden, Fukui Prefecture, dating back to the Jômon period, suggesting that these plants could also have been used for clothing. Some pottery pattern imprints depict also fine mat designs, proving their weaving techniques. Since bone needles were also found, it is assumed that they wore dresses that were sewn together.

The Textile Trade in the Ancient World

The exchange of luxury textiles was predominant on the Silk Road, a series of ancient trade and cultural transmission routes that were central to cultural interaction through regions of the Asian continent connecting East and West by linking traders, merchants, pilgrims, monks, soldiers, nomads and urban dwellers from China to the Mediterranean Sea during various periods of time. The trade route was initiated around 114 BC by the Han Dynasty, although earlier trade across the continents had already existed. Geographically, the Silk Road or Silk Route is an interconnected series of ancient trade routes between Chang'an (today's Xi'an) in China, with Asia Minor and the Mediterranean extending over 8,000 km (5,000 mi) on land and sea. Trade on the Silk Road was a significant factor in the development of the great civilizations of China, Egypt, Mesopotamia, Persia, the Indian subcontinent, and Rome, and helped to lay the foundations for the modern world.

Classical Antiquity

Dress in classical antiquity favored wide, unsewn lengths of fabric, pinned and draped to the body in various ways.

Ancient Greek clothing consisted of lengths of wool or linen, generally rectangular and secured at the shoulders with ornamented pins called fibulae and belted with a sash. Typical garments were the peplos, a loose robe worn by women; the chlamys, a cloak worn by men; and the chiton, a tunic worn by both men and women. Men's chitons hung to the knees, whereas women's chitons fell to their ankles. A long cloak called a himation was worn over the peplos or chlamys.

The toga of ancient Rome was also an unsewn length of wool cloth, worn by male citizens draped around the body in various fashions, over a simple tunic. Early tunics were two simple rectangles joined at the shoulders and sides; later tunics had sewn sleeves. Women wore the draped stola or an ankle-length tunic, with a shawl-like palla as an outer garment. Wool was the preferred fabric, although linen, hemp, and small amounts of expensive imported silk and cotton were also worn.

Iron Age Europe

The Iron Age is broadly identified as stretching from the end of the Bronze Age around 1200 BC to 500 AD and the beginning of the Medieval period. Bodies and clothing have been found from this period, preserved by the anaerobic and acidic conditions of peat bogs in northwestern Europe. A Danish recreation of clothing found with such bodies indicates woven wool dresses, tunics and skirts. These were largely unshaped and held in place with leather belts and metal brooches or pins. Garments were not always plain, but incorporated decoration with contrasting colours, particularly at the ends and edges of the garment.

Men wore breeches, possibly with lower legs wrapped for protection, although Boucher states that long trousers have also been found. Warmth came from woollen shawls and capes of animal skin, probably worn with the fur facing inwards for added comfort. Caps were worn, also made from skins, and there was an emphasis on hair arrangements, from braids to elaborate Suebian knots. Soft laced shoes made from leather protected the foot.

Medieval Clothing and Textiles

The history of Medieval European clothing and textiles has inspired a good deal of scholarly interest in the 21st century. Elisabeth Crowfoot, Frances Pritchard, and Kay Staniland authored *Textiles and Clothing: Medieval Finds from Excavations in London, c.1150-c.1450* (Boydell Press, 2001). The topic is also the subject of an annual series *Medieval Clothing and Textiles* (Boydell Press) edited by Robin Netherton and Professor Gale R. Owen-Crocker of Anglo-Saxon Culture at the University of Manchester.

Byzantium

The Byzantines made and exported very richly patterned cloth, woven and embroidered for the upper classes, and resist-dyed and printed for the lower. By Justinian's time the Roman toga had been replaced by the tunica, or long *chiton,* for both sexes, over which the upper classes wore various other garments, like a *dalmatica* (dalmatic), a heavier and shorter type of tunica; short and long cloaks were fastened on the right shoulder.

Leggings and hose were often worn, but are not prominent in depictions of the wealthy; they were associated with barbarians, whether European or Persian.

Early Medieval Europe

European dress changed gradually in the years 400 to 1100. People in many countries dressed differently depending on whether they identified with the old Romanised population, or the new invading populations such as Franks, Anglo-Saxons, and Visigoths. Men of the invading peoples generally wore short tunics, with belts, and visible trousers, hose or leggings. The Romanised populations, and the Church, remained faithful to the longer tunics of Roman formal costume.

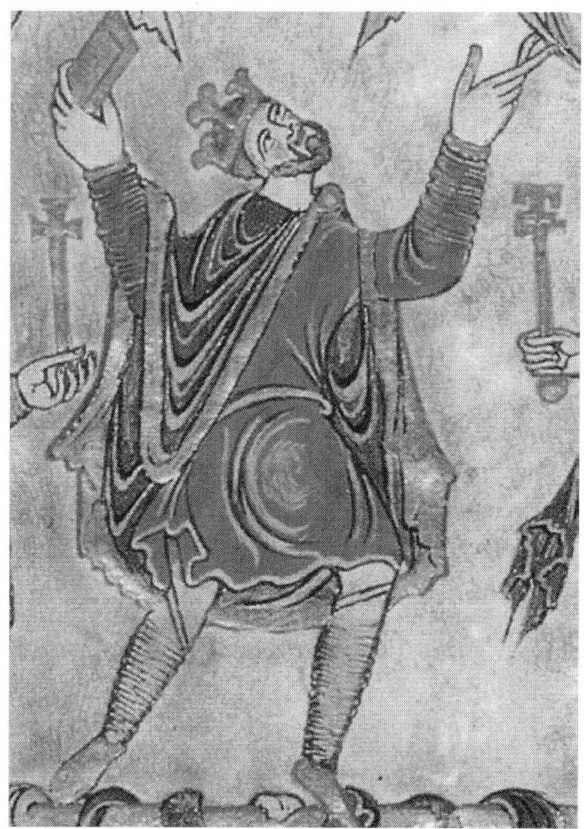

***Figure:** Edgar I of England in short tunic, hose, and cloak, 966*

The elite imported silk cloth from the Byzantine, and later Muslim worlds, and also probably cotton. They also could afford bleached linen and dyed and simply patterned wool woven in Europe itself. But embroidered decoration was probably very widespread, though not usually detectable in art. Lower classes wore local or homespun wool, often undyed, trimmed with bands of decoration, variously embroidery, tablet-woven bands, or colorful borders woven into the fabric in the loom.

High Middle Ages and The Rise of Fashion

Clothing in 12th and 13th century Europe remained very simple for both men and women, and quite uniform across the subcontinent. The traditional combination of short tunic with hose for working-class men and long tunic with overgown for women and upper class men remained the norm. Most clothing, especially outside the wealthier classes, remained little changed from three or four centuries earlier.

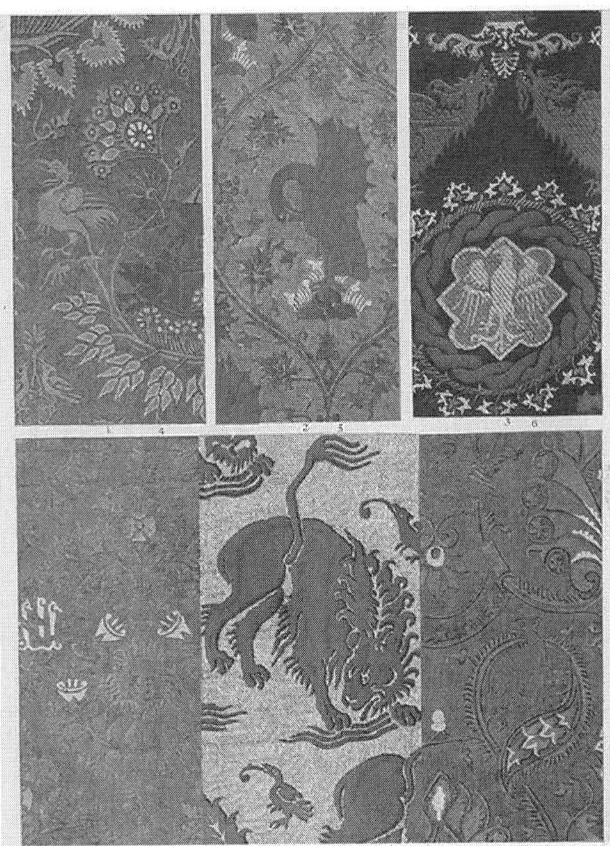

Figure: *14th-century Italian silk damasks*

The 13th century saw great progress in the dyeing and working of wool, which was by far the most important material for outer wear. Linen was increasingly used for clothing that was directly in contact with the skin. Unlike wool, linen could be laundered and bleached in the sun. Cotton, imported raw from Egypt and elsewhere, was used for padding and quilting, and cloths such as buckram and fustian.

Crusaders returning from the Levant brought knowledge of its fine textiles, including light silks, to Western Europe. In Northern Europe, silk was an imported and very expensive luxury. The well-off could afford woven brocades from Italy or even further afield. Fashionable Italian silks of this period featured repeating patterns of roundels and animals, deriving from Ottoman silk-weaving centres in Bursa, and ultimately from Yuan Dynasty China via the Silk Road.

Cultural and costume historians agree that the mid-14th century marks the emergence of recognizable "fashion" in Europe. From this century onwards Western fashion changes at a pace quite unknown to other civilizations, whether ancient or contemporary. In most other cultures only major political changes, such as the Muslim conquest of India, produced radical changes in clothing, and in China, Japan, and the Ottoman Empire fashion changed only slightly over periods of several centuries.

In this period the draped garments and straight seams of previous centuries were replaced by curved seams and the beginnings of tailoring, which allowed clothing to more closely fit the human form, as did the use of lacing and buttons. A fashion for *mi-parti* or *parti-coloured* garments made of two contrasting fabrics, one on each side, arose for men in mid-century, and was especially popular at the English court. Sometimes just the hose would be different colours on each leg.

1100–1200 in Fashion

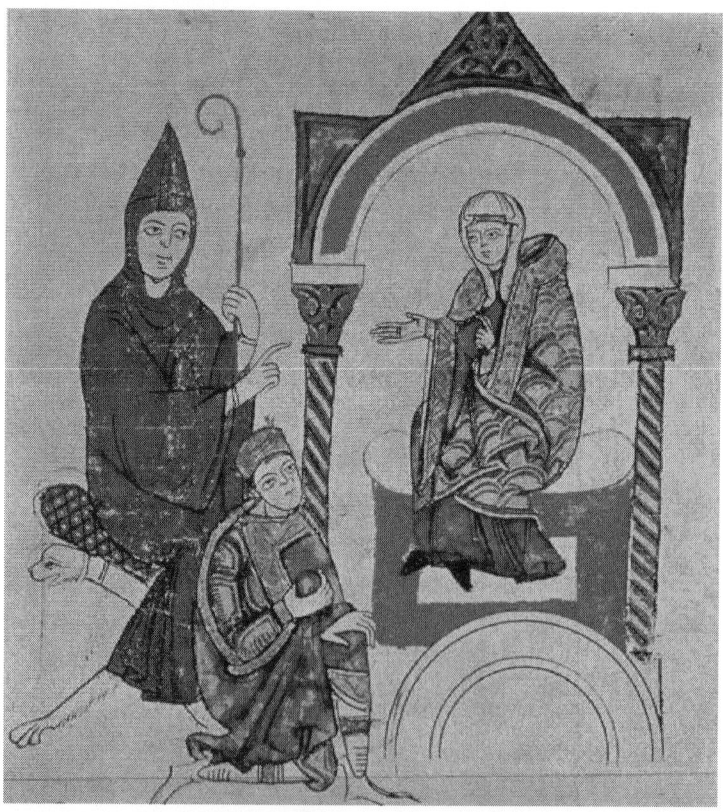

Costume during the twelfth century in Europe was simple and differed only in details from the clothing of the preceding centuries. Men wore knee-length tunics for most activities, and men of the upper classes wore long tunics, with hose and mantles or cloaks. Women wore long tunics or gowns. A close fit to the body, full skirts, and long flaring sleeves were characteristic of upper class fashion for both men and women.

Hugh, Abbot of Cluny, Emperor Henry IV, and Countess Matilda of Tuscany, 1115. The Emperor and the countess wear overgowns and mantles trimmed with bands of gold embroidery. The countess wears a linen veil draped over her hair.

As in the previous centuries, two styles of dress existed side-by-side for men: a short (knee-length) costume deriving from a melding of the everyday dress of the later Roman Empire and the short tunics worn by the invading barbarians, and a long (ankle-length) costume descended from the clothing of the Roman upper classes and influenced by Byzantine dress.

Fabrics and Furs

Wool remained the primary fabric for clothing of all classes, while linen undergarments, which were more comfortable against the skin and could be washed and then bleached in the sun, were increasingly worn.

Silk, although extremely expensive, was readily available to wealthy people of consequence. Silks from Byzantium were traded in Pavia by way of Venice, and silks from Andalusia reached France via Spain. In the last decade of the previous century, the Norman reconquest of Sicily and the First Crusade had opened additional routes for Eastern fabrics and style influences into Europe.

Fur was worn as an inside lining for warmth. Vair, the fur of the squirrel, was particularly popular and can be seen in many illuminated manuscript illustrations, where it is shown as a white and blue-grey softly striped or checkered pattern lining the mantles of the wealthy.

The Bliaut

A new French fashion for both men and women was the *bliaut* or *bliaud,* a long outer tunic with full skirts from the hip and sleeves that fitted tightly to the elbow and then flared into a trumpet shape. Early bliauts were moderately fitted and bloused slightly over the belt at the waist.

Later the bliaut was fitted tightly to the body from shoulder to hip, and the belt, or girdle was wrapped twice around the waist and knotted in front of the abdomen.

Men's Clothing

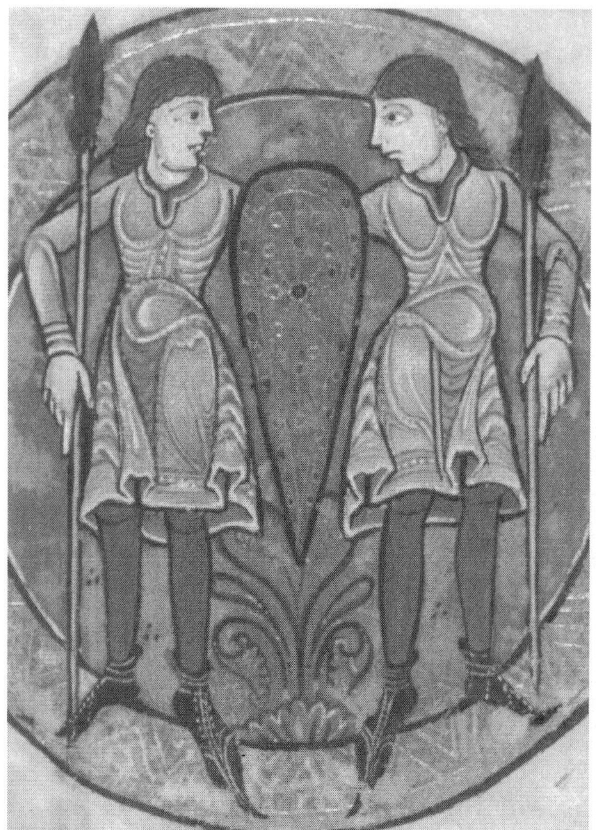

Figure: *"Gemini" from the* Hunterian Psalter *shows the twins in knee-length tunics over chausses and shoes with pointed toes. England, c. 1170*

Shirt, Braies, and Chausses

Underclothes consisted of an inner tunic (French *chainse*) or shirt with long, tight sleeves, and drawers or *braies*, usually of linen. Tailored cloth leggings called *chausses* or hose, made as separate garments for each leg, were often worn with the tunic; striped hose were popular.

During this period, beginning with the middle and upper classes, hose became longer and more fitting, and they reached above the knees. Previously, they were looser and worn with drawers that ranged from knee- to ankle-length. The new type of hose was worn with drawers that reached the knees or above, and they were wide enough at the top to allow the drawers to be tucked into them. They were held up in place by being attached to the girdle of the drawers.

The better fit and girdle attachment of this new hose eliminated the need for the leg bands often worn with earlier hose. In England, however, leg bands continued to be worn by some people, both rich and poor, right up to the reign of Richard I. After 1200, they were largely abandoned.

Outer Tunics and Doublets

Over the undertunic and hose, men wore an outer tunic that reached to the knees or ankles, and that was fastened at the waist with a belt. Fitted bliauts, of wool or, increasingly, silk, had sleeves that were cut wide at the wrist and gored skirts. Men wore bliauts open to the waist front and back or at the side seams.

Newly fashionable were short, fitted garments for the upper body, worn under the tunic: the doublet, made of two layers of linen, and an early form of quilted and padded *jupe* or *gipon.*

The sleeveless surcoat or *cyclas* was introduced during this period as protective covering for armour (especially against the sun) during the Crusades. By the next century, it would become widely adopted as civilian dress.

Rectangular and circular cloaks were worn over the tunic. These fastened on the right shoulder or at the center front.

Headgear

Men of the upper classes often went hatless. The chaperon in the form of hood and attached shoulder-length cape was worn during this period, especially by the rural lower classes, and the fitted linen coif tied under the chin appeared very late in the century. Small round or slightly conical caps with rolled brims were worn, and straw hats were worn for outdoor work in summer.

1. Illustration of the Anti-christ shows long and short tunics and hose or leggings. The king wears a red mantle lined in vair (squirrel fur) fastened on one shoulder, c. 1180.
2. Richard the Lionheart is portrayed in a long tunic with tight sleeves and a mantle, late 12th century.
3. Man feasting wears a cap with a rolled brim and a tunic with wide turned-back cuffs, England, c. 1170.
4. Monument of Geoffrey of Anjou (d. 1151) depicts him in a calf-length overtunic and long undertunic, with a blue mantle lined in vair. He wears a cap with his coat of arms.

Women's Clothing

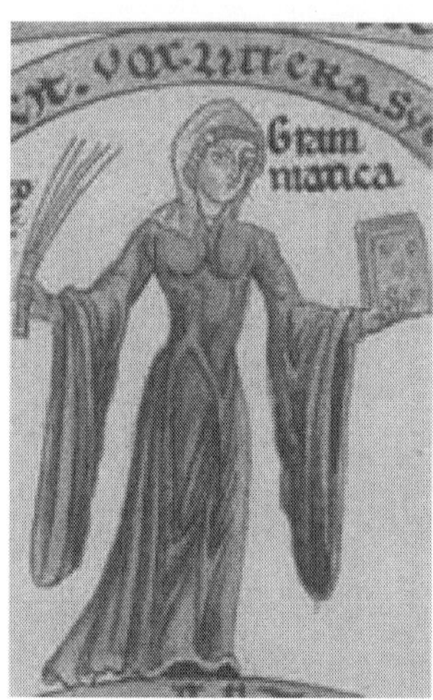

Figure: *of Grammatica showing the trumpet-sleeved bliaut characteristic of the later 12th century, from the Hortus Deliciarum, c. 1180*

Chemise and Tunic

Women's clothing consisted of an undertunic called a chemise, *chainse* or smock, usually of linen, over which was worn one or more ankle-to-floor length tunics (also called gowns or kirtles).

Working class women wore their tunics ankle-length and belted at the waist.

Women of the French court wore a loosely fitted tunic called a *cotte* or the form-fitting bliaut over a full chemise with tight sleeves. The bliaut had a flaring skirt and sleeves tight to the elbow and then widening to wrist in a trumpet shape.

A bliaut apparently cut in one piece from neckline to hem depicted on a column figure of a woman at the Cathedral of St. Maurice at Angers has visible side-lacing and is belted at the natural waistline. A new fashion, the *bliaut gironé*, arose in mid-century: this dress is cut in two pieces, a fitted upper portion with a finely pleated skirt attached to a low waistband.

The fitted bliaut was sometimes worn with a long belt or cincture (in French, *ceinture*) that looped around a slightly raised waist and was knotted over the abdomen; the cincture could have decorative tassels or metal tags at the ends.

In England, the fashionable gown was wide at the wrist but without the trumpet-shaped flare from the elbow seen in France.

Hairstyles and Headdresses

Married women, in keeping with Christian custom, wore veils over their hair, which was often parted in the center and hung down in long braids that might be extended with false hair or purchased hair from the dead, a habit decried by moralists.

The wimple was introduced in England late in the century. It consisted of a linen cloth that covered the throat (and often the chin as well), and that was fastened about the head, under the veil.

1. Woman wears a bliaut cut in one piece from neck to hem and laced at the sides, over a chemise with tight sleeves. Overall she wears a mantle tied with a double cord. Cathédrale Saint-Maurice d'Angers, between 1130 and 1160.
2. Bliaut gironé has a finely pleated skirt attached to a decorative waistband at hip level. The bliaut is worn with a knotted girdle or cincture, Cathédrale Notre-Dame de Chartres, between 1130–1160.
3. Detail of the knotted girdle worn with the bliaut gironé at Chartres. The waistband of the skirt can be seen above the knotted girdle.
4. Eve spinning in a long gown with straight sleeves and a linen veil, c. 1170.
5. Two women from the *Hunterian Psalter*. The woman on the left wears a veil and mantle. The young woman on the right wears her hair uncovered, and her gown sleeves are wide at the wrist as seen in English fashion c. 1170.
6. Queen Leonor of England, sitting on the far left, wears a veil that covers most of her body.

1200–1300 in Fashion

Costume during the thirteenth century in Europe was very simple for both men and women, and quite uniform across the continent. Male and female clothing were relatively similar, and changed very slowly, if at all. Most clothing, especially outside the wealthier classes, remained little changed from three or four centuries earlier. The century saw great progress in the dyeing and working of wool, which was by far the most important material for outer wear. For the rich, colour was very important. Blue was introduced and became very fashionable, being adopted by the Kings of France as their heraldic colour.

Men's Clothing

Men wore a tunic, *cote* or *cotte* with a surcoat over a linen shirt. One of these surcoats was the cyclas, which began as a rectangular piece of cloth with a hole in it for the head. Over time the sides were sewn together to make a long, sleeveless tunic. When sleeves and sometimes a hood were added, the cyclas became a ganache (a cap-sleeved surcoat, usually shown with hood of matching color) or a gardcorps (a long, generous-sleeved traveling robe, somewhat resembling a modern academic robe). A mantle was worn as a formal wrap. Men also wore hose, shoes, and headdress. The clothing of royalty was set apart by its rich fabric and luxurious furs. Hair and beard were moderate in length, and men generally wore their hair in a "pageboy" style, curling under at necklength. Shoes were slightly pointed, and embroidered for royalty and higher clergy.

Working Men's Clothing

Working men wore a short cotte, or tunic, with a belt. It was slit up the center of the front so that they could tuck the corners into their belt to create more freedom of movement. They wore long braies or leggings with legs of varying length, often visible as they worked with their cotte tucked into their belt. Hose could be worn over this, attached to the drawstring or belt at the waist. Hats included poolog a round cap with a slight brim, the beret (just like modern French ones, complete with a little tab at the top), the coif (a little tight white hood with strings that tied under the chin), the straw hat (in widespread use among farmworkers), and the chaperon, then still a hood that came round the neck and over the shoulders. Apart from aprons for trades like smithing, and crude clothes tied round the neck to hi hold seed for sowing, special clothes were not worn for working.

1. Men working in linen braies, tunics, and coifs, from the Maciejowski Bible, c. 1250. The man on the left wears green hose over his braies.
2. Man in a coif and shirt (camisa) with gussets at the hem, from the *Cantigas de Santa Maria,* Spain, mid-13th century.
3. Falconers wear belted tunics and coifs, 1240s.
4. Young Merlin wears a short tunic with a rectangular cloak or mantle and hose. King Vortigern wears a mantle draped over both shoulders over a long overgown or tunic and shoes with straps at the instep. From a manuscript of Geoffrey of Monmouth's *Prophetia Merlini,* c. 1250–70.

5. Man in the short, hooded cape called a *cappa* or *chaperon*, c. 1250–70.
6. Musicians wear two long tunics, one over the other. The tunic on the left is an early example of *mi-parti* or particolored clothing, made from two fabrics. *Cantigas de Santa Maria*, mid-13th century, Spain.
7. Pan-pipe players wear tunics with hanging sleeves over long-sleeved undertunics. Both wear coifs. *Cantigas de Santa Maria*, mid-13th century, Spain.

Women's Clothing

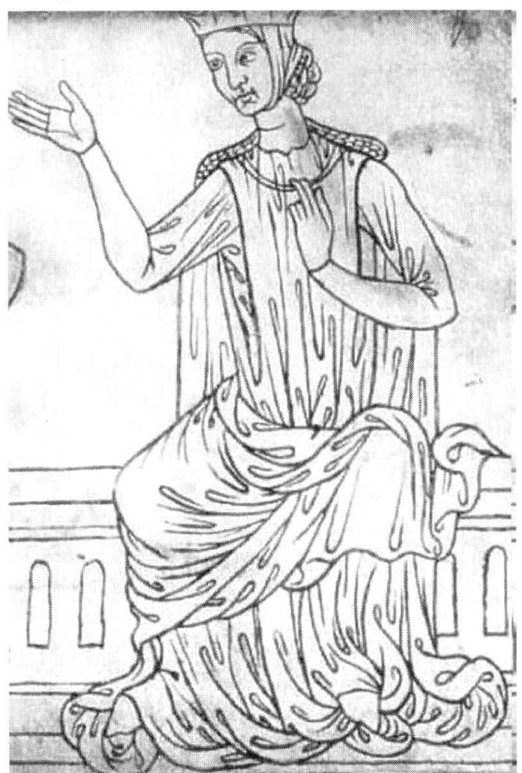

Figure: *Woman in a barbette and coif, sleeveless surcoat, gown and mantle. Sketch by Villard de Honnecourt, c.1230*

Overview

Dress for women was restrained. A floor length, loosely-fitted gown, with long, tight sleeves and a narrow belt was uniform. Over this was worn the *cyclas* or sleeveless surcoat (also worn by men). Richer women wore more embroidery, and the mantle, held in place by a cord across the chest, might be lined with fur. Women also wore hose and leather shoes, like men.

Headdresses and Hairstyles

Individuality in women's costume was expressed through their hair and headdress. One distinctive part of 13th-century women's headwear was the barbette, a chin band to which a hat or various other headdress might be attached. This hat might be a "woman's coif", which more nearly resembled a pillbox hat, severely plain or fluted. The hair was often confined by a net called a crespine or crespinette, visible only at the back. Later in the century the barbette and coif were reduced to narrow strips of cloth, and the entire hairdress might be covered with the crespine, the hair fashionable bulky over the ears. Coif and barbette were white, while the crespine might be colored or gold. The wimple and veil of the 12th century (still seen on nuns today) was still worn, mainly by older women and widows.

Sumptuary Laws

The Fourth Council of the Lateran of 1215 ruled that Jews and Muslims must be distinguishable by their dress, beginning the process that transformed the conical or pointed Jewish hat from something worn as a voluntary mark of difference to an enforced one. Previously it had been worn but had been regarded by European Jews as "an element of traditional garb, rather than an imposed discrimination". A law in Breslau in 1267 said that since Jews had stopped wearing the pointed hats they used to wear, this would be made compulsory. The Yellow badge also dates from this century, although the hat seems to have been much more widely worn.

Sumptuary laws covering prostitutes were introduced (following Ancient Roman precedent) in the 13th century: in Marseilles a striped cloak, in England a striped hood, and so on. Over time these tended to be reduced to distinctive bands of fabric attached to the arm or shoulder, or tassels on the arm.

These probably reflected both a growing concern for control over the increasing urban populations, and the increasing effectiveness of the Church's control over social issues across the continent.

1300–1400 in Fashion

Fashion in fourteenth-century Europe was marked by the beginning of a period of experimentation with different forms of clothing. Costume historian James Laver suggests that the mid-14th century marks the emergence of recognizable "fashion" in clothing, in which Fernand Braudel concurs. The draped garments and straight seams of previous centuries were replaced by curved seams and the beginnings of tailoring, which allowed clothing to more closely fit the human form. Also, the use of lacing and buttons allowed a snugger fit to clothing.

General Trends

In the course of the century the length of female hem-lines progressively reduced, and by the end of the century it was fashionable for men to omit the long loose over-garment of previous centuries (whether called tunic, kirtle, or other names) altogether, putting the emphasis on a tailored top that fell a little below the waist—a silhouette that is still reflected in men's costume today.

Fabrics and Furs

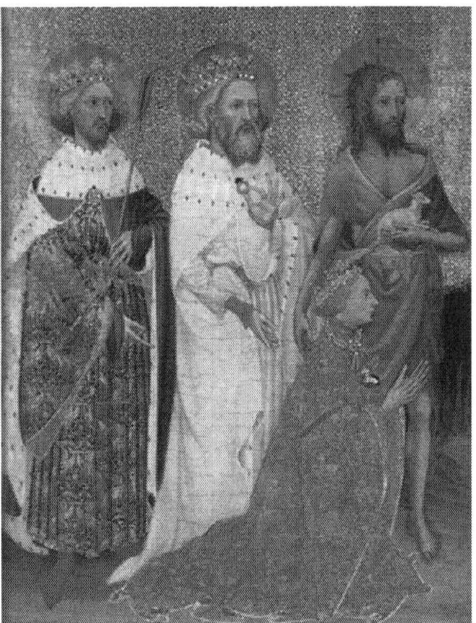

Figure: *The young Richard II of England, kneeling, wears a Houppelande of silk brocade with the badge of his livery. St John the Baptist wears his iconographical clothes, but the sainted English kings Edward the Confessor and Edmund the Martyr are in contemporary royal dress. The Wilton Diptych 1395–99*

Wool was the most important material for clothing, due to its numerous favorable qualities, such as the ability to take dye and its being a good insulator. This century saw the beginnings of the Little Ice Age, and glazing was rare, even for the rich (most houses just had wooden shutters for the winter). Trade in textiles continued to grow throughout the century, and formed an important part of the economy for many areas from England to Italy. Clothes were very expensive, and employees, even high-ranking officials, were usually supplied with, typically, one outfit per year, as part of their remuneration.

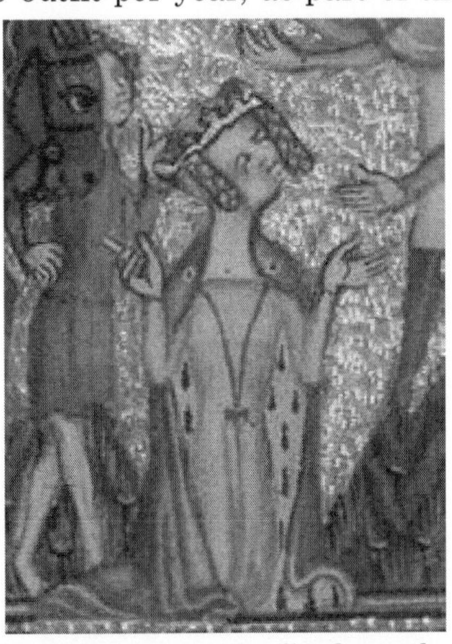

Figure: *Mary de Bohun wears an ermine-lined mantle tied with red strings. Her servant wears a* mi-parti *tunic. From an English psalter, 1380–85*

Woodblock printing of cloth was known throughout the century, and was probably fairly common by the end; this is hard to assess as artists tended to avoid trying to depict patterned cloth due to the difficulty of doing so. Embroidery in wool, and silk or gold thread for the rich, was used for decoration.

Edward III established an embroidery workshop in the Tower of London, who presumably produced the robes he and his Queen wore in 1351 of red velvet "embroidered with clouds of silver and eagles of pearl and gold, under each alternate cloud an eagle of pearl, and under each of the other clouds a golden eagle, every eagle having in its beak a Garter with the motto *hony soyt qui mal y pense* embroidered thereon."

Silk was the finest fabric of all. In Northern Europe, silk was an imported and very expensive luxury. The well-off could afford woven brocades from Italy or even further afield. Fashionable Italian silks of this period featured repeating patterns of roundels and animals, deriving from Ottoman silk-weaving centres in Bursa, and ultimately from Yuan Dynasty China via the Silk Road.

A fashion for *mi-parti* or *parti-coloured* garments made of two contrasting fabrics, one on each side, arose for men in mid-century, and was especially popular at the English court. Sometimes just the hose would be different colours on each leg.

Checkered and plaid fabrics were occasionally seen; a parti-colored cotehardie depicted on the St. Vincent altarpiece in Catalonia is reddish-brown on one side and plaid on the other, and remains of plaid and checkered wool fabrics dating to the 14th century have also been discovered in London.

Fur was mostly worn as an inner lining for warmth; inventories from Burgundian villages show that even there a fur-lined coat (rabbit, or the more expensive cat) was one of the most common garments. Vair, the fur of the squirrel, white on the belly and grey on the back, was particularly popular through most of the century and can be seen in many illuminated manuscript illustrations, where it is shown as a white and blue-grey softly striped or checkered pattern lining cloaks and other outer garments; the white belly fur with the merest edging of grey was called miniver. A fashion in men's clothing for the dark furs sable and marten arose around 1380, and squirrel fur was thereafter relegated to formal ceremonial wear. Ermine, with their dense white winter coats, was worn by royalty, with the black tipped tails left on to contrast with the white for decorative effect, as in the Wilton Diptych above.

Men's Clothing

Shirt, Doublet and Hose

The innermost layer of clothing were the *braies* or breeches, a loose undergarment, usually made of linen, which was held up by a belt. Next came the shirt, which was generally also made of linen, and which was considered an undergarment, like the breeches.

Hose or chausses made out of wool were used to cover the legs, and were generally brightly colored, and often had leather soles, so that they did not have to be worn with shoes. The shorter clothes of the second half of the century required these to be a single garment like modern tights, whereas otherwise they were two separate pieces covering the full length of each leg. Hose were generally tied to the breech belt, or to the breeches themselves, or to a doublet.

A doublet was a buttoned jacket that was generally of hip length. Similar garments were called cotehardie, *pourpoint*, *jaqueta* or *jubón*. These garments were worn over the shirt and the hose.

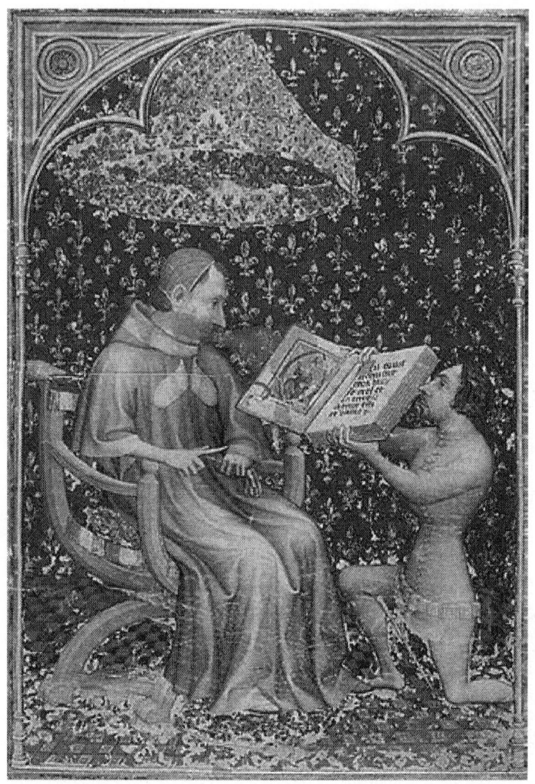

Figure: *Jean de Vaudetar, chamberlain of king Charles V of France, presents his gift of a manuscript to the King, by Jean Bondol, 1372. For this very formal occasion, he is shown without anything over his tightly tailored top. The king wears a coif*

Tunic and Coteheardie

An overgown, tunic, or kirtle was usually worn over the shirt or doublet. As with other outer garments, it was generally made of wool. Over this, a man might also wear an over-kirtle, cloak, or a hood. Servants and working men wore their kirtles at various lengths, including as low as the knee or calf. However the trend during the century was for hem-lengths to shorten for all classes.

However, in the second half of the century, courtiers are often shown, if they have the figure for it, wearing nothing over their closely tailored cotehardie. A French chronicle records: "Around that year (1350), men, in particular noblemen and their squires, took to wearing tunics so short and tight that they revealed what modesty bids us hide. This was a most astonishing thing for the people" This fashion may well have derived from military clothing, where long loose overgowns were naturally not worn in action. At this period, the most dignified figures, like King Charles in the illustration, continue to wear long overgowns—although as the Royal Chamberlain, de Vaudetar was himself a person of very high rank. This abandonment of the gown to emphasise a tight top over the torso, with breeches or trousers below, was to become the distinctive feature of European men's fashion for centuries to come. Men had carried purses up to this time because tunics did not provide pockets.

The funeral effigy and "achievements" of Edward, the Black Prince in Canterbury Cathedral, who died in 1376, show the military version of the same outline. Over armour he is shown wearing a short fitted *arming-coat* or *jupon* or *gipon*, the original of which was hung above and still survives. This has the quartered arms of England and France, with a rather similar effect to a parti-coloured jacket. The "charges", of the arms are embroidered in gold on linen pieces, appliquéd onto coloured silk velvet fields. It is vertically quilted, with wool stuffing and a silk satin lining. This type of coat, originally worn out of sight under armour, was in fashion as an outer garment from about 1360 until early the next century. Only this and a child's version (Chartres Cathedral) survive. As an indication of the rapid spread of fashion between the courts of Europe, a manuscript chronicle illuminated in Hungary by 1360 shows very similar styles to Edward's English version.

Edward's son, King Richard II of England, led a court that, like many in Europe late in the century, was extremely refined and fashion-conscious. He himself is credited with having invented the handkerchief; "little pieces [of cloth] for the lord King to wipe and clean his nose," appear in the Household Rolls (accounts), which is the first documentation of their use. He distributed jewelled livery badges with his personal emblem of the white hart (deer) to his friends, like the one he himself wears in the Wilton Diptych (above). In the miniature (left) of Chaucer reading to his court both men and women wear very high collars and quantities of jewellery. The King (standing to the left of Chaucer; his face has been defaced) wears a patterned gold-coloured costume with matching hat. Most of the men wear chaperon hats, and the women have their hair elaborately dressed. Male courtiers enjoyed wearing fancy-dress for festivities; the disastrous Bal des Ardents in 1393 in Paris is the most famous example. Men as well as women wore decorated and jewelled clothes; for the entry of the Queen of France into Paris in 1389, the Duke of Burgundy wore a velvet doublet embroidered with forty sheep and forty swans, each with a pearl bell round its neck.

A new garment, the Houppelande, appeared around 1380 and was to remain fashionable well into the next century. It was essentially a robe with fullness falling from the shoulders, very full trailing sleeves, and the high collar favored at the English court. The extravagance of the sleeves was criticised by moralists.

Headgear and Accessories

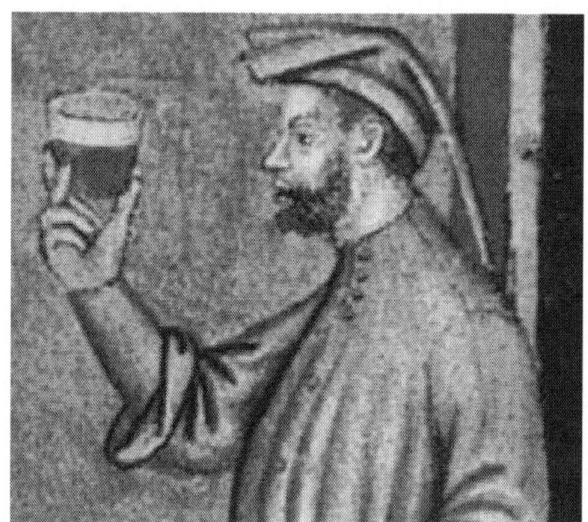

Figure: *Man wearing a chaperon, Italy, late 14th century*

During this century, the chaperon made a transformation from being a utilitarian hood with a small cape to becoming a complicated and fashionable hat worn by the wealthy in town settings. This came when they began to be worn with the opening for the face placed instead on the top of the head. Belts were worn below waist at all times, and very low on the hips with the tightly fitted fashions of the latter half of the century. Belt pouches or purses were used, and long daggers, usually hanging diagonally to the front.

In armour, the century saw increases in the amount of plate armour worn, and by the end of the century the full suit had been developed, although mixtures of chain mail and plate remained more common. The visored bascinet helmet was a new development in this century. Ordinary soldiers were lucky to have a mail hauberk, and perhaps some *cuir-boulli* ("boiled leather") knee or shin pieces.

1. Braies are worn rolled over a belt at the waist. Catalonia.
2. Shirt is made of rectangles with gussets at shoulder, underarm, and hem.

3. Serving man wears a knee-length tunic with long, tight sleeves over hose. Wears a belt with a waist-pouch or purse. His shoes are pointed. From the Luttrell Psalter, England, c. 1325–35.
4. Bridegroom wears a red cotehardie, hose, and hood, Italy, 1350s.
5. Man in a particolored cotehardie of reddish brown and plaid fabric, 2nd half of the 14th century, Catalonia. The cotehardie fits snugly and is buttoned up the front. A narrow belt is worn around the hips.
6. Huntsman wears side-lacing boots, late 14th century.
7. Man walking in a brisk wind wears a chaperon that has been caught by a gust. He wears a belt pouch and carries a walking stick, late 14th century.
8. Older man (chiding an indiscreet young woman) wears a long, loose houppelande. The fashionable young men wear short tunics, one with dagged edges. The man on the right wears shoes with long pointed toes, late 14th century.

Women's Clothing

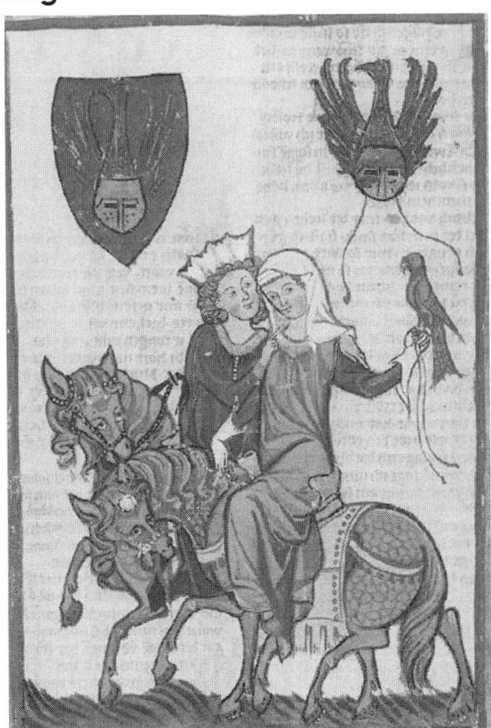

Figure: *For hawking, this woman wears a pink sleeveless gown over a green kirtle, with a linen veil and white gloves. Codex Manesse, 1305–40.*

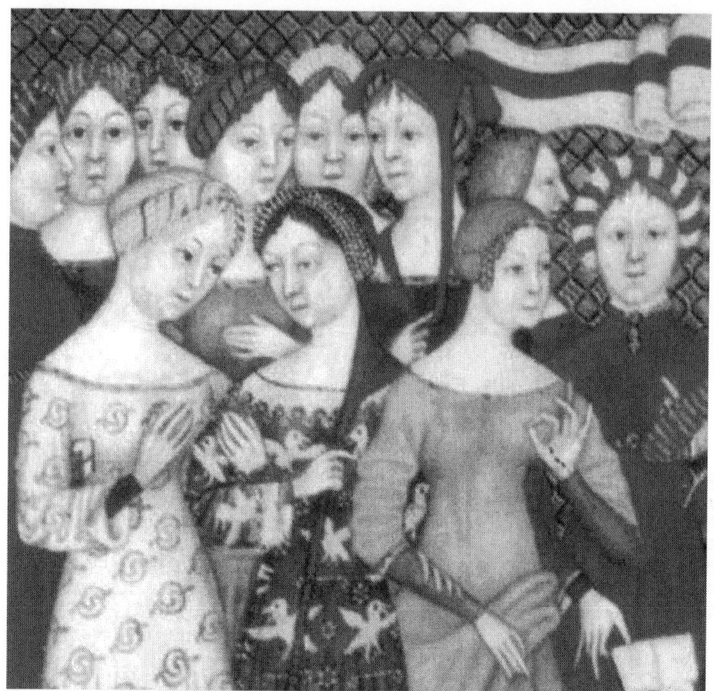

Figure: *Many Italian women wear their hair twisted with cord or ribbon and bound around their heads, c. 1380*

Underwear

The innermost layer of a woman's clothing was a linen or woolen chemise or smock, some fitting the figure and some loosely garmented, although there is some mention of a "breast girdle" or "breast band" which may have been the precursor of a modern bra.

Women also wore hose or stockings, although women's hose generally only reached to the knee.

All classes and both sexes are usually shown sleeping naked—special nightwear only became common in the 16th century —yet some married women wore their chemises to bed as a form of modesty and piety. Many in the lower classes wore their undergarments to bed because of the cold weather at night-time and since their beds usually consisted of a straw mattress and a few sheets, the undergarment would act as another layer.

Gowns and Outerwear

Over the chemise, women wore a loose or fitted gown called a *cotte* or kirtle, usually ankle or floor-length, and with trains for formal occasions. Fitted kirtles had full skirts made by adding triangular gores to widen the hem without adding bulk at the waist. Kirtles also had long, fitted sleeves that sometimes reached down to over the knuckles.

Various sorts of overgowns were worn over the kirtle, and are called by different names by costume historians. When fitted, this garment is often called a cotehardie (although this usage of the word has been heavily criticized) and might have hanging sleeves and sometimes worn with a jewelled or metalworked belt. Over time, the hanging part of the sleeve became longer and narrower until it was the merest streamer, called a *tippet*, then gaining the floral or leaflike daggings in the end of the century.

Sleeveless overgowns or tabards derive from the cyclas, an unfitted rectangle of cloth with an opening for the head that was worn in the 13th century. By the early 14th century, the sides began to be sewn together, creating a sleeveless overgown or surcoat.

Outdoors, women wore cloaks or mantles, often lined in fur. The Houppelande was also adopted by women late in the century. Women invariably wore their Houppelandes floor-length, the waistline rising up to right underneath the bust, sleeves very wide and hanging, like angel sleeves.

Headdresses

Northern and western Europe: Married women in Northern and Western Europe wore some type of headcovering. The *barbet* was a band of linen that passed under the chin and was pinned on top of the head; it descended from the earlier wimple (in French, *barbe*), which was now worn only by older women, widows, and nuns. The barbet was worn with a linen fillet or headband, or with a linen cap called a coif, with or without a *couvrechef* (kerchief) or veil overall. It passed out of fashion by mid-century. Unmarried girls simply just braided the hair to keep the dirt out.

The barbet and fillet or barbet and veil could also be worn over the *crespine*, a thick hairnet or snood. Over time, the crespine evolved into a mesh of jeweler's work that confined the hair on the sides of the head, and even later, at the back.

This metal crespine was also called a *caul*, and remained stylish long after the barbet had fallen out of fashion. For example it was used in Hungary until the beginning of the second half of the 15th century, as it was used by the Hungarian queen consort Barbara of Celje around 1440.

Italy

Uncovered hair was acceptable for women in the Italian states. Many women twisted their long hair with cords or ribbons and wrapped the twists around their heads, often without any cap or veil. Hair was also worn braided. Older women and widows wore a veil and wimple, and a simple knotted kerchief was worn while working. In the image at right, one woman wears a red hood draped over her twisted and bound hair.

Renaissance and early modern period

Renaissance Europe: Wool remained the most popular fabric for all classes, followed by linen and hemp. Wool fabrics were available in a wide range of qualities, from rough undyed cloth to fine, dense broadcloth with a velvety nap; high-value broadcloth was a backbone of the English economy and was exported throughout Europe. Wool fabrics were dyed in rich colours, notably reds, greens, golds, and blues.

Silk-weaving was well established around the Mediterranean by the beginning of the 15th century, and figured silks, often silk velvets with silver-gilt wefts, are increasingly seen in Italian dress and in the dress of the wealthy throughout Europe. Stately floral designs featuring a pomegranate or artichoke motif had reached Europe from China in the previous century and became a dominant design in the Ottoman silk-producing cities of Istanbul and Bursa, and spread to silk weavers in Florence, Genoa, Venice, Valencia and Seville in this period.

As prosperity grew in the 15th century, the urban middle classes, including skilled workers, began to wear more complex clothes that followed, at a distance, the fashions set by the elites. National variations in clothing increased over the century.

Early Modern Europe

By the first half of the 16th century, the clothing of the Low Countries, German states, and Scandinavia had developed in a different direction than that of England, France, and Italy, although all absorbed the sobering and formal influence of Spanish dress after the mid-1520s.

Elaborate slashing was popular, especially in Germany. Black was increasingly worn for the most formal occasions. Bobbin lace arose from passementerie in the mid-16th century, probably in Flanders. This century also saw the rise of the ruff, which grew from a mere ruffle at the neckline of the shirt or chemise to immense cartwheel shapes. At their most extravagant, ruffs required wire supports and were made of fine Italian reticella, a cutwork linen lace. By the turn of the 17th century, a sharp distinction could be seen between the sober fashions favored by Protestants in England and the Netherlands, which still showed heavy Spanish influence, and the light, revealing fashions of the French and Italian courts.

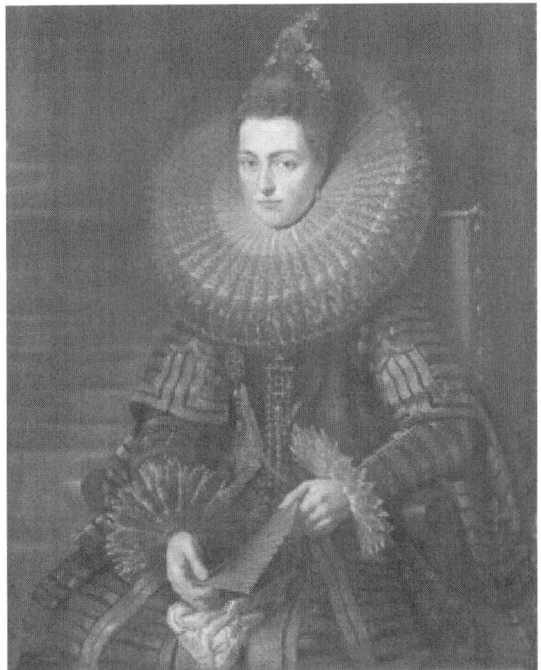

Figure: *A French reinterpretation of Spanish fashion, with elaborate reticella ruff, **1609***

The great flowering of needlelace occurred in this period. Geometric reticella deriving from cutwork was elaborated into true needlelace or *punto in aria* (called in England "point lace"), which reflected the scrolling floral designs popular for embroidery. Lacemaking centers were established in France to reduce the outflow of cash to Italy.

According to Dr. Wolf D. Fuhrig, "By the second half of the 17th century, Silesia had become an important economic pillar of the Habsburg monarchy, largely on the strength of its textile industry."

Enlightenment and the Colonial Period

During the eighteenth century, distinction was made between *full dress* worn at Court and for formal occasions, and *undress* or everyday, daytime clothes. As the decades progressed, fewer and fewer occasions called for full dress which had all but disappeared by the end of the century. Full dress followed the styles of the French court, where rich silks and elaborate embroidery reigned. Men continued to wear the coat, waistcoat and breeches for both full dress and undress; these were now sometimes made of the same fabric and trim, signalling the birth of the three-piece suit.

Women's silhouettes featured small, domed hoops in the 1730s and early 1740s, which were displaced for formal court wear by side hoops or panniers which later widened to as much as three feet to either side at the court of Marie Antoinette. Fashion reached heights of fantasy and abundant ornamentation, before new enthusiasms for outdoor sports and country pursuits and a long-simmering movement toward simplicity and democratization of dress under the influence of Jean-Jacques Rousseau and the American Revolution led to an entirely new mode and the triumph of British woollen tailoring following the French Revolution.

For women's dresses, Indian cottons, especially printed chintzes, were imported to Europe in large numbers, and towards the end of the period simple white muslin gowns were in fashion.

Industrial Revolution

During the industrial revolution, fabric production was mechanised with machines powered by waterwheels and steam-engines. Production shifted from small cottage based production to mass production based on assembly line organisation. Clothing production, on the other hand, continued to be made by hand.

Sewing machines emerged in the 19th century streamlining clothing production.

In the early 20th century workers in the clothing and textile industries became unionised. Later in the 20th century, the industry had expanded to such a degree that such educational institutions as UC Davis established a Division of Textiles and Clothing, The University of Nebraska-Lincoln also created a Department of Textiles, Clothing and Design that offers a Masters of Arts in Textile History, and Iowa State University established a Department of Textiles and Clothing that features a History of costume collection, 1865–1948. Even high school libraries have collections on the history of clothing and textiles.

Alongside these developments were changes in the types and style of clothing produced. During the 1960s, had a major influence on subsequent developments in the industry.

Textiles were not only made in factories. Before this that they were made in local and national markets. Dramatic change in transportation throughout the nation is one source that encouraged the use of factories. New advances such as steamboats, canals, and railroads lowered shipping costs which caused people to buy cheap goods that were produced in other places instead of more expensive goods that were produced locally. Between 1810 and 1840 the development of a national market prompted manufacturing which tripled the output's worth. This increase in production created a change in industrial methods, such as the use of factories instead of hand made woven materials that families usually made.

The vast majority of the people who worked in the factories were women. Women went to work in textile factories for a number of reasons. Some women left home to live on their own because of crowding at home; or to save for future marriage portions. The work enabled them to see more of the world, to earn something in anticipation of marriage, and to ease the crowding within the home. They also did it to make money for family back home. The money they sent home was to help out with the trouble some of the farmers were having. They also worked in the millhouses because they could gain a sense of independence and growth as a personal goal.

Textile Manufacture During the Industrial Revolution

Textile manufacture during the Industrial Revolution in Britain was centred on Greater Manchester, in southern Lancashire and the small towns both sides of the Pennines. In Germany in the Wupper Valley, Ruhr Region and Upper Silesia. In the United States it was in New England. The four key drivers of the industrial revolution were textile manufacturing, iron founding, steam power and cheap labour.

The Prior to the 18th century, the manufacture of goods was performed on a limited scale by individual workers, in the premises where they lived – and goods were transported around the country by horse, or by river. Rivers navigations and some contour following canals had been constructed in the early 18th century. In the mid-18th century, artisans were inventing ways to become more productive. Silk, Wool, Fustian, the traditional fibres, were being eclipsed by cotton which was became the most important textile. This set the foundations for the changes, right though textile industry.

Innovations in carding and spinning enabled by advances in cast iron ever larger spinning mules and water frames were constructed.

They were housed in water driven mills on numerous streams. The need for more power stimulated the production of steam driven beam engines, and then rotative mill engines. The line shaft transmitted this power to each floor of the mill. Surplus power capacity encouraged the construction of ever more sophisticated power looms working in weaving sheds. The scale of production in the mill towns round Manchester created a need for a commercial structure; for a cotton exchange and warehousing. These earned Manchester the sobriquet Cottonopolis.

The technology was applied to other fibres causing the construction of woollen and worsted mills in neighbouring West Yorkshire.

Elements of the Industrial Revolution

The commencement of the Industrial Revolution is closely linked to a small number of innovations, made in the second half of the 18th century:

- Textiles – Cotton spinning using Richard Arkwright's water frame, James Hargreaves's Spinning Jenny, and Samuel Crompton's Spinning Mule (a combination of the Spinning Jenny and the Water Frame). This was patented in 1769 and so came out of patent in 1783. The end of the patent was rapidly followed by the erection of many cotton mills. Similar technology was subsequently applied to spinning worsted yarn for various textiles and flax for linen.
- Steam power – The improved steam engine invented by James Watt and patented in 1775 was initially mainly used for pumping out mines, but from the 1780s was applied to power machines. This enabled rapid development of efficient semi-automated factories on a previously unimaginable scale in places where waterpower was not available.
- Iron founding – In the Iron industry, coke was finally applied to all stages of iron smelting, replacing charcoal. This had been achieved much earlier for lead and copper as well as for producing pig iron in a blast furnace, but the second stage in the production of bar iron depended on the use of potting and stamping (for which a patent expired in 1786) or puddling (patented by Henry Cort in 1783 and 1784).

These represent three 'leading sectors', in which there were key innovations, which allowed the economic take off by which the Industrial Revolution is usually defined. This is not to belittle many other inventions, particularly in the textile industry. Without earlier ones, such as the spinning jenny and flying shuttle in the textile industry and the smelting of pig iron with coke, these achievements might have been impossible. Later inventions such as the power loom and Richard Trevithick's high pressure steam engine were also important in the growing industrialisation of Britain. The application of steam engines to powering cotton mills and ironworks enabled these to be built in places that were most convenient because other resources were available, rather than where there was water to power a watermill.

Industry and Invention

Before the 1760s, textile production was a cottage industry using mainly flax and wool. In a typical house, the girls and women could make enough yarn for the man's loom. The knowledge of textile production had existed for centuries, and the manual methods had been adequate to provide enough cloth. Cotton started to be imported and the balance of demand and supply was upset.

Two systems had developed for spinning: the Simple Wheel, which used an intermittent process and the more refined, Saxony wheel which drove a differential spindle and flyer with heck, in a continuous process. But neither of these wheels could produce enough thread for the looms after the invention by John Kay of the flying shuttle (which made the loom twice as productive). The first moves towards manufactories called mills were made in the spinning sector, and until the 1820s cotton, wool and worsted was spun in mills, and this yarn went to outworking weavers who continued to work in their own homes.

Early Inventions

During the second half of the 17th century, cotton goods were imported from India. Because of the competition with the wool and the linen industries, in 1700, the government placed a ban on imported cotton goods. Cotton had become popular, however, and a home-based cotton industry sprung up using the raw material imported from the colonies. Since much of the imported cotton came from New England, ports on the west coast of Britain, such as Liverpool, Bristol and Glasgow, became important in determining the sites of the cotton industry. Of course, the wool and linen manufacturers made sure that many restrictions were imposed on the import of cotton, but, as cotton had become fashionable, there was little they could do to stop the trend.

Lancashire became a centre for the cotton industry because the damp climate was better for spinning the yarn. Also, because the cotton thread was not strong enough, "fustian" wool or linen had to be used to make the warp for weaving. Lancashire was also a wool centre.

Two processes are necessary in the production of cotton goods from the raw material - spinning and weaving. At first, these were very much home-based, "cottage" industries. The spinning process, using the spinning wheel, was slow and the weavers were often held up by the lack of thread. In the 1760s, James Hargreaves improved thread production when he invented the Spinning Jenny. By the end of the decade, Richard Arkwright had developed the Water Frame. This invention had two important consequences. Firstly, it improved the quality of the thread, which meant that the cotton industry was no longer dependent on wool or linen to make the warp. Secondly, it took spinning away from the home-bases to specific areas where fast-flowing streams could provide water power for the larger machines. The west Pennines of Lancashire became the centre for the cotton industry. Not long after the invention of the Water Frame, Samuel Crompton combined the principals of the Spinning Jenny and the Water Frame to produce his Spinning Mule. This provided even tougher and finer cotton thread.

These inventions turned the tables, and it was the weavers who found it hard to keep up with the supply of thread. In 1770, John Kay's Flying Shuttle loom, which had been invented in 1733 and doubled a weaver's productivity and was widely in use. In conjunction with the Spinning Frame, this new loom was used in factories built in Derbyshire, Lancashire and Scotland.

The textile industry was also to benefit from other developments of the period. As early as 1691, Thomas Savery had made a vacuum steam engine. His design, which was unsafe, was improved by Thomas Newcomen in 1698. In 1765, James Watt further modified Newcomen's engine to design an external condenser steam engine. Watt continued to make improvements on his design, producing a separate condenser engine in 1774 and a rotating separate condensing engine in 1781. Watt formed a partnership with a businessman called Matthew Boulton, and together they manufactured steam engines which could be used by industry.

In 1785, the Reverend Edmund Cartwright invented the power loom. His invention was perfected over a ten year period by William

Horrocks. Henry Cort replaced the early wooden machines with new machines made of iron. These new iron machines needed coal, rather than charcoal, to produce the steam to drive them.

In 1734 in Bury, Lancashire, John Kay invented the flying shuttle — one of the first of a series of inventions associated with the cotton industry. The flying shuttle increased the width of cotton cloth and speed of production of a single weaver at a loom. Resistance by workers to the perceived threat to jobs delayed the widespread introduction of this technology, even though the higher rate of production generated an increased demand for spun cotton.

In 1738, Lewis Paul (one of the community of Huguenot weavers that had been driven out of France in a wave of religious persecution) settled in Birmingham and with John Wyatt, of that town, they patented the Roller Spinning machine and the flyer-and-bobbin system, for drawing wool to a more even thickness. Using two sets of rollers that travelled at different speeds yarn could be twisted and spun quickly and efficiently. This was later used in the first cotton spinning mill during the Industrial Revolution.

1742: Paul and Wyatt opened a mill in Birmingham which used their new rolling machine powered by donkey; this was not profitable and was soon closed.

1743: A factory opened in Northampton, fifty spindles turned on five of Paul and Wyatt's machines proving more successful than their first mill. This operated until 1764.

1748: Lewis Paul invented the hand driven carding machine. A coat of wire slips were placed around a card which was then wrapped around a cylinder. Lewis's invention was later developed and improved by Richard Arkwright and Samuel Crompton, although this came about under great suspicion after a fire at Daniel Bourn's factory in Leominster which specifically used Paul and Wyatt's spindles. Bourn produced a similar patent in the same year.

1758: Paul and Wyatt based in Birmingham improved their roller spinning machine and took out a second patent. Richard Arkwright later used this as the model for his water frame.

Start of the Revolution

In 1761, the Duke of Bridgewater's canal connected Manchester to the coal fields of Worsley and in 1762, Matthew Boulton opened the Soho Foundry engineering works in Handsworth, Birmingham. His partnership with Scottish engineer James Watt resulted, in 1775, in the commercial production of the more efficient Watt steam engine which used a separate condensor.

In 1764, James Hargreaves is credited as inventor of the spinning jenny which multiplied the spun thread production capacity of a single worker — initially eightfold and subsequently much further. Others credit the original invention to Thomas Highs. Industrial unrest and a failure to patent the invention until 1770 forced Hargreaves from Blackburn, but his lack of protection of the idea allowed the concept to be exploited by others. As a result, there were over 20,000 Spinning Jennies in use by the time of his death. Again in 1764, Thorp Mill, the first water-powered cotton mill in the world was constructed at Royton, Lancashire, England. It was used for carding cotton.

Richard Arkwright used waterwheels to power textile machinery. His first spinning mill, Cromford Mill, Derbyshire, was built in 1771. It contained his invention the water frame. Frame is another name for the machinery for spinning or weaving. The water frame was developed from the spinning frame that Arkwright had developed with (a different) John Kay, from Warrington. The original design was again claimed by Thomas Highs, which he claimed he had patented in 1769. Initial attempts at driving the frame had used horse power, but the innovation of using a waterwheel demanded a location with a ready supply of water, hence the mill at Cromford. This mill is preserved as part of the Derwent Valley Mills in some ways it was modelled on Matthew Boulton and John Fothergill's Soho Manufactory. Arkwright protected his investment from industrial rivals and potentially disruptive workers. He generated jobs and constructed accommodation for his workers, this led to a sizeable industrial community. Arkwright expanded his operations to other parts of the country.

Samuel Crompton of Bolton combined elements of the spinning jenny and water frame in 1779, creating the spinning mule. This mule produced a stronger thread than the water frame could. Thus in 1780, there were two viable hand operated spinning system that could be easily adapted to run by power of water. As early mules were suitable for producing yarn for use in the manufacture of muslin, and which were known as the muslin wheel or the Hall i' th' Wood (pronounced Hall-ith-wood) wheel. As with Kay and Hargreaves, Crompton was not able to exploit his invention for his own profit, and died a pauper.

In 1783 a mill was built in Manchester at Shudehill, at the highest point in the city away from the river. Shudehill Mill was powered by a 30 ft diameter waterwheel. Two storage ponds were built, and the water from one passed from one to the other turning the wheel. A steam driven pump returned the water to the higher reservoir. The steam engine was of the atmospheric type. An improvement devised by Joshua Wrigley, trialled in Chorlton-upon-Medlock used two Savery engines to supplement the river in driving on overshot waterwheel.

In 1784, Edmund Cartwright invented the power loom, and produced a prototype in the following year. His initial venture to exploit this technology failed, although his advances were recognised by others in the industry. Others such as Robert Grimshaw (whose factory was destroyed in 1790 as part of the growing reaction against the mechanization of the industry) and Austin [4] – developed the ideas further.

In the 1790s industrialists, such as John Marshall at Marshall's Mill in Leeds, started to work on ways to apply some of the techniques which had proved so successful in cotton to other materials, such as flax. In 1803, William Radcliffe invented the dressing frame which was patented under the name of Thomas Johnson which enabled power looms to operate continuously.

Later Developments

With the Cartwright Loom, the Spinning Mule and the Boulton & Watt steam engine, the pieces were in place to build a mechanised textile industry. From this point there were no new inventions, but a continuous improvement in technology as the mill-owner strove to reduce cost and improve quality. Developments in the transport infrastructure - the canals and, after 1831, the railways - facilitated the import of raw materials and export of finished cloth.

Firstly, the use of water power to drive mills was supplemented by steam driven water pumps, and then superseded completely by the steam engines. For example Samuel Greg joined his uncle's firm of textile merchants, and, on taking over the company in 1782, he sought out a site to establish a mill. Quarry Bank Mill was built on the River Bollin at Styal in Cheshire. It was initially powered by a water wheel, but installed steam engines in 1810. In 1830, the average power of a mill engine was 48 hp, but Quarry Bank mill installed an new 100 hp water wheel. This was to change in 1836, when Horrocks & Nuttall, Preston took delivery of 160 hp double engine. William Fairbairn addressed the problem of line-shafting and was responsible for improving the efficiency of the mill. In 1815 he replaced the wooden turning shafts that drove the machines at 50rpm, to wrought iron shafting working at 250 rpm, these were a third of the weight of the previous ones and absorbed less power.

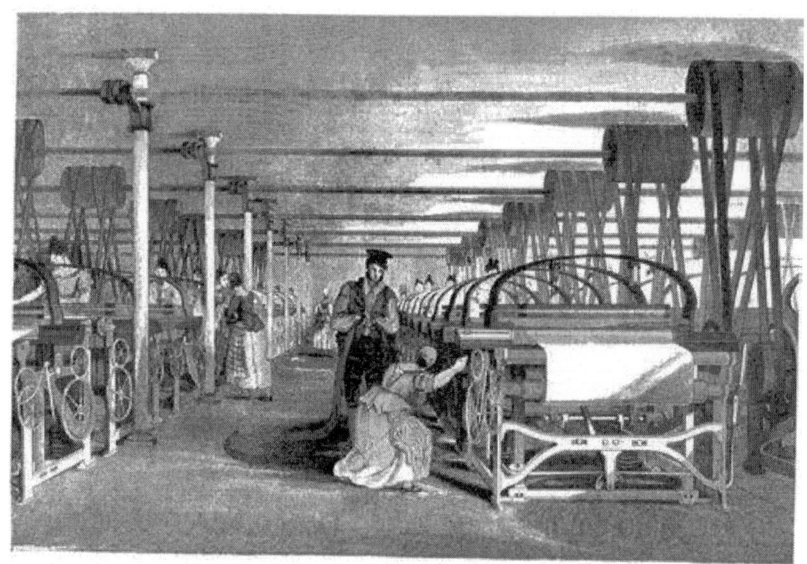

Figure: *A Roberts loom in a weaving shed in 1835. Note the wrought iron shafting, fixed to the cast iron columns*

Secondly, in 1830, using a 1822 patent, Richard Roberts manufactured the first loom with a cast iron frame, the Roberts Loom. In 1842 James Bullough and William Kenworthy, made the Lancashire Loom . It is a semi automatic power loom. Although it is self-acting, it has to be stopped to recharge empty shuttles. It was the mainstay of the Lancashire cotton industry for a century, when the Northrop Loom invented in 1894 with an automatic weft replenishment function gained ascendancy.

Number of Looms in UK

Year	1803	1820	1829	1833	1857
Looms	2400	14650	55500	100000	250000

Thirdly, also in 1830, Richard Roberts patented the first self-acting mule. Stalybridge mule spinners strike was in 1824, this stimulated research into the problem of applying power to the winding stroke of the mule. The draw while spinning had been assisted by power, but the push of the wind had been done manually by the spinner, the mule could be operated by semiskilled labour. Before 1830, the spinner would operate a partially powered mule with a maximum of 400 spindles after, self-acting mules with up to 1300 spindles could be built.

The savings that could be made with this technology were considerable. A worker spinning cotton at a hand-powered spinning wheel in the 18th century would take more than 50,000 hours to spin 100 lb of cotton; by the 1790s, the same quantity could be spun in 300 hours by mule, and with a self-acting mule it could be spun by one worker in just 135 hours.

Spinning Mule

The spinning mule is a machine used to spin cotton and other fibres in the mills of Lancashire and elsewhere. They were used extensively from the late eighteenth to the early twentieth century. Mules were worked in pairs by a minder, with the help of two boys: the little piecer and the big or side piecer. The carriage carried up to 1320 spindles and could be 150 feet (46 m) long, and would move forward and back a distance of 5 feet (1.5 m) four times a minute. It was invented between 1775 and 1779 by Samuel Crompton. The self-acting (automatic) mule was patented by Richard Roberts in 1825. At its peak there were 50,000,000 mule spindles in Lancashire alone. Modern versions are still in niche production and are used to spin woollen yarns from noble fibers such as cashmere, ultra-fine merino and alpaca for the knitware market.

The spinning mule spins textile fibres into yarn by an intermittent process. In the draw stroke, the roving is pulled through rollers and twisted; on the return it is wrapped onto the spindle. Its rival, the throstle frame or ring frame uses a continuous process, where the roving is drawn, twisted and wrapped in one action. The mule was the most common spinning machine from 1790 until about 1900 and was still used for fine yarns until the early 1980s. In 1890, a typical cotton mill would have over 60 mules, each with 1,320 spindles, which would operate four times a minute for 56 hours a week.

Before the 1770s, textile production was a cottage industry using flax and wool. Weaving was a family activity. The children and women would card the fibre, which the women would spin into yarn; the male weaver would use a frame loom to weave this into cloth. This was then tentered in the sun to bleach it. The same production system was attempted with cotton, but the demand was too high, and with the invention by John Kay of the flying shuttle, which made the loom twice as productive, more cotton yarn was being woven than the traditional spinners could supply. There were two types of spinning wheel: the Simple Wheel, which uses an intermittent process, and the more refined Saxony wheel, which drives a differential spindle and flyer with a heck (an apparatus that guides the thread to the reels) in a continuous process. These two wheels became the starting point of technological development. Businessmen such as Richard Arkwright employed inventors to find solutions that would increase the amount of yarn spun, then took out the relevant patents.

The spinning jenny allowed a group of eight spindles to be operated together. It mirrored the simple wheel; the rovings were clamped and a frame moved forward stretching and thinning the roving. A wheel was rapidly turned as the frame was pushed back, and the spindles rotated, twisted the rovings into yarn and collecting it on the spindles.

The throstle and the later water frame pulled the rovings through a set of attenuating rollers, spinning at differing speeds these pulled the thread continuously and it was twisted by the heck as it was wound on the heavy spindles. Eight or sixteen of these were mounted in parallel on a static frame driven usually by a water wheel. It was ideas from these two system that inspired the spinning mule. It was the water frame that inspired the ring frame.

The increased supply of yarn inspired developments in loom design such as Edmund Cartwright's power loom. Some spinners and handloom weavers opposed the perceived threat to their livelihood: there were frame-breaking riots and, in 1811–3, the Luddite riots. The preparatory and associated tasks allowed many children to be employed until this was regulated.

The hand-operated mule was a breakthrough in yarn production and the machines were copied by Samuel Slater, who founded the cotton industry in Rhode Island. Development over the next century and a half led to an automatic mule and to finer and stronger yarn. The ring frame, originating in New England in the 1820s, was little used in Lancashire until the 1890s. It required more energy and could not produce the finest counts. —>

The First Mule

Samuel Crompton invented the spinning mule or mule jenny in 1779, so called because it is a hybrid of Arkwright's water frame and James Hargreaves' spinning jenny in the same way that mule is the product of crossbreeding a female horse with a male donkey. The spinning mule has a fixed frame with a creel of bobbins to hold the roving, connected through the headstock to a parallel carriage with the spindles. On the outward motion, the rovings are paid out through attenuating rollers and twisted. On the return, the roving is clamped and the spindles reversed to take up the newly spun thread.

Crompton built his mule from wood. Although he used Hargreaves' ideas of spinning multiple threads and of attenuating the roving with rollers, it was he who put the spindles on the carriage and fixed a creel of roving bobbins on the frame. Both the rollers and the outward motion of the carriage remove irregularities from the rove before it is wound on the spindle. When Arkwright's patents expired, the mule was developed by several manufacturers. Crompton's first mule had 48 spindles and could produce 1 lb of 60s thread a day. This demanded a spindle speed of 1700 rpm, and a power input of 1/16 hp.

The mule produced strong, thin yarn, suitable for any kind of textile. It was first used to spin cotton, then other fibres.

Samuel Crompton could not afford to patent his invention. He sold the rights to David Dale and returned to weaving. Dale patented the mule and profited from it.

Improvements

Crompton's machine was largely built of wood, using bands and pulley for the driving motions. After his machine was public, he had little to do with its development. Henry Stones, a mechanic from Horwich, constructed a mule using toothed gearing and, importantly, metal rollers. Baker of Bury worked on drums, and Hargreaves used parallel scrolling to achieve smoother acceleration and deceleration.

In 1790, William Kelly of Glasgow used a new method to assist the draw stroke. First animals and then water was used as the prime mover. Wright of Manchester moved the head stock to the centre of the machine, allowing twice as many spindles; a squaring band was added to ensure the spindles came out in a straight line He was in conversation with John Kennedy about the possibility of a self-acting mule. Kennedy, a partner in McConnell & Kennedy machine makers in Ancoats, was concerned with building ever larger mules. McConnell & Kennedy ventured into spinning when they were left with two unpaid-for mules; their firm prospered and eventually merged into the Fine Spinners & Doublers Association. In 1793, John Kennedy was addressing the problem of fine counts. With these counts, the spindles on the return traverse needed to rotate faster than on the outward traverse. He attached gears and a clutch to implement this motion.

William Eaton, in 1818, improved the winding of the thread by using two faller wires and performing a backing off at the end of the outward traverse. All these mules had been worked by the strength of the operatives. The next improvement was a fully automatic mule.

Roberts' Self-acting Mule

Richard Roberts took out his first patent in 1825 and a second in 1830. The task he had set himself was to design a self-actor, a self-acting or automatic spinning mule. Roberts is also known for the Roberts Loom, which was widely adopted because of its reliability. The mule in 1820 still needed manual assistance to spin a consistent thread; a self-acting mule would need:

- A reversing mechanism that would unwind a spiral of yarn on the top of each spindle, before commencing the winding of a new stretch
- A faller wire that would ensure the yarn was wound into a predefined form such as a cop
- An appliance to vary the speed of revolution of the spindle, in accordance with the diameter of thread on that spindle

A counter faller under the thread was made to rise to take in the slack caused by backing off. This could be used with the top faller wire to guide the yarn to the correct place on the cop. These were controlled by levers and cams and an inclined plane called the shaper. The spindle speed was controlled by a drum and weighted ropes, as the headstock moved the ropes twisted the drum, which using a tooth wheel turned the spindles. None of this would have been possible using the technology of Crompton's time, fifty years earlier. With the invention of the self actor, the hand operated mule was increasingly referred to as a mule-jenny.

Oldham Counts

Oldham counts refers to the medium thickness cotton that was used for general purpose cloth. Roberts didn't profit from his self-acting spinning mule, but on the expiry of the patent other firms took forward the development, and the mule was adapted for the counts it spun. Initially Robert's self-actor was used for coarse counts (Oldham Counts), but the mule-jenny continued to be used for the very finest counts (Bolton counts) until the 1890s and beyond.

Bolton Counts

Bolton specialised in fine count cotton, its mules ran slower to put in the extra twist. The mule jenny allowed for this gentler action but in the twentieth century additional mechanisms were added to make the motion more gentle, leading to mules that used two or even three driving speeds. Fine counts needed a softer action on the winding, and relied on manually adjustment to wind the chase or top of the perfect cop,

Woollen Mules

Spinning wool was very different: the staple was naturally twisted and easily adhered to other staples. The yarn could be bulked out by pressing in short fibres that would have been consider too short to spin if cotton. The mule could be far simpler in its construction.

Condenser Spinning

Condenser spinning or cotton waste spinning is akin to spinning wool, and the mules are similar. Helmshore was a cotton waste mule spinning mill.

Current Usage

Mules are still in use for spinning woolen and alpaca, and being produced across the world. In Italy for example by Bigagli and Cormatex

Operation of a Mule

Mule spindles rest on a carriage that travels on a track a distance of 60 inches (1.5 m), while drawing out and spinning the yarn. On the return trip, known as putting up, as the carriage moves back to its original position, the newly spun yarn is wound onto the spindle in the form of a cone-shaped cop. As the mule spindle travels on its carriage, the roving which it spins is fed to it through rollers geared to revolve at different speeds to draw out the yarn.

Marsden in 1885 described the processes of setting up and operating a mule. Here is his description, edited slightly.

The creel holds bobbins containing rovings. The rovings are passed through small guide-wires, and between the three pairs of drawing-rollers.

- The first pair takes hold of the roving, to draw the roving or sliver from the bobbin, and deliver it to the next pair.
- The motion of the middle pair is slightly quicker than the first, but only sufficiently so to keep the roving uniformly tense
- The front pair, running much more quickly, draws out (attenuates) the roving so it is equal throughout.

Connection is then established between the attenuated rovings and the spindles. When the latter are bare, as in a new mule, the spindle-driving motion is put into gear, and the attendants wind upon each spindle a short length of yarn from a cop held in the hand. The drawing-roller motion is placed in gear, and the rollers soon present lengths of attenuated roving. These are attached to the threads on the spindles, by simply placing the threads in contact with the untwisted roving. The different parts of the machine are next simultaneously started, when the whole works in harmony together.

The back rollers pull the sliver from the bobbins, and passing it to the succeeding pairs, whose differential speeds attenuate it to the required degree of fineness. As it is delivered in front, the spindles, revolving at a rate of 6,000–9,000 rpm twist the hitherto loose fibres together, thus forming a thread.

Whilst this is going on, the spindle carriage is being drawn away from the rollers, at a pace very slightly exceeding the rate at which the roving is coming forth. This is called the gain of the carriage, its purpose being to eliminate all irregularities in the fineness of the thread. Should a thick place in the roving come through the rollers, it would resist the efforts of the spindle to twist it; and, if passed in this condition, it would seriously deteriorate the quality of the yarn, and impede subsequent operations. As, however, the twist, spreading itself over the level thread, gives firmness to this portion, the thick and untwisted part yields to the draught of the spindle, and, as it approaches the tenuity of the remainder, it receives the twist it had hitherto refused to take. The carriage, which is borne upon wheels, continues its outward progress, until it reaches the extremity of its traverse, which is 63 inches (160 cm) from the roller beam. The revolution of the spindles cease, the drawing rollers stop.

Backing-off commences. This process is the unwinding of the several turns of the yarn, extending from the top of the cop in process of formation to the summit of the spindle. As this proceeds, the faller-wire, which is placed over and guides the threads upon the cop, is depressed ; the counter-faller at the same time rising, the slack unwound from the spindles is taken up, and the threads are prevented from running into snarls. Backing-off is completed.

The carriage commences to run inwards; that is, towards the rollerbeam. This is called putting up. The spindles wind on the yarn at a uniform rate. The speed of revolution of the spindle must vary, as the faller is guiding the thread upon the larger or smaller diameter of the cone of the cop. Immediately the winding is finished, the depressed faller rises, the counter-faller is put down.

These movements are repeated until the cops on each spindle are perfectly formed: the ' set is completed. A stop-motion paralyzes every action of the machine, rendering it necessary to doff or strip the spindles, and to commence anew.

Doffing is performed by the piercers thrutching, that is raising, the cops partially up the spindles, whilst the carriage is out. The minder then depressing the faller, so far as to guide the threads upon the bare spindle below. A few turns are wound onto the spindle, to fix the threads to the bare spindles for a new set. The cops are removed and collected into cans or baskets, and subsequently delivered to the warehouse. The remainder of the "draw" or "stretch," as the length of spun yarn is called when the carriage is out, is then wound upon the spindles as the carriage is run up to the roller beam. Work then commences anew. The doffing took only a few minutes, the piecers would run the length of the mule gate thrutching five spindles a time, and the doffing involved lifting four cops from the spindles with the right hand and piling them on the left forearm and hand. To get a firm cop bottom, the minder would whip the first few layers of yarn. After the first few draws the minder would stop the mule at the start of an inward run and take it in slowly depressing and releasing the faller wire several times. Alternatively, a starch paste could be skillfully applied to the first few layers of yarn by the piecers – and later a small paper tube was dropped over spindle – this slowed down the doffing operation and extra payment was negotiated by the minders.

Duties of the Operatives

A pair of mules would be manned by a man called the minder and two boys called the side piecer and the little piecer. They worked barefoot in humid temperatures, the minder and the little piecer worked the minder's half of the mule. The minder would make minor adjustments to his mules to the extent that each mule worked differently. They were specialists in spinning, and were only answerable to the gaffer and under-gaffer who were in charge of the floor and with it the quantity and quality of the yarn that was produced. Bobbins of rovings came from the carder in the blowing room delivered by a bobbin carrier who was part of the carder's staff, and yarn was hoisted down to the warehouse by the warehouseman's staff. Delineation of jobs was rigid and communication would be through the means of coloured slips of paper written on in indelible pencil.

Creeling involved replacing the rovings bobbins in a section of the mule without stopping the mule. On very coarse counts a bobbin lasted two days but on fine count it could last for 3 weeks. To creel, the creeler stood behind the mule, he placed new bobbins on the shelf above the creel. As the bobbin ran empty he would pick it off its skewer in the creel unreeling 30 cm or so of roving, and drop it into a skip. With his left hand, he would place on the new bobbin onto the skewer from above and with his right hand twist in the new roving into the tail of the last.

Piecing involved repairing sporadic yarn breakages. At the rollers, the broken yarn would be caught on the underclearer (or fluker rod on Bolton mules), while at the spindle it would knot itself into a whorl on the spindle tip. If the break happened on the winding stroke the spindle might have to be stopped while the thread was found. The number of yarn breakages was dependent on the quality of the roving, and quality cotton led to fewer breakages. Typical 1200 spindle mules of the 1920s would experience 5 to 6 breakages a minute. The two piecers would thus need to repair the thread within 15 to 20 seconds while the mule was in motion but once they had the thread it took under three seconds. The repair actually involved a slight rolling of the forefinger against the thumb.

Doffing has Already been Described

Cleaning was important and until a formal ritual had been devised it was a dangerous operation. The vibration in a mule threw a lot of short fibres (or fly) into the air. It tended to accumulate on the carriage behind the spindles and in the region of the drafting rollers. Piking the stick meant placing the hand though the yarnsheet, and unclipping two sticks of underclearer rollers from beneath the drafting rollers, drawing them through the 1 ¼ in gap between two ends, stripping them of fly and replacing them on the next inward run. Cleaning the carriage top was far more dangerous. The minder would stop the mule on the outward run, and raise his hands above his head. The piecers would enter under the yarn sheet with a scavenger cloth on the carriage spindle rail and a brush on the roller beam, and run bent double the entire length of the mule, avoiding the rails and draw bands, and not letting themselves touch the yarn sheet. When they had finished they would run to agreed positions of safety where the minder could see both of them, and the minder would unclip the stang and start the mule. Before this ritual was devised, boys had been crushed. The mule was 130 feet (40 m) long, the minder's eyesight might not have been good, the air in the mill was clouded with fly and another minder's boys might have been mistaken for his. The ritual became encoded in law.

Key Components

- Drawing rollers
- Faller and counter faller
- Quadrant

Terminology

Social and economic:

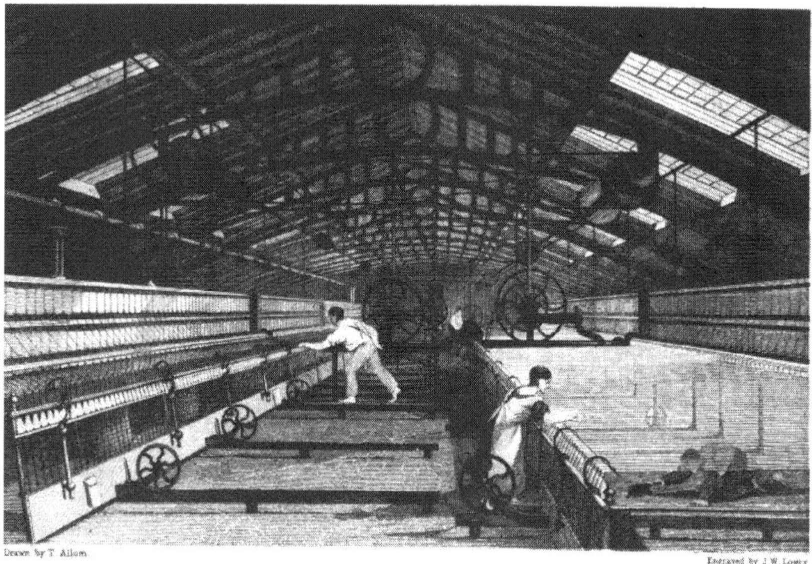

Figure: *Mules operating in a Cotton mill.*

The spinning inventions were significant in enabling a great expansion to occur in the production of textiles, particularly cotton ones. Cotton and iron were leading sectors in the Industrial Revolution. Both industries underwent a great expansion at about the same time, which can be used to identify the start of the Industrial Revolution.

The 1790 mule was operated by brute force: the spinner drawing and pushing the frame while attending to each spindle. Home spinning was the occupation of women and girls, but the strength needed to operate a mule caused it to be the activity of men. Hand loom weaving, however, had been a man's occupation but in the mill it could and was done by girls and women. Spinners were the bare-foot aristocrats of the factory system.

Mule spinners were the leaders in unionism within the cotton industry; the pressure to develop the self-actor or self-acting mule was partly to open the trade to women. It was in 1870 that the first national union was formed.

The wool industry was divided into woollen and worsted. It lagged behind cotton in adopting new technology. Worsted tended to adopt Arkwright water frames which could be operated by young girls, and woollen adopted the mule.

Mule-spinners' Cancer

About 1900 there was a high incidence of scrotal cancer detected in former mule spinners. It was limited to cotton mule spinners and did not affect woollen or condenser mule spinners. The cause was attributed to the blend of vegetable and mineral oils used to lubricate the spindles. The spindles when running threw out a mist of oil at crotch height, that was captured by the clothing of anyone piecing an end. In the 1920s much attention was given to this problem. Mules had used this mixture since the 1880s, and cotton mules ran faster and hotter than the other mules, and needed more frequent oiling. The solution was to make it a statutory requirement to only use vegetable oil or white mineral oils, which were believed to be non-carcinogens. By then cotton mules had been superseded by the ring frame and the industry was contracting, so it was never established whether these measures were effective.

Workers

Working conditions in some early British textile factories were unfavorable relative to modern standards. Children, men, and women regularly volunteered for 68-hour work weeks. Factories often were not well ventilated and became very hot in the summer. Worker health and safety regulations were non-existent. Textile factories organized workers' lives much differently from craft production. Handloom weavers worked at their own pace, with their own tools, and within their own cottages. Factories set hours of work, and the machinery within them shaped the pace of work. Factories brought workers together within one building to work on machinery that they did not own. Factories also increased the division of labor. They narrowed the number and scope of tasks and included children and women within a common production process. As Manchester mill owner Friedrich Engels decried, the family structure itself was "turned upside down" as women's wages undercut men's, forcing men to "sit at home" and care for children while the wife worked long hours.

Factories flourished over manual craftsmanship because they had more efficient production output per worker, keeping prices down for the public, and they had much more consistent quality of product. The work-discipline was forcefully instilled upon the workforce by the factory owners, and he found that the working conditions were below the national average, and poverty levels were at an unprecedented high. Engels was appalled and his research in Derby, played a large role in his and Marx's 'Das Kapital'.

At times, the workers rebelled against poor wages. The first major industrial action in Scotland was that of the Calton weavers in Glasgow, who went on strike for higher wages in the summer of 1787. In the ensuing disturbances, troops were called in to keep the peace and three of the weavers were killed. There was continued unrest. In Manchester in May 1808, 15,000 protesters gathered on St George's Fields and were fired on by dragoons, with one man dying. A strike followed, but was eventually settled by a small wage increase. In the general strike of 1842, half a million workers demanded the Charter and an end to pay cuts. Again, troops were called in to keep the peace, and the strike leaders were arrested, but some of the worker demands were met.

The early textile factories employed a large share of children, but the share declined over time. In England and Scotland in 1788, two-thirds of the workers in 143 water-powered cotton mills were described as children. Sir Robert Peel, a mill owner turned reformer, promoted the 1802 Health and Morals of Apprentices Act, which was intended to prevent pauper children from working more than 12 hours a day in mills. Children had started in the mills at around the age of four, working as mule scavengers under the working machinery until they were eight, they progressed to working as little piecers which they did until they were 15. During this time they worked 14 to 16 hours a day, being beaten if they fell asleep. The children were sent to the mills of Derbyshire, Yorkshire and Lancashire from the workhouses in London and other towns in the south of England. A well documented example was that of Litton Mill. Further legislation followed. By 1835, the share of the workforce under 18 years of age in cotton mills in England and Scotland had fallen to 43%. About half of workers in Manchester and Stockport cotton factories surveyed in 1818 and 1819 had begun work at under ten years of age. Most of the adult workers in cotton factories in mid-19th-century Britain were workers who had begun work as child labourers. The growth of this experienced adult factory workforce helps to account for the shift away from child labour in textile factories.

A Representative Early Spinning mill 1790–1825

Cromford Mill was an early Arkwright mill and was the model for future mills The site at Cromford had year-round supply of warm water from the sough which drained water from nearby lead mines, together with another brook. It was a five storey mill. Starting in 1772, the mills ran day and night with two 12 hour shifts.

It started with 200 workers, more than the locality could provide so Arkwright built housing for them nearby, one of the first manufacturers to do so. Most of the employees were women and children, the youngest being only 7 years old. Later, the minimum age was raised to 10 and the children were given 6 hours of education a week, so that they could do the record keeping their illiterate parents could not. Initially the first stage of the process was hand carding, but in 1775 he took out a second patent for a water-powered carding machine and this led to increased output. He was soon building further mills on this site and eventually employed 1,000 workers at Cromford. By the time of his death in 1792, he was the wealthiest untitled person in Britain.

The gate to Cromford Mill was shut at precisely 6am and 6pm every day and any worker who failed to get through it not only lost a day's pay but was fined another day's pay. In 1779, Arkwright installed a cannon, loaded with grapeshot, just inside the factory gate, as a warning to would-be rioting textile workers, who had burned down another of his mills in Birkacre, Lancashire. The cannon was never used.

A Representative Mid-century Spinning Mill 1840

Brunswick Mill, Ancoats is a cotton spinning mill in Ancoats, Manchester, Greater Manchester. It was built around 1840, part of a group of mills built along the Ashton Canal, and at that time it was one of the country's largest mill. It was built round a quadrangle, a seven storey block faced the canal. It was taken over by the Lancashire Cotton Corporation in the 1930s and passed to Courtaulds in 1964. Production finished in 1967.

The Brunswick mill was built around 1840 in one phase. The main seven storey block that faces the Ashton Canal was used for spinning. The preparation was done on the second floor and the self-acting mules with 400 spindles were arranged transversely on the floors above on the upper floor. The wings contained some spinning and ancillary processes like winding. The mill is of fireproof construction and was built by David Bellhouse, but it is suspected that William Fairbairn was involved in the design. It was powered by a large double beam engine.

In 1850 the mill had some 276 carding machines, and 77,000 mule spindles, 20 drawing frames, fifty slubbing frames and eighty one roving frames.

Export of Technology

> *While profiting from expertise arriving from overseas (e.g. Louis Paul), Britain was very protective of home-grown technology. In particular, engineers with skills in constructing the textile mills and machinery were not permitted to emigrate — particularly to the fledgeling America.* Horse power (1780–1790)

The earliest cotton mills in the United States were horse powered. The first mill to use this method was the Beverly Cotton Manufactory, built in Beverly, Massachusetts. It was started August 18, 1788 by entrepreneur John Cabot and brothers. It was operated in joint by Moses Brown, Israel Thorndike, Joshua Fisher, Henry Higginson, and Deborah Higginson Cabot. The Salem Mercury reported that in April 1788 that the equipment for the mill was complete, consisting of a spinning jenny, a carding machine, warping machine, and other tools. That same year the mill's location was finalized and built in the rural outsets of North Beverly. The location had the presence of natural water, but it was cited the water was used for upkeep of the horses and cleaning of equipment, and not for mass-production.

Much of the internal designs of the Beverly mill were hidden due to concerns of competitors stealing designs. The beginning efforts were all researched behind closed doors, even to the point that the owners of the mill set up milling equipment on their estates to experiment with the process. There were no published articles describing exactly how their process worked in detail. Additionally, the mill's horse powered technology was quickly dwarfed by new water-powered methods.

Slater

Following the creation of the United States, an engineer who had worked as an apprentice to Arkwright's partner Jedediah Strutt evaded the ban. In 1789, Samuel Slater took his skills in designing and constructing factories to New England, and he was soon engaged in reproducing the textile mills that helped America with its own industrial revolution. Local inventions spurred this on, and in 1793 Eli Whitney invented and patented the cotton gin, which sped up the processing of raw cotton by over 350 times.

Contemporary Technology

Synthetic fibers such as nylon were invented during the 20th century and synthetic fibers have been added to many natural fibers.

Type of Fabrics

Fabrics are manufactured from various raw-materials which are available from nature or artificially generated or mix of both. Fabrics can be classified based on the origin of fibers and its processes or its end usage. Natural fabrics are those which are created from the fibers of animals coats, the cocoons of silkworms, and plants seeds, leaves and stems. It is breathable and never cause rashes apart from being soft and durable. Natural fabric is the best choice for everyone. It does not change color from UV light and there is no warming until the material looses its tensile strength.

Synthetic or man-made fabrics are made from fibers which are either completely made from inorganic materials or organic materials combined with chemicals. Synthetic fabrics have numerous properties with the purpose for which it is produced and finished. Some are lightweight with ultra sheer while others are moisture wicking and fast drying. Few are very luxurious to imitate some other natural fabrics and some are very strong and tough.

2

Fabrics from Man-made Fibers

Acetate Fabric

Made from the cellulose and obtained by reconstructing cotton or wood pulp, Acetate fabric is resistant to shrinkage, moth and mildew. Acetate fabric is fabric which gives extremely soft and luxurious look just like silk fabric.

Chiffon Fabric

Chiffon basically refers to a light plain woven sheer fabric with a soft drape. Chiffon fabric can be manufactured using different fibers like silk or synthetic, cotton etc. but chiffon is generally associated with fibers like nylon or silk. Chiffon fabric can easily be dyed in contrast to any desired shade. Chiffon is used for bridal gowns and also appears in evening dresses, prom dresses, and scarves. Chiffon can be made using various materials like silk, polyester, or rayon. Chiffon fabric is a classic choice for manufacturing blouses and various types of dresses. Chiffon fabric adds a magical look to the dress and wearer's personality.

Acrylic Fabric

Acrylic fabrics is a kind of the synthetic fibre that is artificially manufactured. Acrylic fabrics can also be referred as the imitation of wool. Acrylic fabrics is used to make loads of apparels and many other things. The main use of the Acrylic fabrics is in outfits like shirts and many other ladies outfits. Also, Acrylic fabrics is used in seats of chairs and sofas as well. Acrylic fabrics are known for their stiffness and ability of wear and tear resistance. Acrylic also does not losses the glaze for a longer period of time.

Acrylic fabrics is available mainly in two forms that are 'Courtelle' and 'Orlon'. These fabrics are known for their durability and especially Orlon is reckoned for its light weightiness. These kinds of Acrylic fabrics serve plenty of option in shapes and designs. In the market, there are several manufacturers and suppliers in the business of the Acrylic fabrics. That shows the popularity of Acrylic fabrics amidst masses. People prefer the Acrylic fabrics as they are available at the low rates than any other fabrics. In addition, these fibers are wear resistant stays for longer period of time. Acrylic fabrics is the finest example of the invention of the mankind in the fabric industry. And thence is looked up with a great value of pride when put on.

Organza Fabric

Organza basically refers to a thin, plain weave, a sheer fabric which is made out of continuous filament of silk yarn worms. In modern fashion era many organzas are woven with synthetic filament fibers like nylon and polyester but most of the stylish organzas are woven in silk. The most popular item made of organza fabric are bags. Various designs and shapes of organza fabric bags are attracting people towards them. Adding a nice touch with sophistication and uniqueness Organza fabric is the choice of millions.

Lastex Fabric

Lastex fabric basically refers to an elastic fiber that is made from Latex. Moreover, lastex fabric is used with other complex fibers with a intent to made different fabrics like spandex and foundation garments.

Nylon Fabric

The term nylon is derived from the New York and London. Nylon is yet another form of synthetic fibre that is commonly used amidst the masses. Fabric composed of nylon, called nylon fibre is used in variety of uses like clothing, sheets, covers, and many other domestic and industrial appliances. Nylon fabric is preferred amidst all other fabrics as it is really strong and has a strong ability of stretchiness. High elasticity of nylon fabrics makes it prime use in like of luggage baggage, wallets and many more. In addition, nylon fabrics are easy to maintain as gets cleaned and dried without any special effort.

Nylon Fabrics are availed in the latest forms that are much more stiff and lighter in weight. Since it is highly durable, nylon fabric makes the cloth or the other long lasting and wears and tears resistant. Nylon is the polymer of amide, termed as polyamide extracted from the petroleum. Nylon is an easy product to manufacture as it needs less time and also lesser attention. That is indeed makes nylon fabrics a nice product to trade and make money. The increasing uses and popularity of Nylon fabrics have made the finest product to trade

Velvet Fabric

Velvet is one of the smoothest and softest amidst all the other kinds of fabrics. Velvets are specially manufactured and process because of its distinctive properties. Velvet fabrics are used in variety of appliances like clothing including trousers, shirts, and many more. Also, velvet fabric is used in bed sheets, covers, curtains and etc. Velvet fabric is no less than silk in any assessments whether be glossiness or be the unending glaze. Velvet fabric, due to its high class looks and price viability has made it the most preferred fabrics.

In the modern times, velvet fabrics are availed in the multifarious designs and colors. And also are stronger and elastic than the previous times. The newer velvet fabrics needs less maintenance and can be easily washed and dried. Use of modern innovations in the composition of the velvet fabrics have made it more easily accessible to the common masses. Today in the market, there are numerous brands for velvet fabrics, and many more are too coming. With the healthy competition in the market, brands are offering new designs and colors for the velvet fabrics and that too at the least rates. That is why; market considers the velvet fabrics industry safer and secure place for investment

Polyester Fabric

Polyester is a type of fabric that is not found naturally. The polyester fabric is man made. The polyester fabric is widely used in various applications and is very much in demand in markets. This fabric has various qualities due to those it is so popular like wrinkle resistance and springing back into its smooth shape. The polyester fabric is very strong and soft as well.

The polyester fabric can also be mixed with other fabrics to make a strong and durable fabric or to achieve any other motive. For example, In upholstery, polyester is generally blended with wool to eliminate crushing and reduce fading. There are various uses of polyester fabric like it is used in casement curtains, draperies, floor coverings, throw rugs, bedding, and as a cushioning or insulating material.

Taffeta Fabric

Taffeta fabric is a crisp, soft and smooth plain woven fabric which with its slight sheen manufactured out of different fibers like rayon, silk or nylon. Taffeta fabric is widely used in manufacturing of women's garments. The taffeta fabric has a unique rippled or wavy pattern which exhibits similarity to a water stain or mark, with dull and lustrous areas that reflect light differently.

The word 'Taffeta' has its origin from Persia, and means "twisted woven". It is generally made with a plain weave, fine warp yarns and heavier filling yarns. A good quality taffeta fabric represents the artwork in optimum manner.

Denim Fabric

Denim fabric is a rugged cotton twill. In denim fabric the weft passes under two or more than two warp fibers that produces the common diagonal ribbing which is identifiable on the back of the fabric. The diagonal ribbing separates the existence of denim fabric from cotton duck. The denim fabric is generally colored with indigo dye to create blue jeans though jean denoted a distinct lighter cotton textile.

Denim fabric is used at a large scale all over the world economies. Its vivid texture and ability to provide extreme comfort makes it one of demanding fashion entities all over. With blissful shopping experience, people are moving toward more purchasing new innovative designs of denim fabric.

Rayon Fabric

Rayon fabric is basically that synthetic textile fiber which is obtained by forcing a cellulose solution through fine spinnerets. In other words, rayon fabric is a final result of solidifying filaments. Rayon is a unique type of fabric that cannot be termed either a synthetic fabric or natural one. The process of making rayon is quite distinct; through which natural raw supplies are transformed to make it practical. Rayon is a fabric that can be woven or knit; further ensuring a versatile use. The efficiency of rayon fabric is comparatively much higher than taffeta or other cotton fabric. It is economical too. Apart from this, its soft texture makes rayon one of the most lovable fabrics. Rayon fabric is widely used in making of number of apparels and home furnishing items.

Spandex Fabric

Because of its great shape retention quality, spandex fabric is widely used as fashion fabric. The important point to note about spandex fabric is that it bounce back to its original structure even after stretching up to 600 times. Highly durable superior strength spandex fabric is resistant to dry heat and oil. Providing great comfort and flexibility it does not put on weight on the body of the wearer. With the characteristics like elasticity, retaining back to original shape, resistance to dry heat and abrasion, spandex fabric feel and fits better when blended and of course make one look better. With its great shape retention qualities, spandex is used in making undergarments and support hose. It creates a less confined feel and becomes more stronger and versatile piece of clothing. Providing resistance to perspiration and body oils spandex fabric is more stable and durable.

Georgette Fabric

Georgette is a sheer and strong silk or silk like clothing fabric that often comes with a dull, creped surface. In simple words, it is a sheer lightweight fabric that provides utmost comfort. This is fabric is usually made out of silk or polyester. As compared to chiffon, it is opaque and slightly heavy. If it comes to least expensive and much practical fabric then a large number of couture prefers georgette. Due to its exquisiteness and uniqueness, a georgette fabric proves a demanding item in the fashion industry.

Viscose Fabric

Since its invention, viscose is widely used for coating fabric. Its development with the passage of time has led to viscose being spun into thread for embroidery and trimmings. As the further development take place, viscose had entirely replaced the old wool and cotton and its being widely used for women's stocking and underwear.

Due to its perishable nature, viscose is often refused to be used in the manufacturing of solid objects like umbrella handles etc. Nowadays, viscose fabric is widely used for lining and furnishing because it provides the staple for towels and table-cloths.

Grey fabric Fabric

Due to its cost effectiveness, exquisiteness and longevity, grey fabric has been widely used for cloth manufacturing. Uniquely woven grey fabric has become increasingly popular in appreciation of increased market demand. Clothes made out of grey fabric can simply be termed as stunning in each and every aspect.

Showcasing immense aesthetics and revealing a tendency of glamor, clothes made using grey fabric are ruling the international market. A blissful shopping could be conducted with the availability of different textures, finishes and sizes of grey fabric.

Polypropylene Fabric

Polypropylene fabric is especially meant for winter seasons, because the only layer of hundred per cent polypropylene rib knit generally stays dry and due to this feature it keeps one's body warmer. A high quality lightweight polypropylene fabric is preferred in winter season because it is allows user to perform any moderate activity in cold weather at ease.

Polypropylene fabric basically consists of hydrophobic which relinquishes any possibility of moisture in such fabric and further its pushes the moisture vapor away from the skin. Entailing a large number of features, polypropylene fabric can simply be termed stunning in each and every aspect.

Satin Fabric

Satin fabric is also said to be the most elegant fabrics. The reason behind is its astonishing looks and smooth surface. Satin fabric is used in loads of apparels and many others things. Especially for women, satin fabric is used in variety of apparels like blouse, panties, gowns, and many more clothing. Also, satin fabric is used for bed sheets, curtains and many other decorative purposes. The glossiness of the satin fabric really makes the material high class. At top of that, satin fabric is availed in multifarious color options like black, red, green, purple, blue and etc.

Satin fabric is generally composed of silk or rayon and that is why it is so smooth. Also, satin fabrics are availed in various weights and normally are very light. Also, satin are very delicate and are manufactured with a great deal of care and attention. Satin fabrics needs a fine set up of manufacturing and processing unit as each and every strand of the satin fabric must be well knitted. Satin fabric s huge demand amidst the masses is not a new thing as has been the most demanded fabric since a long time. In the present too, with the innovative designer apparels, satin fabric usability range has expanded like never before.

Fabrics for Special Uses

Industrial Fabric

Industrial fabric is a fabric which is usually made from man-made fibers like fiberglass, carbon, and aramid fibers. It covers a wide variety of widths, weights and construction particularly made to meet a specific application. Industrial fabric are used for decorative purposes.

Industrial fabric is woven in various thicknesses and constructions in basic weave, namely plain, leno, satin, basket etc. It is primarily used for filtration, marine and recreational products, insulation, electronics, commercial & construction and protective garments etc.

Fiberglass Fabric

Fiberglass is a material that generally consists of extremely fine glass fibers and often used in manufacturing different products like fabric, yarns, insulators and structural objects.

Filter Fabric

A filter fabric is well known for its functionality and longevity. However a filter fabric is known for its high temperature and chemical resistance.

Carbon Fabric

Carbon fabric is generally used in different applications such as Brake linings, Aircraft interiors, Windmill blades, Tooling, Primary and secondary structures, Racing helmets and so on. Widely used in aerospace application, carbon fabric provides maximum degree of stiffness in aircrafts.

An exquisitely created carbon fabric is well known for its light weight and hight strength. A carbon fabric is also characterized by different types of features such as Fire resistant, Dimensionally stable, Lightweight, High strength etc.

Vinyl Fabric

It is well observed that a large number of vinyl fabrics satin and spot resistant. Vinyls fabric is generally created with ultraviolet stabilized pigments and this segment proves much crucial if one's application regarding vinyl fabric involves direct exposure to sunlight.

Plain Fabric

Plain fabrics are well known for their soberness and long lasting durability. Clothing made our of plain fabric can simply be termed as the most impressive and exclusive range of clothing available today. With the available different varieties of plain fabric, the choice is endless. Plain fabrics are also well known for their durability and cost effectiveness.

The clothing made using plain fabric is totally capable of impressing absolute anybody with its unique qualities and aesthetic appeal. A quality that along with its comfort, palin fabric clothes are extremely popular for leisure wear. Among the vast accumulation of available fabric, plain fabric is most popular fabric.

Blended Fabric

Blended Fabrics are the compositions of the strands extracted either from natural resources or artificially by treating chemicals. There are several kinds of fabric like synthetic fabric, natural fabric and many others. Blended fabric is the special form of the fabrics that constitutes two or more elements properties. The specialty of the blended fabric is that it is different in the composition and looks. Also, blended fabric is stiffer and resistant to any kind of depreciation by any means. There are many forms of the blended fabrics, lets have a look on them

- Silk blended fabric: Silk in the blended fabric makes it astonishing in looks and style. It raises the standards of the blended fabrics. Also, silk blended fabrics are known for their smoothness and nonpareil high quality.
- Jute blended fabric: jute is the finest example of the stiffness and durability. Hence the jute blended fabric is also stiffer and sustains the high quality for a longer period of the time. Also, jute blended fabric is used in various purposes as the fabric is capable of holding any kind of weight.
- Apart from the above there are several kinds of the blended fabric. Blended fabrics are scientifically approved and found appropriate for any kind of usability.

PTFE Fabric

A PTFE fabric is well renowned for its excellent non-stick surface that allows user to carry his work smoothly and efficiently. It is well observed that a PTFE fabric is resistant to tears and abrasions. Long lasting durable, PTFE fabric remains stagnant even at high temperatures. PTFE fabric is resistant from chemical, corrosion, and moisture.

The uniqueness and exquisiteness of PTFE fabric capable of impressing absolutely anybody. A high quality PTFE fabric has gained immense popularity in appreciation of increased market demand.

Crewel Fabric

A wide range of crewel fabric come from Kashmir in north-western India. Because of its versatility, a crewel fabric is widely used for the manufacturing of curtains, light upholstery, bedheads, cushions and bed covers and so on. Due to its longevity, exquisiteness and with its aesthetic appeal, crewel fabric has been ruling the international market.

The availability of crewel fabric in subtle lustrous color and rich texture makes it one of the most demanding items. A crewel fabric possess the capability to complement various types of body tones.

Stretch Fabric

Stretch fabric is a fabric referring to the normal fabric, which stretches in all four directions. Simplifying the construction of clothing stretches fabrics are commonly used in swimsuits. They were originally being used in the mid 1980s by large number of fashion designers. Entering mainstream market in the early 1990, Stretch fabrics are widely used in sports wear.

Sometimes Stretch fabric is also termed as Stretch woven fabric when it is blended with stable fiber of cotton, wool or synthetic. When it comes to talk about stretching, then Stretch fabric is very easy to Stretch in one or both directions presenting the traditional look and lot of comfort. Stretch fabric have better shape retention and are wrinkle resistance because of which they are more comfortable to wear.

Reflective Fabric

Reflective fabric is the nicest instance of the expanded usability of the fabrics. This has been all possible just because of the continuous innovation in the science field. Reflective fabric is known for their ability to reflect the light to the farthest distance possible. That is why; reflective fabric is used in countless usability, few of them are listed below:

- In the streets: - the reflectors and the alerts are made up of the reflective fabric. It is generally red in color as red has the largest ability to reflect. Also, it can be visible from the very long distance that makes the traffic flow smoothly. Especially in the night vision, reflective fabrics are proven to be the boon.
- Security- life jackets are made by the reflective fabrics. Also, other apparels are made by the reflective fabrics. Reflective fabrics help in notify the person in the crowd or any kind of situations. Coast guards and even police sometimes have their dresses made up of the reflective life jackets.

There are many other numerous usability of the reflective fibers, making it the finest fabrics that are great in durability and usability as well.

Quilted Fabric

Quilting is the art of covering the fabrics for frontal and back, both the sides. The fabrics composed by the sides are generally said to be the quilting fabric. Quilted fabrics are generally made for products like bags, clothing and mattresses. Quilted fabrics can blend any of the material like cotton, polyesters, silk and many more including the wool. Quilted fabrics have been in the daily uses since ages. With the time, quilted fabric has been innovated and modernized in its composition and designs as well. Quilted fabric is also available in countless colors and shapes. Especially, the variety in the quilted fabric can be witnessed in the jackets and mattresses.

Quilted fabric is now the new status symbol, as masses take a great matter of pride in owning. Apart from the glaze and astounding looks, other reasons of the popularity of the quilted fabric are its unlimited usability. Quilted fabrics are soft in nature and hence can be threaded easily. Also, needs less maintenance, as is easily washable and dryable. The quilted fabrics can sustain the original high quality for the longer period of time than nay other fabrics availed in the market. At top of that, luxurious looking quilted fabric is priced at the most affordable rates for the common people.

Polyethylene Fabric

Polyethylene fabric is a distinct fabric that is highly acclaimed in the domestic and industrial sectors. Polyethylene fabric is known for its unmatchable density and strength that is superior to all others. Polyethylene fabric is a type of a synthetic fabric that is manufactured in the labs. The polymerizing the ethylene results in the stiffer product called polyethylene that is later used for the fabric. Polyethylene fabric is used for loads of purposes:

- Domestic-polyethylene fabric is the finest replacement of the traditional fabrics for all kinds of bags. Polyethylene fabric is able to hold a lot more weight than previous ones. People like it as is very light and is wear and tear resistant. Also, it is highly elastic that makes it stretchy. It is used in various toys like jumping pads.
- Industrial-polyethylene fabric is used for machineries. Also, the tough woven fabric is used in the industries at the large scale. The newest technology in the polyethylene fabric has enhanced the usability of the fabric, like in manufacturing and packaging units.

Polyethylene fabric has many more purposes than above. That s why in the market, the demand of the polyethylene fabric is climbing day by day.

Narrow Fabric

Fabrics are something that we daily come across. With the clothing to the seats, the fabrics are the integral part of the lives. There are several sorts of the fabrics like synthetic fabrics, natural fabrics and many more depending upon their designs and usability. Narrow fabric is also the most commonly utilized fabrics in our daily lives.

Narrow fabrics are the thicker version of the fabrics as its strands are thicker and stronger. That is why; narrow strands are used in the things that are used for heavy duties. The narrow fabric is availed in mainly in the following forms:

- Laces- laces are used in shoes and many other tying purposes. Narrow fabrics in the laces make it strong and easy to grip on. In the recent times, there has been a revolution in the designs and shapes of the laces composed of narrow fabric. Now, laces, like ropes are commonly used in the daily appliances.
- Tapes- narrow fabrics are used to make the tapes. These tapes are great in appearance and stiff in the quality. These tapes are used for wrapping, decorating and many other purposes.

In the modern times, the usability of the narrow fabric has grown as it is light and has a splendid durability. That is why; narrow fabrics are hugely demanded in the global marketplace

Laminated Fabric

Sometimes the apparels, bags, beds are needed to be protected from the dust and other outer particles. This can be carried out through the laminated fabric, used to laminate all kind of clothing, sheets, covers, hand bags and many more. Laminated fabric safeguards the core thing from any kind of external particles that hampers the quality and the glaze. Lamination is carried our by the covering the material with the protective film on all the sides. That does not let water to pass through, making the material completely safe. However it is not completely air tight as moisture is allowed to let in the for the longer life of the fabrics.

Laminated fabric adds the durability and sustains the quality. In the recent developments, laminated fabric designs and shapes have been transformed with the undue assistance of the modern tools and techniques. Also, people have shown a great deal of zeal in the laminate fabrics because of its astounding glossiness and superior style. Today, laminated fabric is one of the prime fabrics used for the decoration and giving the interior a luxurious touch. In addition, the availability of the newest kind of the laminated fabric and those too at the most affordable prices has made it own by anyone

Flocked Fabric

Flocked fabrics are the fabrics composed of several fabrics. The combination of different elements makes the flocked fabric inherit all the nicest properties of them. The flocked fabric is greatly demanded in domestic and international market both making it the most money making fabric in the fabric industry. Flocked fabrics are manufactured and traded by the loads of the people as it is one of the fabrics that's demand is rising day and night. Also, the attractive offers for flocked fabrics have made consumers to make most of the profit.

The reason behind such a reputable fame is its unending usability. Flocked fabric is used in clothing of all kinds and also in many others purposes as well. Flocked fabrics are used in shirts, pants, trousers, inner garments and etc. in addition is used in laces and as other packaging threads as well. Flocked fabrics are known for their extraordinary gripping capabilities and since are the finest material to carve shoes or others. In seats, carpets, the flocked fabric is the best component as it is resistible all kinds of tribulations. Flocked fabric is availed in loads of nonpareil designs and shapes and can be shaped in any kind of moulds easily

Flame Resistant Fabric

Fire and many other casualties are very common in the daily lives. That is why people prefer fabrics that are flame resistible. The concept of the flame resistant fabric was possible due to the long research and experiments in the labs for several years. The first priority of the flame resistant fabric is that it should be convenient for the user. That means it should neither be too heavy nor too thin. Also, it should have a nice look that attracts the user. The good news is that such a high quality flame resistant fabric is now easily available. The latest flame resistant fabric is simply superb in faade and has the longest durability.

Flame resistant fabric is used in variety of apparel and many others like curtains, sheets and many more. The flame resistant fabric is composed of chemicals and other components that make it easily hold in any amount of heat and flame. Also, does not loose the glaze or the quality level for a longer period of time. With the awareness in the masses, flame resistant fabric is becoming globally apt clothing and for many other usability. Also, with the pleasant intrusion of the big brands in the flame resistant fabric, has made it the latest trend amidst masses especially younger generation.

Fabrics from Natural Fibers

Cotton Fabric

The fabric which is believed to be most soothing and safe is called as cotton fabric. Immense use of cotton fabric for infant s dresses or beddings is a live testimony of its softness and skin-friendliness. Cotton fabric has a distinctive feature that it adjusts easily with climatic requirements that is why it is called all-season fabric. In summer season cotton fabric keeps the body cool and absorbs the sweat easily whereas they give a warm feel if worn in winder season.

Silk Fabric

Silk counts to the strongest natural fabric in the world. Known for its softness, luster, beauty and luxurious look, silk fabric is one of the higher grade fabric providing comfort to the wearer in all types of weather. Keeping the body cool in summer and warm in winter, silk was discovered during 2640 B.C. in china. Today there are different variety of silk available in the market like Chiffon, Georgette, Organza, Crepe de Chine, Duponi, Noil, Pongee, Shantung, Tussar, etc. Because of its sheer variety of designs, weaving and quality, Indian silk textile are popular worldwide.

Silk fabric is mainly used for making luxurious and expensive dresses and home furnishings. Indian silk textile is popular worldwide whereas USA is the worlds leading manufacturer of silk products with France and Italy are also involved in the same line producing high value sophisticated silk fabrics in Europe.

Linen Fabric

Linen is called as king of natural fabric. Linen is extensively used for apparel making and home furnishing as well. Linen, being a natural fiber is considered to be safe for all types of skin. Linen fabric is also suggested for sensitive skin as its natural properties makes it resistant for allergies.

Linen fabric do not cause problems like irritation, allergic reaction etc. The natural fiber of linen makes it strong and durable. Linen is an easy maintainable fabric. No special treatments are required for linen; it can be simply washed by hands. Although linen is used for all kinds of clothing, yet mostly used for home furnishing items like table cloth, bedspreads, curtains etc.

Wool Fabric

Soft, strong and very durable wool fabric provide warmth and attractive appearance. It is the fabric which keeps the wearer dry while sweating and cool when it is hot. Wicking away perspiration from the body, wool fabric does not wrinkle easily and is resistant to dirt wear and tear. It is also having the quality of not burning when put over the flame, it only smolder. Felt made of wool fabric is used as covers for piano hammers. It is also used in absorbing odors and noise in machinery and stereo speakers. Wool fabric is being used for clothing for over twelve thousand years does not only come from sheep only, whereas widely used kashmiri sweaters are made from goats.

Wool fabric is equipped with different characteristics like warm, resists to wrinkle, wear and tear, it is light weight and durable which also absorbs moisture. Have been largely used in blankets and carpets, today almost every wardrobe contains garment made of woolen fabric.

Leather Fabric

Comfortable in both hot and cold condition, leather fabric is not affected by surrounding temperature. Adding a classic luxury, pleasant to touch and comfortable, leather fabric is soft , elastic and firm. Leather fabric is blessed with the quality of absorbing water vapor without loosing dryness and retaining to the original shape when stretched.

Ramie Fabric

Ramie fabric having characteristics like moisture absorption, air permeability are valued as a summer fabric which are not harmed by mild acid and are resistant to alkali.

Hemp Fabric

Highly versatile hemp fabric is used in countless number of products like shoes, furniture, apparel, accessories and home furnishing. Hemp fabric is a fabric which is commonly known for its warmth, softness and durability. Providing beautiful lusture, hemp fabric is best for making apparel which can withstand harsh conditions and last longer. UV protected apparel fabric have an insulative quality that allows clothing to be cool in summer. Having characteristics like durability, absorption, insulation, apparel fabric withstand water better then any other textile product. It is obtained from stem of the plant, the finest hemp fabric is produced in Italy. Acting as a great choice for comfortable work clothes, home decoration, hemp fabric is also used in the manufacturing of clothing, curtains, draperies, upholstery, bedspreads, table linens, sheets, dish towels, canvas, etc.

Jute Fabric

Being among the strong and durable fabric, jute fabric is ideally being used as bags or sacks for packing since aging. The jute fabric is much soughed item for fashionable clothes, home furnishing and fashion accessories. Bangladesh counts to the largest cultivator of jute fabric with India as the second largest jute goods manufacturer.

The most important use of the jute fabric is in the manufacturing of carpets, linoleum, cordage and twines. It is sometimes used as webbing to cover inner springs of the auto seats. Sometimes used as fashion accessory used for fashion garments, tapestries, soft luggage, etc.

Elements of Art

Elements of art are the basic properties of a work of art that may be perceived through the senses. In a painting, for instance, the properties that may be perceived through our senses are texture, form, shape, color, line and value (tone). Other elements, for instance sound and time, may be perceived in other art forms such as music and video. The way the elements of an artwork relate to each other and are organised in the artwork are referred to as the principles of art.

Texture

The texture is the quality of a surface, often corresponding to its tactile character, or what may be sensed by touch. Texture may be used, for example, in portraying fabrics. It can be explicitly rendered, or implied with other artistic elements such as lines, shading, and variation of color.

Space

Space is the area provided for a particular purpose. Space includes the background, foreground and middle ground. Space refers to the distances or areas around, between and within things. It has two kinds: negative and positive.

Shape

Shape pertains to the use of areas in two-dimensional space that can be defined by edges, setting one flat specific space apart from another. Shapes can be geometric (e.g.: square, circle, hexagon, etc.) or organic (such as the shape of a puddle, blob, leaf, boomerang, etc.)

Shapes are defined by other elements of art: Space, Line, Texture, Value, Color, shape, form.

Color

Color pertains to the use of hue in artwork and design. Defined as primary colors (red, yellow, blue) which cannot be mixed in pigment from other hues, secondary colours (green, orange, violet) which are directly mixed from combinations of primary colors.

Tone/Value

Value, or tone, refers to the use of light and dark, shade and highlight, in an artwork.

Line

Line is defined as a mark that spans a distance between two points (or the path of a moving point), taking any form along the way. As an art element, line pertains to the use of various marks, outlines and implied lines in artwork and design, most often used to define shape in two-dimensional art work.

Design Elements and Principles

Design elements and principles describe fundamental ideas about the practice of good visual design.

Design Elements

Design elements are the basic units of a painting, drawing, design or other visual piece and include:

Line

A line is a fundamental mark or stroke used in drawing in which the length is longer than the width. Two connected points form a line and every line has a length, width, and direction if it is straight.

Uses:

- A line that defines or bounds an edge, but not always the outside edge, could represent a fold or color change.
- A line that defines the edge of space can also be created by a gap of negative space. Many uses include to separate columns, rows of type, or to show a change in document type.

- Lines are used in linear shapes and patterns to decorate many different substrates, and can be used to create shadows representing tonal value, called hatching.

Color

Color can play a large role in the elements of design with the color wheel being used as a tool, and color theory providing a body of practical guidance to color mixing and the visual impacts of specific color combination.

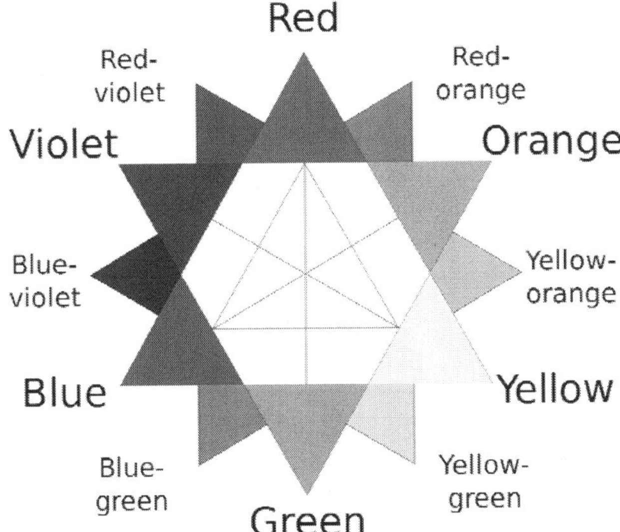

Figure: *Color star containing primary, secondary, and tertiary colors.*

Uses

- Color can aid organization so develop a color strategy and stay consistent with those colors.
- It can give emphasis to create a hierarchy

Attributes

- Hue
- Values and tints and shades of colors that are created by adding black to a color for a shade and white for a tint. Creating a tint or shade of a color reduces the saturation.
- Saturation gives a color brightness or dullness.

Shape

A shape is defined as an area that stands out from the space next to or around it due to a defined or implied boundary, or because of differences of value, color, or texture. All objects are composed of shapes and all other 'Elements of Design' are shapes in some way.

Categories

- Mechanical Shapes or Geometric Shapes are the shapes that can be drawn using a ruler or compass. Mechanical shapes, whether simple or complex, produce a feeling of control or order.
- Organic Shapes are freehand drawn shapes that are complex and normally found in nature. Organic shapes produce a natural feel.

Texture

Meaning the way a surface feels or is perceived to feel. Texture can be added to attract or repel interest to an element, depending on the pleasantness of the texture.

Types of texture

- Tactile texture is the actual three-dimension feel of a surface that can be touched. Painter can use impasto to build peaks and create texture.
- Visual texture is the illusion of the surfaces peaks and valleys, like the tree pictured. Any texture shown in a photo is a visual texture, meaning the paper is smooth no matter how rough the image perceives it to be.

Most textures have a natural feel but still seem to repeat a motif in some way. Regularly repeating a motif will result in a texture appearing as a pattern.

Space

In design, space is concerned with the area deep within the moment of designated design, the design will take place on. For a two-dimensional design space concerns creating the illusion of a third dimension on a flat surface:

- Overlap is the effect where objects appear to be on top of each other. This illusion makes the top element look closer to the observer. There is no way to determine the depth of the space, only the order of closeness.
- Shading adds gradation marks to make an object of a two-dimensional surface seem three-dimensional.
- Highlight, Transitional Light, Core of the Shadow, Reflected Light, and Cast Shadow give an object a three-dimensional look.

- Linear Perspective is the concept relating to how an object seems smaller the farther away it gets.
- Atmospheric Perspective is based on how air acts as a filter to change the appearance of distance objects.

Form

Form is any three dimensional object. Form can be measured, from top to bottom (height), side to side (width), and from back to front (depth). Form is also defined by light and dark. There are two types of form, geometric (man-made) and natural (organic form). Form may be created by the combining of two or more shapes. It may be enhanced by tone, texture and color. It can be illustrated or constructed.

Principles of Design

Principles applied to the elements of design that bring them together into one design. How one applies these principles determines how successful a design may be.

Unity

According to Alex White, author of *The Elements of Graphic Design*, to achieve visual unity is a main goal of graphic design. When all elements are in agreement, a design is considered unified. No individual part is viewed as more important than the whole design. A good balance between unity and variety must be established to avoid a chaotic or a lifeless design.

Methods

- Proximity
- Similarity
- Continuation
- Repetition
- Rhythm is achieved when recurring position, size, color, and use of a graphic element has a focal point interruption.
- Altering the basic theme achieves unity and helps keep interest.

Balance

It is a state of equalized tension and equilibrium, which may not always be calm.

Types

- Symmetry
- Asymmetrical produces an informal balance that is attention attracting and dynamic.

- Radial balance is arranged around a central element. The elements placed in a radial balance seem to 'radiate' out from a central point in a circular fashion.
- Overall is a mosaic form of balance which normally arises from too many elements being put on a page. Due to the lack of hierarchy and contrast, this form of balance can look noisy.

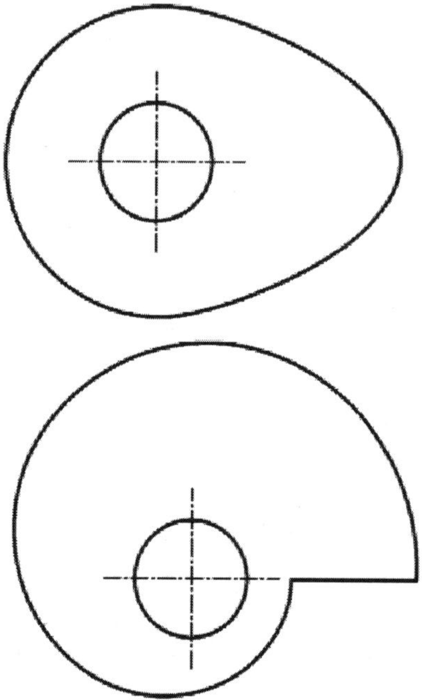

Figure: *The top image has symmetrical balance and the bottom image has asymmetrical balance*

Hierarchy

A good design contains elements that lead the reader through each element in order of its significance. The type and images should be expressed starting from most important to the least.

Scale/Proportion

Using the relative size of elements against each other can attract attention to a focal point. When elements are designed larger than life, scale is being used to show drama.

Dominance/Emphasis

Dominance is created by contrasting size, positioning, color, style, or shape. The focal point should dominate the design with scale and contrast without sacrificing the unity of the whole.

Similarity and Contrast

Planning a consistent and similar design is an important aspect of a designers work to make their focal point visible. Too much similarity is boring but without similarity important elements will not exist and an image without contrast is uneventful so the key is to find the balance between similarity and contrast.

Similar Environment

There are several ways to develop a similar environment:

- Build a unique internal organization structure.
- Manipulate shapes of images and text to correlate together.
- Express continuity from page to page in publications. Items to watch include headers, themes, borders, and spaces.
- Develop a style manual and stick with the format.

Contrasts

- Space
  - o Filled / Empty
  - o Near / Far
  - o 2-D / 3-D
- Position
  - o Left / Right
  - o Isolated / Grouped
  - o Centered / Off-Center
- Form
  - o Simple / Complex
  - o Beauty / Ugly
  - o Whole / Broken
- Direction
  - o Stability / Movement
- Structure
  - o Organized / Chaotic
  - o Mechanical / Hand-Drawn
- Size
  - o Large / Small
  - o Deep / Shallow
  - o Fat / Thin

- Color
  - o Grayscale / Color
  - o Light / Dark
- Texture
  - o Fine / Coarse
  - o Smooth / Rough
  - o Sharp / Dull
- Density
  - o Transparent / Opaque
  - o Thick / Thin
  - o Liquid / Solid
- Gravity
  - o Light / Heavy
  - o Stable / Unstable

Movement is the path the viewer's eye takes through the artwork, often to focal areas. Such movement can be directed along lines edges, shape and color within the artwork.

Looms and Loom Mechanisms

A loom is a device used to weave cloth. The basic purpose of any loom is to hold the warp threads under tension to facilitate the interweaving of the weft threads. The precise shape of the loom and its mechanics may vary, but the basic function is the same.

The word "loom" is derived from the Old English "geloma" formed from ge-(perfective prefix) and loma, a root of unknown origin; this meant utensil or tool of any kind. In 1404 it was used to mean a machine to enable weaving thread into cloth. By 1838 it had gained the meaning of a machine for interlacing thread as in weaving, knitting or lacemaking. In Greek mythology, the loom was the symbol of Athena, and in Roman, Minerva.

Weaving

Weaving is done by intersecting the longitudinal threads, the warp, i.e. "that which is thrown across", with the transverse threads, the weft, i.e. "that which is woven".

The major components of the loom are the warp beam, heddles, harnesses or shafts (as few as two, four is common, sixteen not unheard of), shuttle, reed and takeup roll. In the loom, yarn processing includes shedding, picking, battening and taking-up operations. These are the principal motions.

- Shedding. Shedding is the raising of part of the warp yarn to form a shed (the vertical space between the raised and unraised warp yarns), through which the filling yarn, carried by the shuttle, can be inserted. On the modern loom, simple and intricate shedding operations are performed automatically by the heddle or heald frame, also known as a harness. This is a rectangular frame to which a series of wires, called heddles or healds, are attached. The yarns are passed through the eye holes of the heddles, which hang vertically from the harnesses. The weave pattern determines which harness controls which warp yarns, and the number of harnesses used depends on the complexity of the weave. Two common methods of controlling the heddles are dobbies and a Jacquard Head.

Shuttles:

- Picking. As the harnesses raise the heddles or healds, which raise the warp yarns, the shed is created. The filling yarn in inserted through the shed by a small carrier device called a shuttle. The shuttle is normally pointed at each end to allow passage through the shed. In a traditional shuttle loom, the filling yarn is wound onto a quill, which in turn is mounted in the shuttle. The filling yarn emerges through a hole in the shuttle as it moves across the loom. A single crossing of the shuttle from one side of the loom to the other is known as a pick. As the shuttle moves back and forth across the shed, it weaves an edge, or selvage, on each side of the fabric to prevent the fabric from ravelling.
- Battening. Between the heddles and the takeup roll, the warp threads pass through another frame called the reed (which resembles a comb). The portion of the fabric that has already been formed but not yet rolled up on the takeup roll is called the fell. After the shuttle moves across the loom laying down the fill yarn, the weaver uses the reed to press (or batten) each filling yarn against the fell. Conventional shuttle looms can operate at speeds of about 150 to 160 picks per minute.

There are two secondary motions, because with each weaving operation the newly constructed fabric must be wound on a cloth beam. This process is called taking up. At the same time, the warp yarns must be let off or released from the warp beams. To become fully automatic, a loom needs a tertiary motion, the filling stop motion. This will brake the loom, if the weft thread breaks. An automatic loom requires 0.125 hp to 0.5 hp to operate.

Types of Looms

Back strap loom: A simple loom which has its roots in ancient civilizations comprising two sticks or bars between which the warps are stretched. One bar is attached to a fixed object and the other to the weaver usually by means of a strap around the back. On traditional looms, the two main sheds are operated by means of a shed roll over which one set of warps pass, and continuous string heddles which encase each of the warps in the other set. The weaver leans back and uses his body weight to tension the loom. To open the shed controlled by the string heddles, the weaver relaxes tension on the warps and raises the heddles. The other shed is usually opened by simply drawing the shed roll toward the weaver. Both simple and complex textiles can be woven on this loom. Width is limited to how far the weaver can reach from side to side to pass the shuttle. Warp faced textiles, often decorated with intricate pick-up patterns woven in complementary and supplementary warp techniques are woven by indigenous peoples today around the world. They produce such things as belts, ponchos, bags, hatbands and carrying cloths. Supplementary weft patterning and brocading is practiced in many regions. Balanced weaves are also possible on the backstrap loom. Today, commercially produced backstrap loom kits often include a rigid heddle.

Warp-weighted Loom

The warp-weighted loom is a vertical loom that may have originated in the Neolithic period. The earliest evidence of warp-weighted looms comes from sites belonging to the Starèevo culture in modern Hungary and from late Neolithic sites in Switzerland. This loom was used in Ancient Greece, and spread north and west throughout Europe thereafter. Its defining characteristic is hanging weights (loom weights) which keep bundles of the warp threads taut. Frequently, extra warp thread is wound around the weights. When a weaver has reached the bottom of the available warp, the completed section can be rolled around the top beam, and additional lengths of warp threads can be unwound from the weights to continue. This frees the weaver from vertical size constraints.

Drawloom

A drawloom is a hand-loom for weaving figured cloth. In a drawloom, a "figure harness" is used to control each warp thread separately. A drawloom requires two operators, the weaver and an assistant called a "drawboy" to manage the figure harness.

Handloom

Elements of a foot-treadle floor loom

1. Wood frame
2. Seat for weaver
3. Warp beam- let off
4. Warp threads
5. Back beam or platen
6. Rods – used to make a shed
7. Heddle frame - heald frame - harness
8. Heddle- heald - the eye
9. Shuttle with weft yarn
10. Shed
11. Completed fabric
12. Breast beam
13. Batten with reed comb
14. Batten adjustment
15. Lathe
16. Treadles
17. Cloth roll- takeup

A handloom is a simple machine used for weaving. In a wooden vertical-shaft looms, the heddles are fixed in place in the shaft. The warp threads pass alternately through a heddle, and through a space between the heddles (the shed), so that raising the shaft raises half the threads (those passing through the heddles), and lowering the shaft lowers the same threads—the threads passing through the spaces between the heddles remain in place.

Flying Shuttle

The flying shuttle was one of the key developments in the industrialization of weaving. It allowed a single weaver to weave much wider fabrics, and it could be mechanized, allowing for automatic machine looms. It was patented by John Kay (1704–c. 1779) in 1733.

Before the Flying Shuttle

In order to understand the importance of this invention, it is useful to review the action of weaving prior to it. In a typical frame loom, the operator sits with the newly woven cloth before him or her. Using treadles or some other mechanism, the heddles are raised and lowered to open the shed in the warp threads. The operator must then reach forward, holding the shuttle in one hand, and pass it through the shed; the shuttle carries a bobbin for the weft. The shuttle must then be caught in the other hand, the shed closed, and the beater pulled forward to push the weft into place. This action (called a "pick") requires a lot of bending forward over the fabric; more importantly, however, the coordination between the throwing and catching of the shuttle requires more than one operator if the width of the fabric exceeds that which can be reasonably reached across (typically 60 inches (150 cm) or less).

How the Flying Shuttle Works

- Watch video #1: Demonstration of fly shuttle

In one respect, the term is somewhat misleading, as the shuttle itself is only a component in a new system attached to the loom as part of the beater. A board called the "race" runs along the front of the beater, from side to side, forming a track on which the shuttle runs. At each end of the race, there is a box which catches the shuttle at the end of its journey, and which contains a mechanism for propelling the shuttle on its return trip. The shuttle itself has some subtle differences from the older form. The ends of the shuttle are bullet-shaped and metal-capped, and the shuttle generally has rollers to reduce friction. The weft thread is made to exit from the end rather than the side, and the thread is stored on a pirn (a long, conical, one-ended, non-turning bobbin) to allow it to feed more easily. Finally, the flying shuttle is generally somewhat heavier, so as to have sufficient momentum to carry it all the way through the shed.

In manual operation, a cord runs to each box from a handle held by the operator. To start the pick, the shed is opened as before; however, instead of throwing the shuttle, the operator jerks the cord for the box containing the shuttle. This causes the mechanism in the box to shoot the shuttle along the race to the other box; then the shed is closed and the beater is used to complete the pick as before. The operator does not need to touch the shuttle until it needs to be reloaded, so fabrics of great width can be woven; but more importantly, the movements needed are greatly reduced.

Even more important was the fact that this mechanism could be automated and powered; all the operator needed to do was monitor the machine for failures and keep it supplied with pirns of weft thread, a job that was simplified with the invention of the Northrop Loom, which reloaded the shuttle automatically. Kay's son developed a modification that allowed the use of an array of different shuttles.

Social Effects

The increase in production due to the flying shuttle exceeded the capacity of the spinning industry of the day, and prompted development of powered spinning machines, beginning with the spinning jenny and the waterframe, and culminating in the spinning mule, which could produce strong, fine thread in the quantities needed. These innovations transformed the textile industry in Great Britain. All were attacked as threats to the livelihood of spinners and weavers, and Kay's patent was largely ignored. It is often incorrectly written that Kay was attacked and fled to France, but in fact he simply moved there to attempt to rent out his looms, a business model that had failed him in England. The flying shuttle itself produced a new source of injuries; if deflected from its path, it could be shot clear of the machine, potentially striking workers. Turn of the century injury reports abound with instances in which eyes were lost or other injuries sustained, and in several instances (for example, an extended exchange in 1901) the British House of Commons was moved to take up the issue of installing guards and other contrivances to reduce these injuries.

Obsolescence

The flying shuttle dominated commercial weaving through the middle of the twentieth century. By that time, other systems began to supplant it. The heavy shuttle was noisy and energy-inefficient (since the energy used to throw it was largely lost in the catching); also, its inertia limited the speed of the loom. Projectile and rapier looms eliminated the need to take the bobbin/pirn of thread through the shed; later, air- and water-jet looms reduced the weight of moving parts further. Flying shuttle looms are still used for some purposes, and old models remain in use.

Hand weavers could only weave a cloth as wide as their armspan. If cloth needed to be wider, two people would do the task (often this would be an adult with a child). John Kay (1704–1779) patented the flying shuttle in 1733. The weaver held a picking stick that was attached by cords to a device at both ends of the shed. With a flick of the wrist, one cord was pulled and the shuttle was propelled through the shed to the other end with considerable force, speed and efficiency. A flick in the opposite direction and the shuttle was propelled back. A single weaver had control of this motion but the flying shuttle could weave much wider fabric than an arm's length at much greater speeds than had been achieved with the hand thrown shuttle. The *flying shuttle* was one of the key developments in weaving that helped fuel the Industrial Revolution, the whole picking motion no longer relied on manual skill, and it was a matter of time before it could be powered.

Haute-lisse *and* Basse-lisse *Looms*

Looms used for weaving traditional tapestry are classified as *haute-lisse* looms, where the warp is suspended vertically between two rolls, and the *basse-lisse* looms, where the warp extends horizontally between the rolls.

Inkle Weaving

Inkle weaving is a type of warp-faced weaving where the shed is created by manually raising or lowering the warp yarns, some of which are held in place by fixed heddles on a loom known as an inkle loom. Inkle weaving was referred to in Shakespeare's *Love's Labour's Lost*. It was brought to the United States in the 1930s, but predates this by many centuries in other countries. The term "Inkle" simply means "ribbon" or "tape" and probably refers to a similarly structured woven good that could have been made on different types of looms, such as a box-loom.

Inkle weaving is commonly used for narrow work such as trims, straps and belts.

Equipment

Inkle looms are constructed in both floor and table-top models. Either model is characterized by a wooden framework upon which dowels have been fastened. These dowels will hold the warp threads when the loom has been dressed. One of the dowels, or a paddle, is constructed so that its position can be adjusted. This tensioning device will be taken in as weaving commences and the warp threads become shorter. Additional equipment includes yarn of the weaver's choice, yarn or thread for forming heddles and a shuttle to hold the weft. A notebook is also handy for charting weaving diagrams.

Process

The inkle loom is threaded with warp threads according to the weaver's design, alternating between yarn that can be raised and lowered and yarn that is secured in place through the use of the heddles. The raising and lowering of these warp threads creates the shed through which the weft thread will be carried on a shuttle. The weaver should make one pass with the shuttle with each opening of a shed through the raising and lowering of threads.

A simple raising and lowering of threads creates a plain-weave band in which warp threads are slightly offset. Weft threads are only visible at the edges of the band and the weaver may wish to take this into account by warping threads that will form the edges in the same color as the weft.

As the weaving commences, the warp threads will shorten on the loom and the weaver will need to adjust the tension periodically. As the inkle band progresses, it will also get closer to the heddles. The weaver will also need to advance the warp thread along the bottom of the loom to open up new weaving space. In her book "Inkle Weaving," Helene Bress recommends loosening the tension when you are ready to advance the warp. Once you have done so, tighten the tension again and resume your weaving.

There are other more advanced techniques in which, instead of merely allowing warp threads to alternate in their up or down positions, individual threads are brought to the surface to form what is called a "pick up" pattern. One side of the band will show the exposed surfaces of warp threads while, on the other side of the pattern, the weft thread will be visible. Using a supplemental weft thread that will come up over the top of certain warp threads, brocaded designs can also be worked into the inkle band.

An inkle loom is also useful in the practice of tablet weaving for its added portability. Simply thread the warp onto the loom but use cards instead of alternating between free-hanging and heddle-secured yarn.

Uses for Inkle Weaving

The narrow bands that inkle weaving forms are ideal for use as belts, trims, straps, ribbons, or garment hem decorations, for instance. The many varieties of color and pattern are limited only by the weaver's imagination. Some modern uses include guitar straps and camera straps, colorful shoelaces, and there have been recent sightings of inkle bands as canoe tie-down straps.

3

Traditional Looms

Several other types of hand looms exist, including the simple frame loom, pit loom, free-standing loom, and the pegged loom. Each of these can be constructed, and provide work and income in developing societies.

The Simple Frame Loom

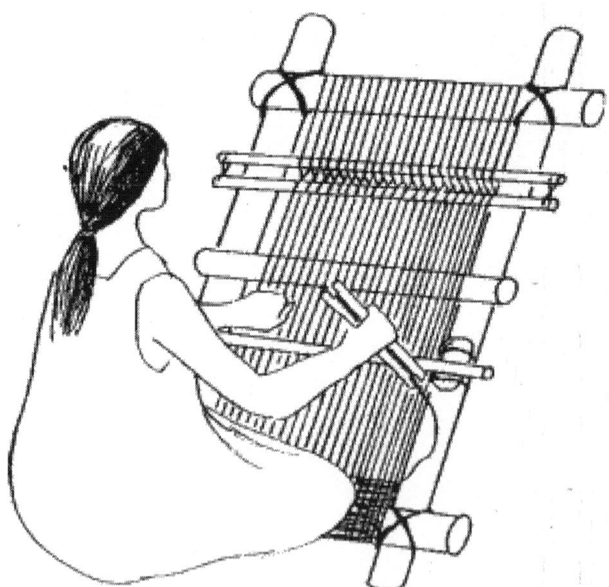

No dimensions are given since there is no real limit on the size of the loom. The smallest practical size, however, is probably about 30cm in either direction. While it is possible to build looms smaller than 30cm, it is not practical because weaving narrower than 30cm can be done on the 30cm framework. Therefore, loom size can vary from one made small enough to hold in the lap (30 by 60cm is a good size) or large enough to weave a room size rug. Such large-size looms must be worked by several weavers at one time.

Materials Needed

For the frame: Two (2) sturdy pieces of wood(*) slightly larger than the desired width of the finished cloth. These will be horizontal pieces of the frame (AB and CD).

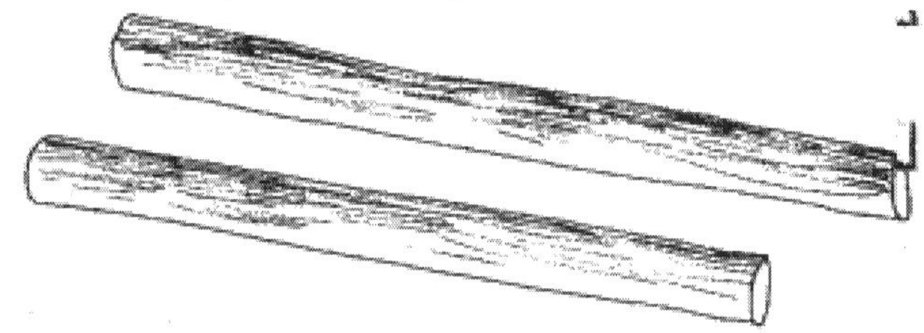

Two (2) sturdy pieces of wood(*) slightly longer than two thirds the desired length of the finished cloth. These will be the vertical pieces (EF and GH).

(*) NOTE: This wood and any other wood used for this loom need not be commercial lumber. Tree limbs with the bark removed may be used instead.

Lashing or Nails to join the frame.

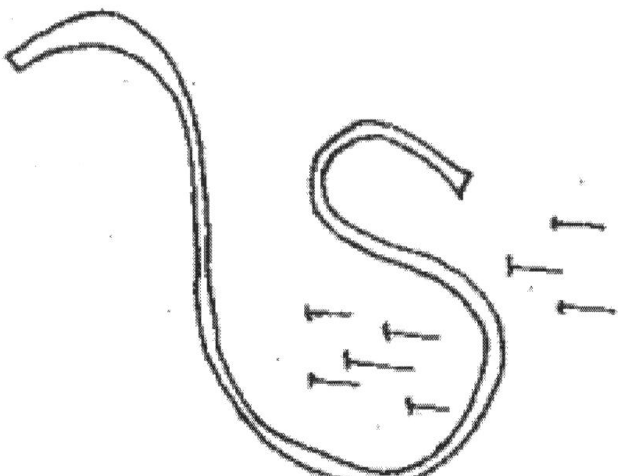

For the heddle: One (1) strong stick, the width of the loom frame.

A length of cotton or synthetic cord (such as is used in fishnets) about four (4) times the width of the loom.

Two (2) blocks of wood or two (2) flat

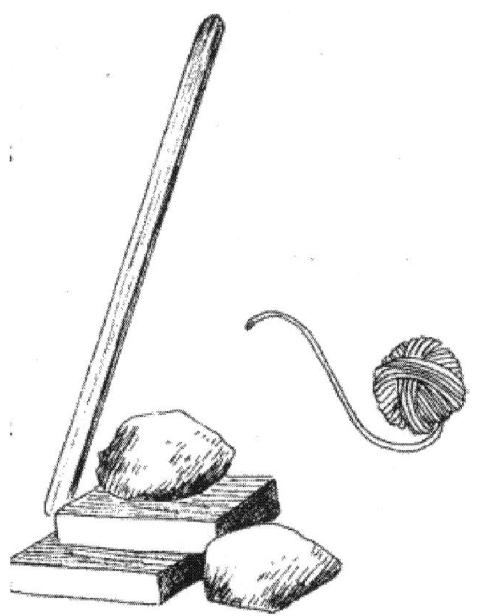

For the shed stick:

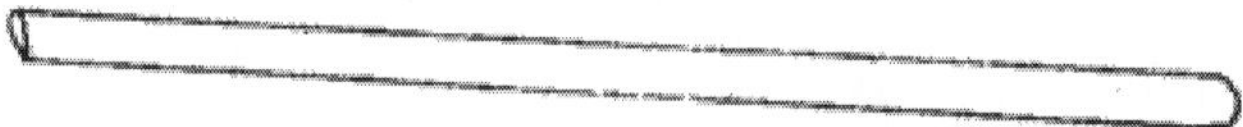

One (1) rounded piece of wood, the width of the loom. For looms between 30 and 60cm wide, it should be about 4cm in diameter; for looms between 60 and 120cm wide, 8cm in diameter; for looms between 120 and 180cm wide, 12cm in diameter, and so on. Increase 4cm for every 60cm in width.

For lease sticks:

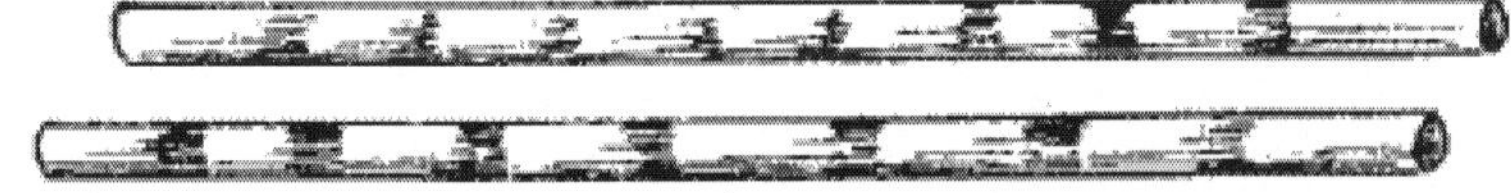

Two (2) lightweight poles, such as reed or bamboo, the width of the loom.

Tools and supplies: Hammer Drill Sharp Knife Sandpaper Oil for Wood

Before beginning to build, please note the following:

1. The wood used must be as straight as possible and well-seasoned so it will not warp during use.
2. Smooth and sand the wood so there are no rough spots that will catch the thread or yarn.

3. Oil the wood rather than use paint or varnish. Oil keeps the wood from drying and cracking, and provides a smooth renewable finish for the yarn to move against.
4. The top and bottom crosspieces (called the cloth and warp beam on the foot-powered loom) must be at right angles to the warp threads and parallel to each other. Measure carefully during construction to make sure they are parallel.

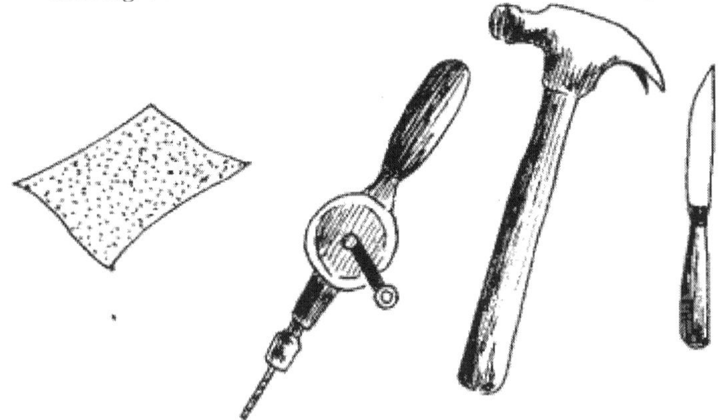

Construction

A. Prepare wood pieces

1. Remove bark if necessary
2. Sand and smooth rough places
3. Oil wood to prevent splitting

B. Build the Frame

1. Join the four pieces of wood to make a rectangular frame.
2. The pieces AB and CD (width) should overlap the pieces EF and GH (length) as shown in the illustration. AB and CD must be on top of EF and GH.
3. Lash or nail the joints together so that the pieces do not move and are at right angles to each other—as shown below left.

C. Prepare the Heddle Stick

1. About 2 to 3cm in from each end of the stick cut a groove 0.3cm deep completely around the circumference.

D. Prepare the Lease Sticks

- About 2cm in from the ends of each stick, drill a hole completely through to the other side. The hole should be large enough to put a piece of string through

Set Up the Loom for Weaving

Before setting up the warp, you may wish to read Chapter 7 , Weaves, Patterns and Finishing Touches. This may help you choose a weave and/or a pattern to set up. Plain weave or a basket weave and/or a striped or plaid pattern are recommended for your first weaving attempt.

A. Warp the Loom

1. Gather the warp into a ball, or in the case of very stiff fibres, into an easily undone skein.
2. Tie one end of the warp, in an easily undone knot such as a half-hitch, to the far inside corner of crosspiece AB (as shown above).

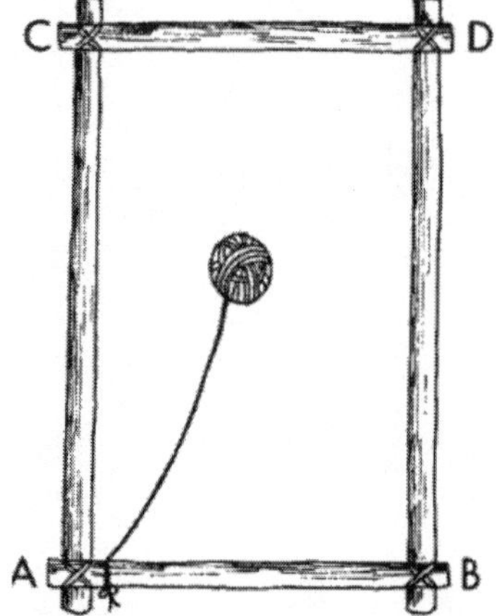

3. Unwind a small length of warp and bring it up and around crosspiece CD (as shown).

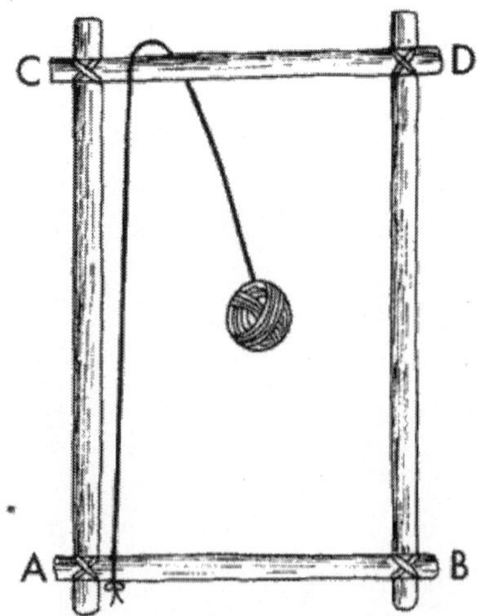

4. Bring the warp down and around AB in the same direction you started as illustrated at bottom left.
5. Continue Steps 2 thru 4 until the desired number of warp threads is reached.

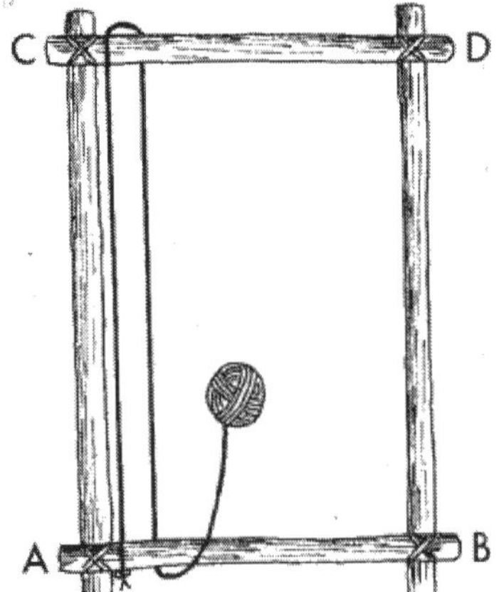

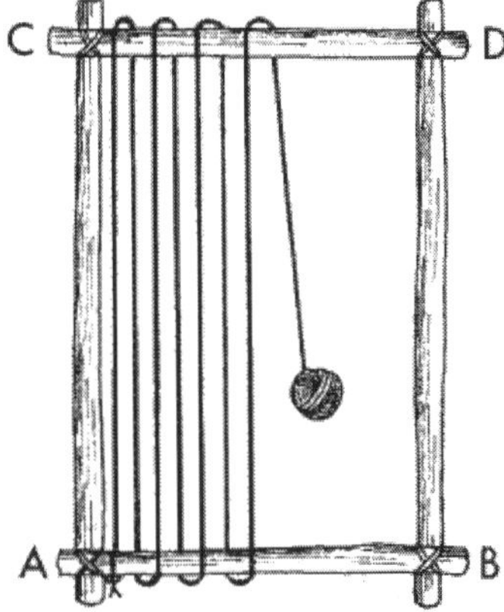

6. Untie the beginning end and join with a square knot to the other end, so that they stretch diagonally across the back of the loom.

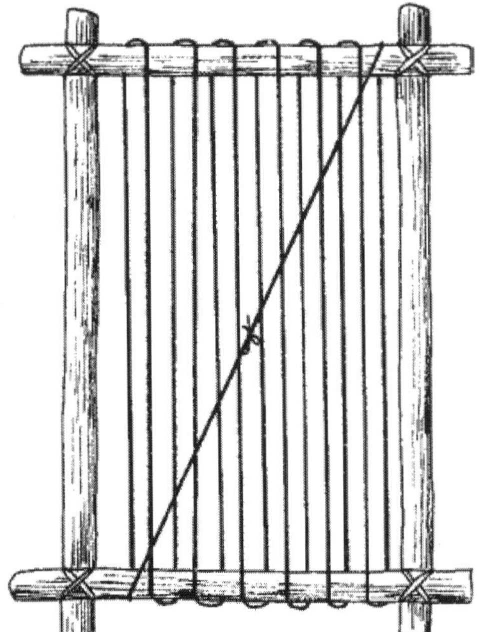

7. Make sure all the warp threads are stretched as taut as possible.

Note: If your pattern calls for several different colour warp threads, such as in a plaid, start warping as indicated in Steps 1 through 4, and then:

a. When the desired number of the first colour warp is reached, do not cut off the extra warp but set aside the whole ball of remaining warp still attached to the loom.
b. Pick up a ball or skein of the next colour.
c. Tie the end of the new colour to AB using a half-hitch.
d. Wrap the new colour around as described in Steps 2 thru 4.
e. When the desired number of threads have been wound, set aside this ball like the first; do not cut it off.
f. Start the next colour in the same way. If you must repeat a colour, just pick up the original ball of that colour, pull it taut and continue winding.
g. When all the required warp is wound around the frame, untie all the beginning ends from AB and hold them in one hand.
h. Pick up the free ends of all the colours of warp and tie both groups together using a square knot. On very wide looms it may be necessary to tie the ends in several groups.

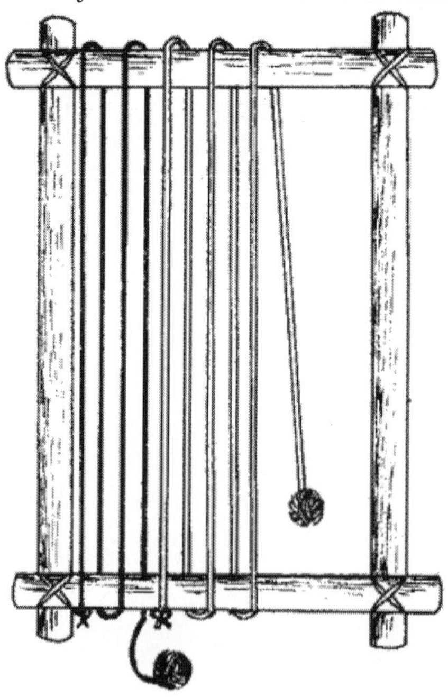

Your Loom is Now Warped

B. Place the Shed Stick on the Loom:

Note: Look at the warped loom frame. Notice that there is one set of warp threads on the top side and another set on the bottom. If you grabbed all the warp on one side and pulled on it, the warp would slide around the loom, so that the side that was in back moves to the front, or top. This is a continuous warp—there is no beginning and no end. In the following directions, you will be attaching the working parts to the loom. They must be attached only to the top side of the warp, so that the warp will continue to slide around freely. When the warp is referred to as being lowered or raised, this refers only to the top warp threads.

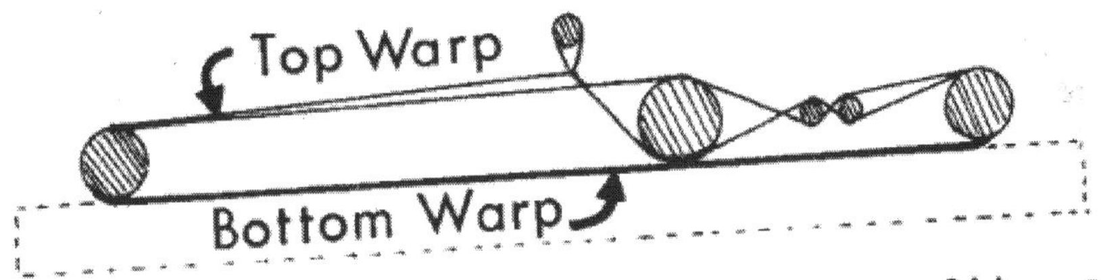

1. Lay the loom flat on a table or the ground.
2. Place the shed stick across the middle of the loom, at right angles to the warp threads.
3. Weave the stick in and out of the top warp threads, going over and under every other top warp for Plain Weave. If you are using another weave check for the proper order.
4. This shed stick will be left in place during the entire weaving process, but it should be free to slide up and down the loom at right angles to the warp.

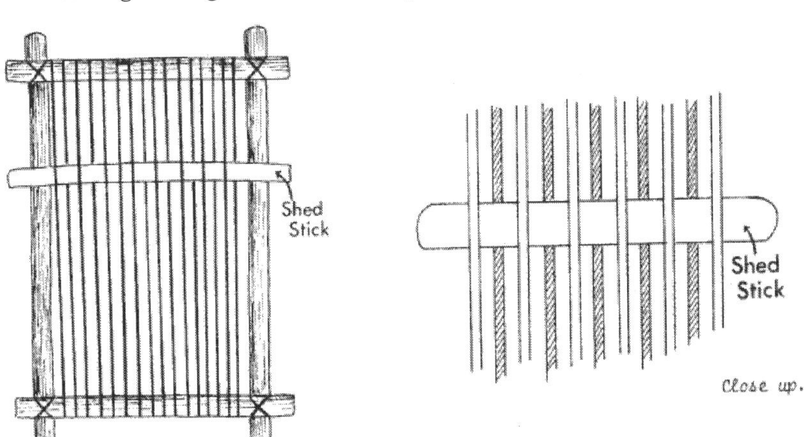

C. Place the Lease Sticks on the Loom

1. Take one of the lease sticks and place it above the shed stick, going over and under the same top warp threads as did the shed stick. (Loom should still be lying flat on ground.)
2. Push this stick towards the top of the loom or crosspiece CD as shown above.

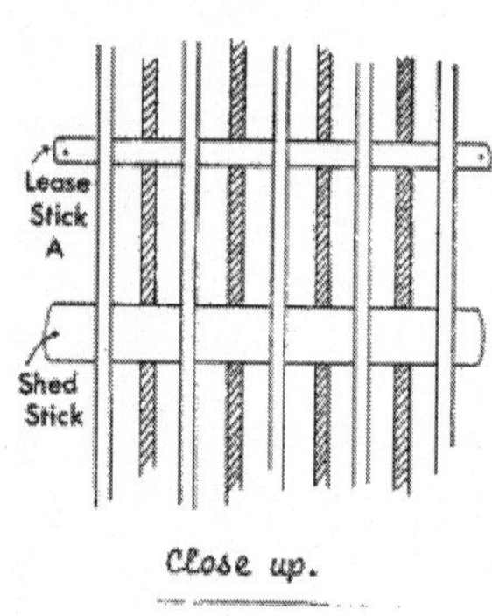

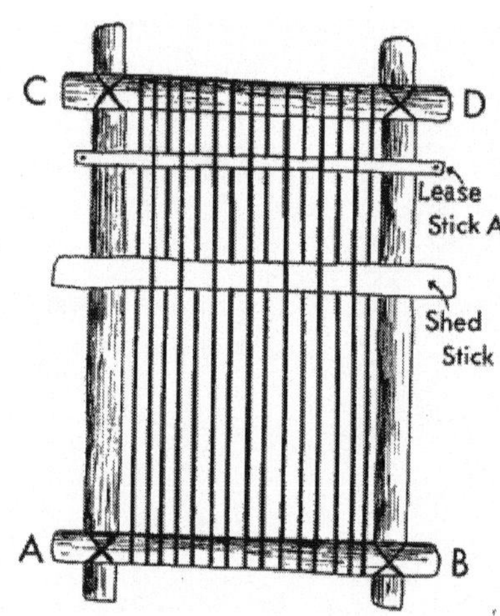

3. Take the other stick and place it in the space between the shed stick and the other lease stick as shown below.
4. Weave the second stick in and out of the top warp, going under the warp threads lowered by the shed stick, and over the ones raised by it. This will tighten the warp on the loom.
5. Slide the two lease sticks together until they are 4 to 8cm apart.

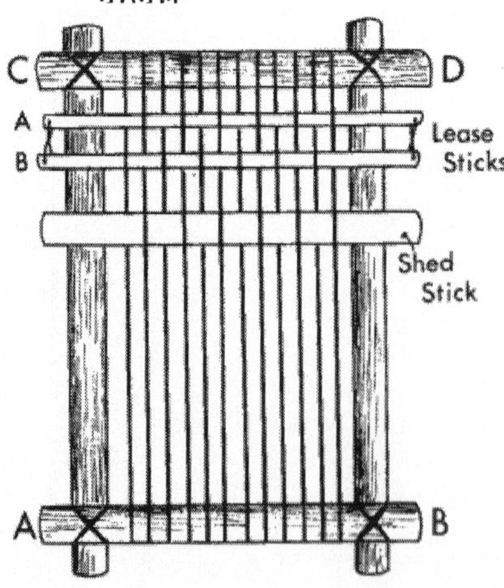

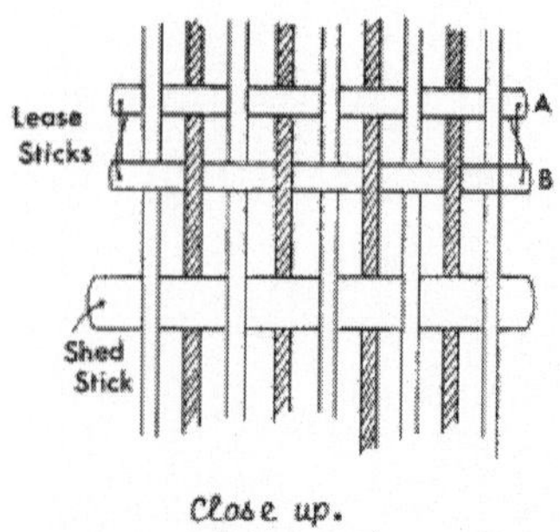

6. Tie them together by putting a string through the holes at each end and tying as illustrated (left) using a square knot. This will keep the sticks together and prevent them from slipping sideways.

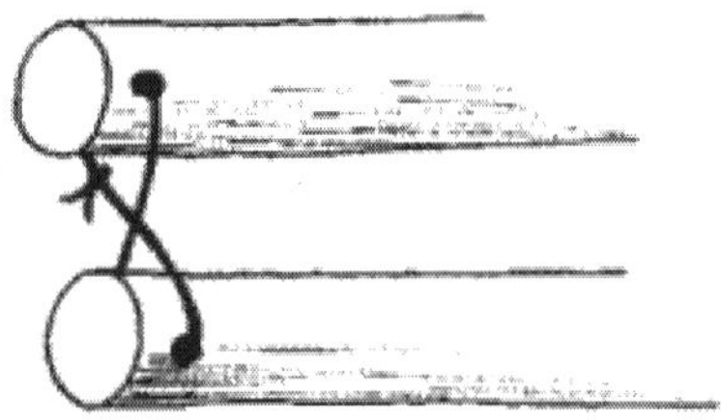

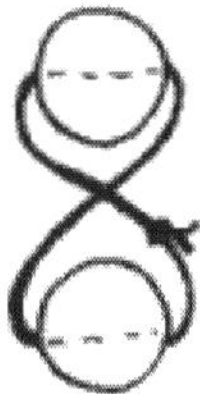

D. Make the Heddle

1. With the loom still lying flat on the ground, lay the heddle rod across the lifted top warp threads that are in front of the shed stick as shown.

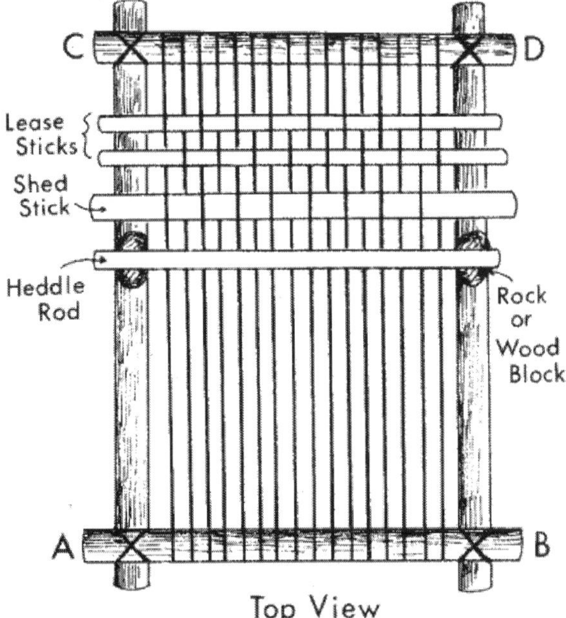

Top View

2. Move the heddle rod closer to the shed stick so that the bottom edge of the heddle stick is even with the top edge of the shed stick. Check this by looking at the loom from the side. The heddle rod should still be resting directly on the raised top warp threads.
3. Place a block of wood or a flat ended stone of the right size at each end of the heddle stick so that the heddle remains at the same height as the shed stick. If the loom will be used on the lap or in an upright position lash the blocks or stones to the frame. Do not permanently fasten them, however, as the heddle rod must move up and down the loom during weaving. A simple lashing that can be untied easily works best. On small looms tape can be used.

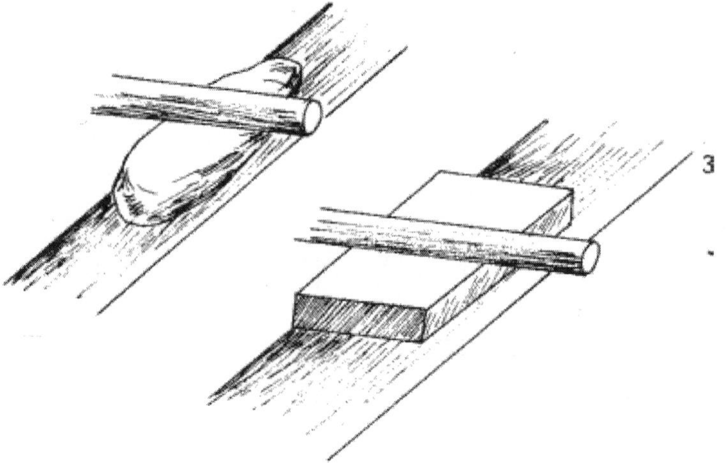

4. Tie the end of the cord of string in the groove at one end of the heddle stick.

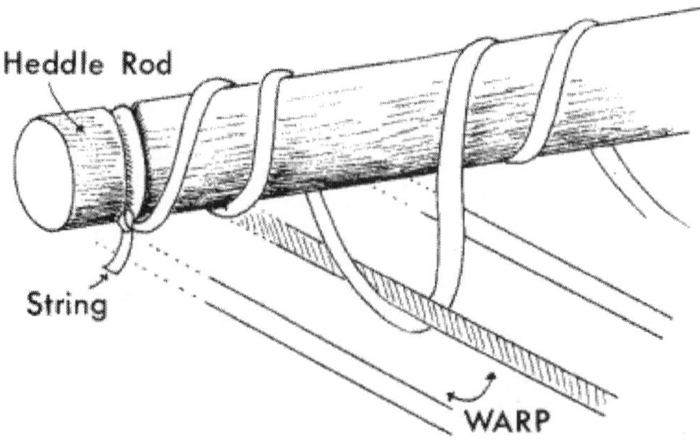

Note: The next Steps 5, 6, 7 and 8 describe the process of attaching the heddle to the warp. Read the directions through and study the illustrations before beginning. Remember that raised and lowered warp refers to the top warp only.

5. Loop the cord once completely around the heddle stick, bring the end of the cord down, under the first lowered warp thread and then back up between the same two raised warp threads.

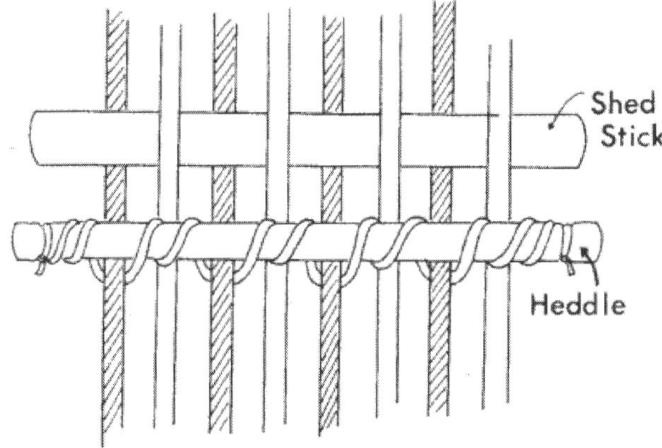

6. Continue the cord over the heddle stick again, and then repeat the process of going between the two raised warp threads, under a lowered one, back up between the same two warps and over and around the heddle stick.
7. As each lowered warp thread is looped by the cord, pull the lowered warp up to the same height as the raised warp threads.
8. Repeat the above process until all the lowered top warp threads are raised to the same height by the cord. Tie the end of the cord in the groove at the other end of the heddle stick.

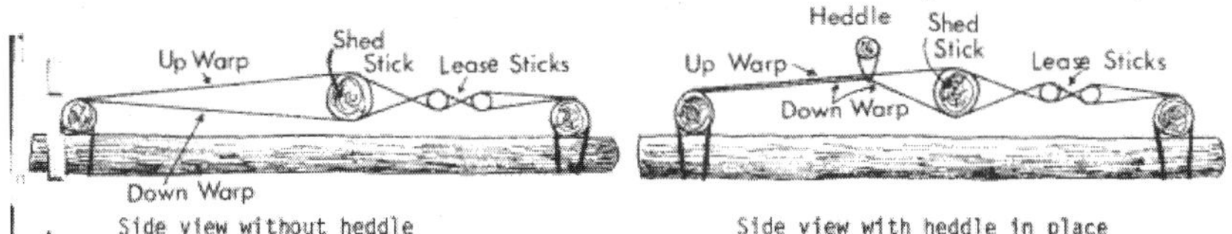

Side view without heddle

Side view with heddle in place

E. Check the Position of Heddle and Shed Stick

1. Position the heddle stick relative to the shed stick so that there is enough room for your fist behind the heddle rod.
2. Press down on the warp behind the heddle with your fist.
3. This should create a shed or space in front of the heddle and between the top warp threads that is large enough to pass your shuttle through.

4. Lift up on the warp threads behind the heddle using your fingers and palm. This should also create a shed big enough for the shuttle.
5. If your shuttle does not fit through easily, adjustments can be made in the size of the shed by moving the heddle and shed stick either further apart or closer together.

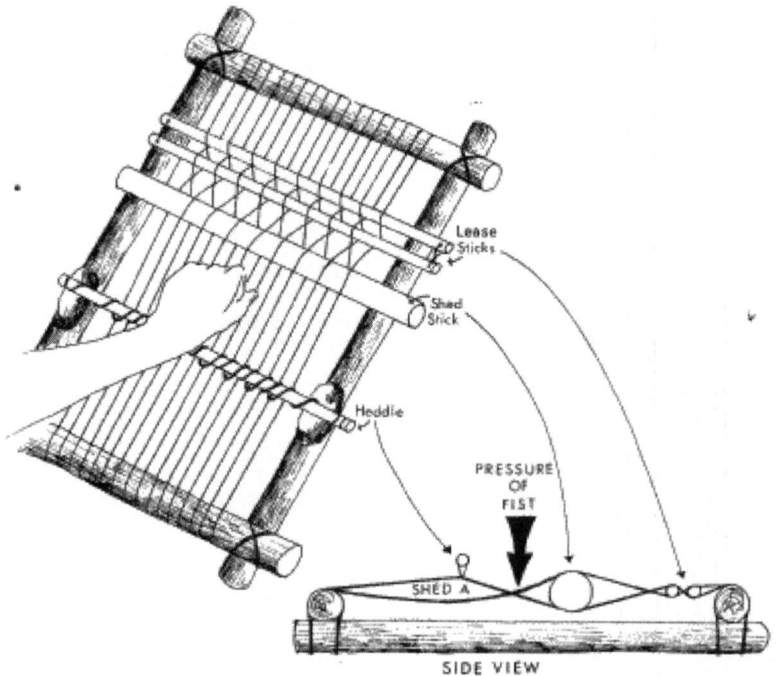

F. Positioning the Loom

1. Depending on the size and shape of the loom it can be used in one of three positions:
   1) Held on the lap
   2) Leaned against a wall or tree, the weaver either sitting on the ground or a stool, or if the loom is tall, standing.
   3) Laid flat on the ground. As the weaving progresses the weaver can sit on the finished cloth.

You Are Now Ready to Weave

How to Weave on a Frame Loom

You will need a Beater, Shuttle and a Stretcher to help you weave. Consult Chapter 6, "The Weaver's Tools" for directions for making these and other helpful tools.

Steps in Weaving

1. Wrap weft on to shuttle.
2. Press down on warp behind heddle with fist.
3. Slide shuttle into shed created in front of heddle.
4. Move fist to next section of warp, press down and slide shuttle along.

   Note: On very large looms you may prefer to use a piece of wood instead of your hand.
5. Repeat this process until shuttle has reached other side of the loom. With practice you will develop a steady rhythm.

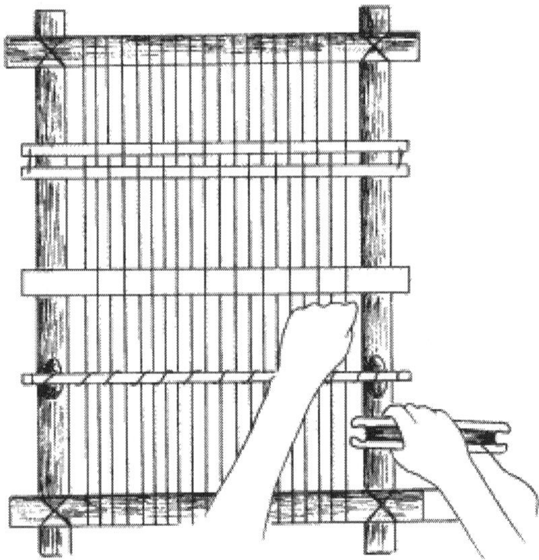

6. Pull shuttle out and beat weft tightly into place with a Beater.
7. Repeat from Step 3, but start at the other side of the loom and instead of pressing down on the warp, lift it up using the fingers and palm.

   Note: On very large looms you may prefer to use a piece of wood instead of your hand.
8. Beat the weft in after each row. Remember to alternate each row - one pushing down, one pulling up.
9. After you have woven about 10cm of fabric, put a Stretcher in position as shown in illustration at left.
10. Continue weaving until you reach the heddle and can no longer fit the shuttle through the shed.

11. Release the tension on the warp by removing the blocks or rocks holding the heddle rod. Holding the finished weaving on both sides, pull down slowly and steadily so that the finished cloth moves down and under the bottom crosspiece AB.

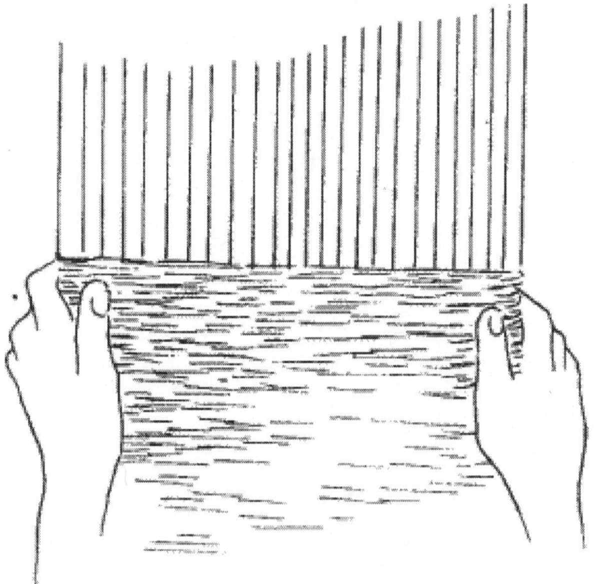

12. Adjust the position of the heddle, shed stick and lease sticks so that the shed is the proper size.
13. Weave as before on the new warp.
14. When you reach the top beam of the loom with the lease sticks and shed stick you can advance the warp by pulling down on all the warp threads so that the finished woven cloth moves under the bottom beam and around to the back side of the loom.

    The unwoven warp will slide over the top beam to the front. Adjust the diagonal warps so they are parallel on the front side. (They will remain twisted on the back) Move the heddle, shed stick and lease sticks into proper position and continue weaving.
15. When the weaving can be advanced no further, or the cloth is the desired length, the weaving is finished.
16. Cut the warp so that there is an equal length of extra warp threads on both ends of the cloth. Remove from loom and tie ends to prevent unraveling.

Variations of the Simple Frame Loom

The Pegged Loom: This loom is suitable for places where the weaver can work outside or where dwellings have earthen floors.

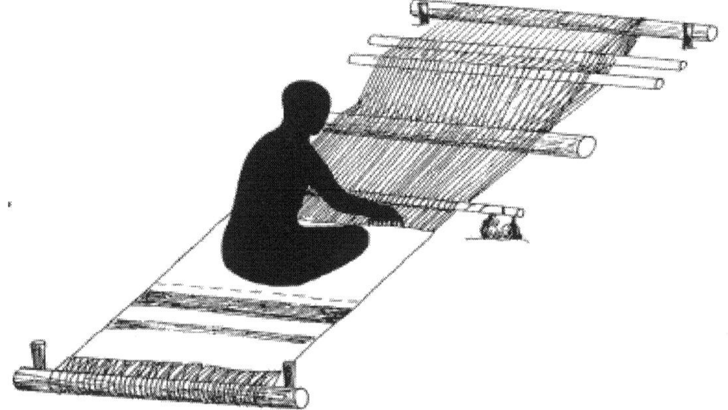

Materials Needed: Same as Frame Loom except instead of four crosspieces only two are needed. These should be slightly longer than the desired width of cloth.

Prepare the materials as described for the frame loom.

Warp the Loom

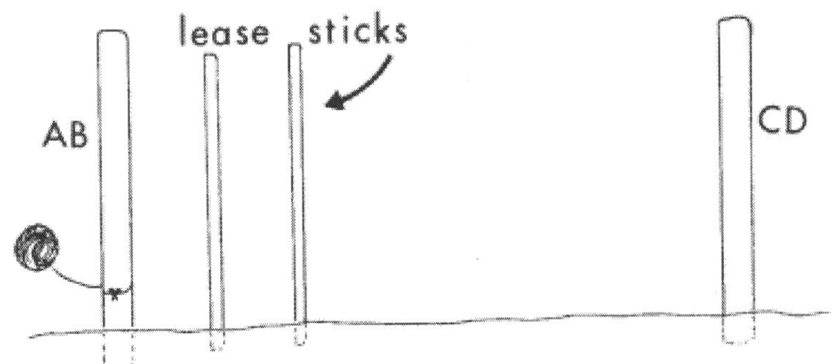

1. Put the two crosspieces upright in the ground, slightly farther apart than the desired length of the weaving.
2. Place the two lease sticks upright in the ground, between the two crosspieces and about 30cm apart.
3. Tie the end of the warp to one crosspiece. Wrap the warp around the four uprights as shown, until the desired number of warp threads are reached.

   Each warp thread is tied to the loom separately.

4. Untie the first warp end and tie it to the other end.
5. Taking care to keep the warp in place, pull up the crosspieces and lease sticks carefully from the ground and lay them flat where the weaving will be done.

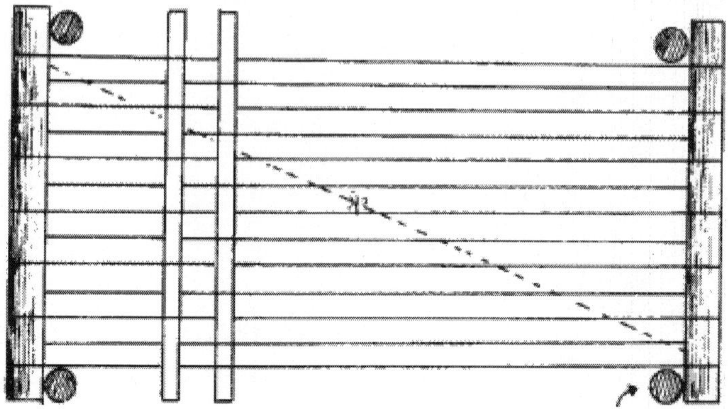

6. Drive stakes on the inside ends of each crosspiece. Make sure the warp is stretched tightly.

   Note: An important difference between the Frame Loom and the Pegged Loom is that the Pegged Loom does not have a continuous warp. This means that all the warp threads both top and bottom will be picked up by the shed stick and heddle as the weaver works.

Place the Shed Stick on the Loom

1. This is done the same way as the Frame Loom except all the warp threads are used.

The Lease Sticks

The sticks are already in position because of the way the loom was warped.

The Heddle:

1. The heddle is put into position the same way as on the Frame Loom.
2. The blocks or stones that support the heddle will rest on the ground, since there is no frame.
3. When looping the lowered warp with the cord, remember to pick up all lowered warp threads.

How to Weave on a Pegged Loom

Weaving progresses in much the same way as it does on the Frame Loom—except that the warp does not move. Instead, as the cloth approaches the heddle, the heddle, shed stick and lease sticks are moved back. The weaver moves forward by sitting on the finished weaving.

The Foot-Powered Loom

There are two versions of the Foot-Powered Loom presented here. Directions are given first for building the frames for the Pit Loom (which can be fixed to a wall or ceiling) and the Free-Standing Loom. Instructions for constructing the moveable parts and for warping and weaving on the looms follow and are the same for both of these foot-powered looms.

Dimensions: Height: 120cm or height from floor to ceiling Width: 100cm Length: 200cm

length of warp held: 200 to 3600cm

width of finished weaving: 2 to 100cm

Materials Needed:

For the Frame of both wall-mounted and ceiling-mounted types:

Four (4) appropriately shaped forked tree branches at least 15cm in diameter at the base, and at least 60cm in length from the base to the bottom of the fork. Commercial lumber, 5x20x75 with a notch cut out as indicated, may be substituted.

For the Frame of the wall-mounted type only:

One (1) forked tree branch at least 15cm in diameter at base and 120cm long. Commercial lumber 5x20x120cm with a notch cut out as indicated, may be substituted.

A. Find a Site:

This loom is permanently built into the house or other building. Locate so that it will not interfere with other activities and where the weaver will be comfortable while working.

1. Locate the loom in a building with an earthen floor. After the loom is constructed the floor may be cemented over.
2. Place the front of the loom in such a way that light from a door or window will come from the weaver's side or over his or her shoulder.
3. Leave clear access to both ends of the loom from at least one side.
4. Build a loom supported by a wall so that one of the long sides of the loom runs along the wall.

5. Build a loom supported by the ceiling so that there is a beam about midway over the loom from which to hang the harnesses.

B. Prepare the Wood:

1. Remove bark
2. Sand and smooth any rough places or edges
3. Put wood preservative on the bases of the five forked posts
4. Oil the wood to prevent splitting

C. Erect the Frame:

1. Mark off a rectangle one meter wide by two meters long on the floor where the loom will be located.
2. Dig a hole in each of the four corners. The hole should be about 30cm deep.
3. Place the four short forked posts in the holes and fill the earth firmly around them. Clay or mixed clay soils will provide the firmest base. Make sandy soils firmer by adding clay or cement.

D. Build the Pit:

1. Mark off a second rectangle 20cm in from the front of the loom, 60cm wide, 80cm long.
2. Dig the pit 40 to 50cm deep, about the length of the weaver's leg from the back of the knee to the sole of the foot.

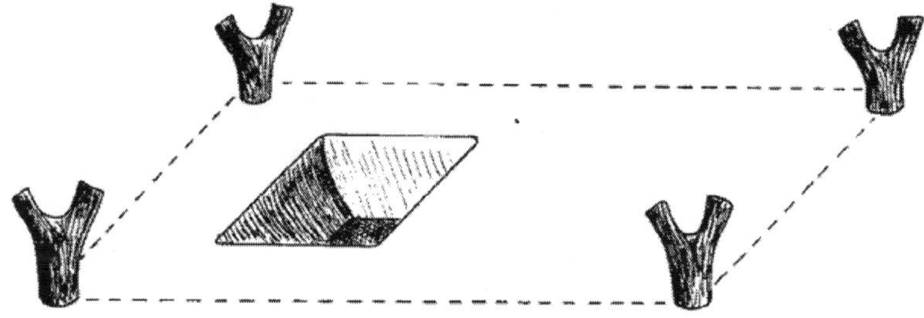

E. Attach the Wall-Supports for the Wall-Supported Type

1. Dig a hole 30cm deep midway along the outside edge of the rectangle.
2. Place the end of the 120cm forked post in hole and fill as described earlier.
3. Place the meter length of wood in the fork and push until it touches the wall. It should be parallel to the ground and at right angles with the wall. Mark the wall where it touches.
4. Remove pole and make a hole in the wall at that spot, the same diameter as the stick.

5. Put pole back into the fork and push until it is firmly in the wall.
6. Seal with plaster or cement.

The Wall Supported Frame is Now Complete.

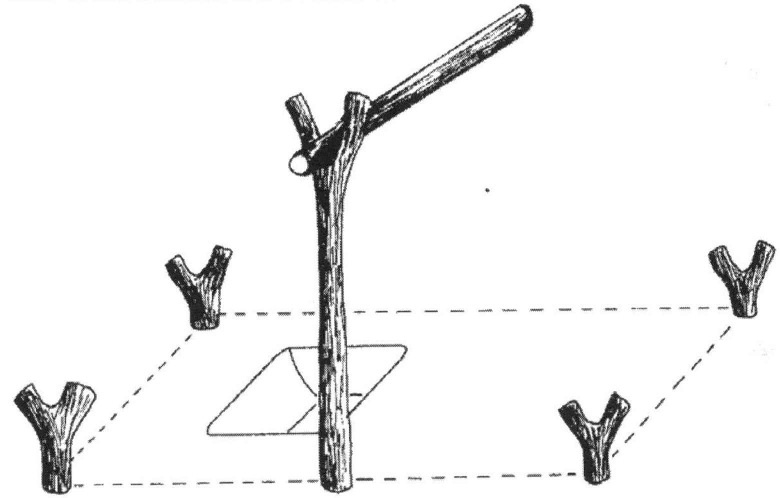

Optional: If desired the floor and pit can be coated with a smooth layer of cement.

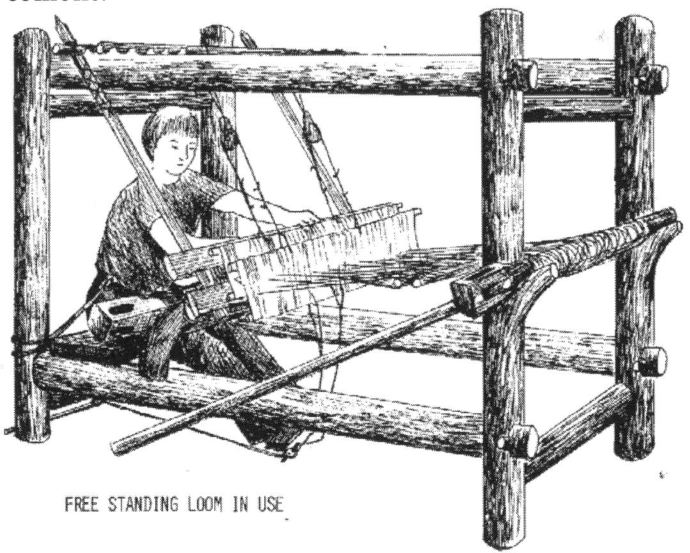

FREE STANDING LOOM IN USE

Dimensions:

Height: 130cm

Width: 98cm

Length: 200cm

length of warp held: 200 to 3600cm

width of cloth woven: 2 to 90cm

Saw 26

Tools and supplies:

Hammer Sandpaper

Drill Wood Glue

Wood Screws

Rasp Oil for Wood

Screwdriver

Materials Needed:

For Frame: (Letters are used to identify pieces in text)

(A) Four pieces of wood - 110cm long, 6cm in diameter OR 4x6x110

(B) Four pieces of wood - 132cm long, 8cm in diameter OR 8x8x132

(C) Two pieces of wood - 5x10x30

(D) Two pieces of wood - 200cm long, 8cm in diameter OR 6x8x200

(E) Two pieces of wood - 4x9x30cm

(F) Two pieces of wood - 200cm long, 6cm in diameter OR 3x6x200

(G) Two pieces of wood - 3x4x55

(H) One board - 32x110, thickness ranging from 2 to 5cm

(J) Two poles or sticks - 110cm long, 2cm in diameter

Fourteen (14) wooden pegs or dowels 15cm long, 3cm in diameter

Free-Standing Loom Construction

A. Prepare the Wood

1. Remove bark of unmilled tree limbs
2. Sand and smooth all rough spots and edges
3. Oil wood to prevent splitting

B. Build the Frame (all dimensions in centimeters)

1. Trim both ends of pieces A as illustrated.
2. Cut four slots in each of the four B pieces using the dimensions indicated. Slots must go completely through piece.
3. Shape piece C as illustrated. Drill hole as diagramed. Sand inside until smooth.

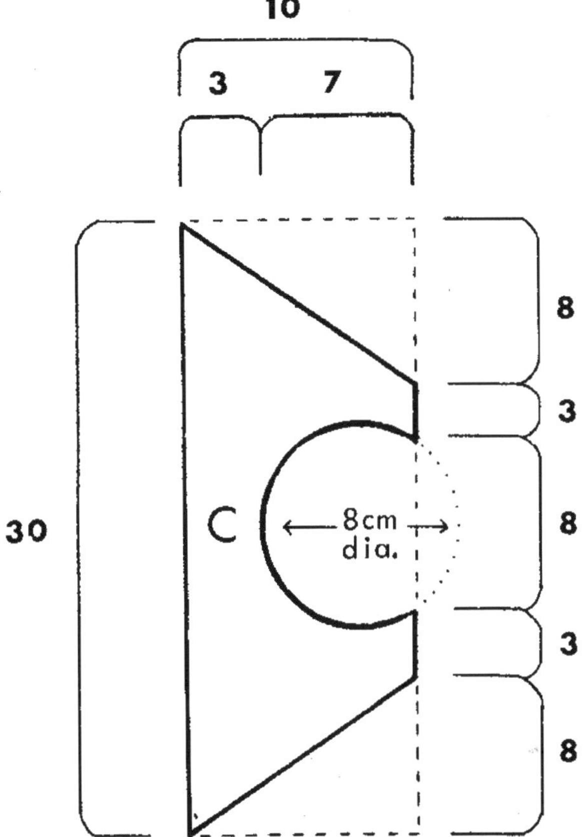

4. Trim ends of piece D as illustrated. Cut a slot 2x7cm 32cm in from one end of each piece D. Slot should be 7cm long.
5. Trim bottom ends of E as shown. Cut out notch as shown on pattern. Sand inside until smooth.
6. Trim ends of each piece F as illustrated.

C. Join the Frame

1. Attach each piece C to piece B in the position diagramed using two wooden pegs and glue.
2. Place the trimmed end of piece E in the slot in piece D. The notch must face toward the shorter end as shown.

   Glue and peg in place. Make sure it is securely attached: this piece undergoes great stress during weaving.
3. Place pieces A into the corresponding slots of pieces B. Note the position pieces C in illustration glue and screw together.

4. Place the trimmed ends of D and F into the appropriate slots in pieces B. Hammer them so that the trimmed end projects as far as possible.
5. Drill a hole 2cm in diameter, as close as possible to the crosspiece at each point where the trimmed ends project.
6. Taper the remaining eight pegs so that they are 3cm at the top and 2cm at the bottom.
7. Drive the tapered peg into the drilled holes.
8. Place Piece H, the seat, between the end of the loom and piece E.

D. Make and Attach the Rod Holder

1. Cut ten semi-circular notches out of the top edge of piece G with the dimensions illustrated.
2. Smooth inside edges of cutouts with rasp and sandpaper.
3. Glue and screw pieces G to the top of pieces F in the location illustrated.
4. Place pieces J, the rods, across the top of the loom frame, resting in the notches of piece G.

The Moveable Parts for Both Loom Designs

The following parts—the beams, beater, comb and heddles—are designed to be interchangeable for both foot-powered looms. These parts are not a permanent part of the loom frame. When necessary they can be removed—even when there is still cloth being woven—and stored away. This means that more people can weave than might be possible otherwise; it is not necessary for each weaver to have his or her own frame. It is possible to construct a set of moveable parts for each weaver so that several people can share the same loom frame.

I. Cloth Beam

A. Materials Needed:

One (1) straight tree limb - 125cm long, 10cm in diameter, or milled lumber - 10 x 10 - 125cm.

B. Construction

1. Trim the piece of wood to 6cm in diameter for 115cm of its length.
2. Leave the remaining 10cm in diameter, but drill and chisel a hole 2cm by 5cm completely through one side.
3. Drill a similar hole from the other side at right angles to the first.

4. Cut a notch 2cm by 90cm completely through the beam in the 6cm diameter section.

The Cloth Beam is Now Complete.

II. The Warp Beam

A. Materials Needed:

One (1) straight tree limb, 125cm long, 10cm in diameter, or milled lumber 10x10x125cm.

B. Construction

1. Construction proceeds as described for the cloth beam from Step 1 to Step 3.
2. Cut groove 2 x 90cm only to a depth of 2cm; do not cut completely through the beam.

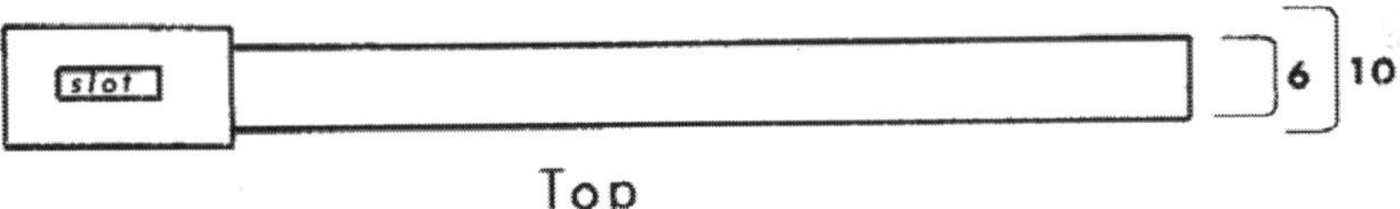

Top

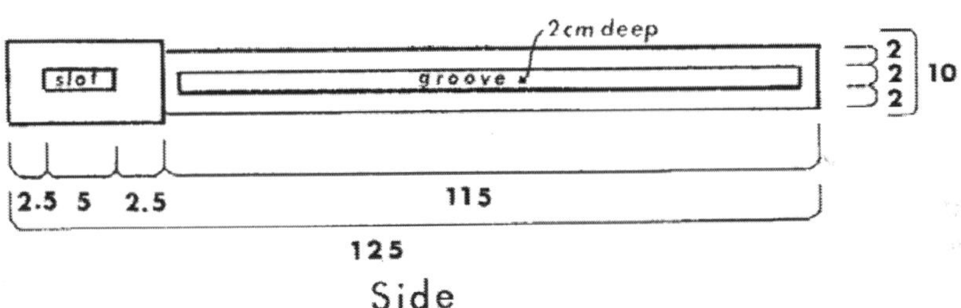

Side

The Warp Beam Is Now Complete.

III. The Beater

A. Materials Needed:

Two (2) pieces of wood - 5 x 5 x 120cm (labelled A).

Two (2) pieces of wood - 1 x 4 x 120cm (labelled B).

Two (2) pieces of wood - 1 x 2 x 4cm (labelled C).

B. Construction

1. Drill and chisel a hole 1cm by 4cm in each end of both pieces A. Smooth the insides of the holes.
2. Carve a groove 1cm deep the length of both pieces A between the two holes as shown.
3. Nail piece C to the bottom of each piece B.

4. Sand and smooth each piece B. Taper the top end to a point, to ease assembly.
5. Slide pieces B into the holes in pieces A so that the grooved edges of pieces A face one another.

The Beater Is Now Complete.

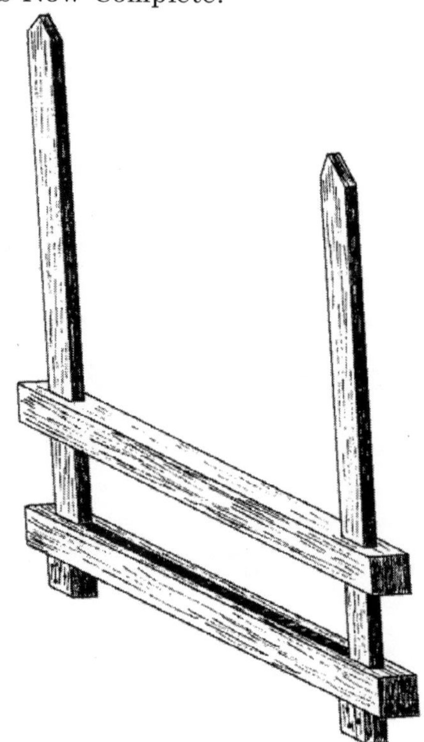

C. Attach the Beater to the Loom

Pit Loom

1. Ceiling type: suspend a rod one (1) meter long from 2 hooks in a ceiling beam.
2. Wall type: suspend from a crosspiece which is attached to the wall and supported by a fork.
3. Free-Standing: Attach to rod (J) which rests across top of frame on pieces G.
   a) Tie arms of beater to rod as illustrated. A leather shoe sole may be used to create a simple hinge.
   b) The beater should swing freely at the same height as the top edge of the cloth beam.

IV. The comb

A. Materials Needed:

1. Four (4) pieces of lightweight wood - 0.2 x 0.8 x 100cm.
2. Reed - 220 pieces - 0.3 x 0.5 x 12cm for heavy two-ply warp.

   or

   - 380 pieces - 0.15 x 0.5 x 12cm for medium cotton warp.

   or

   - 500 pieces - 0.1 x 0.5 x 12cm for fine cotton warp.

Note: The size and number of reed pieces is determined by the diameter of the warp thread used. You may have to make adjustments in the above recommendations to suit your particular warp.

3. Two pieces of wood - 0.5 x 2 x 12cm
4. Cotton string, about 20 meters, and the same diameter as that of the warp to be used.
5. A sharp knife.

B. Construction

1. Take two of the pieces A and one piece C and place them together sandwich style as shown.

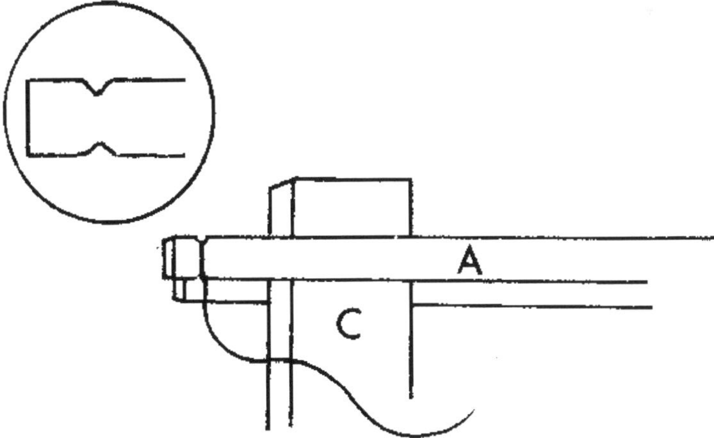

2. Securely knot the end of the cotton string around one piece A at the end as shown. A small notch can be made with the knife to prevent slipping if necessary.
3. Loop in and out of the two ends of pieces A in a figure eight about six times
4. Bring the string parallel to piece A on one side past piece C.

5. Holding it in that position with one finger, bring the rest of the string under and up around the top of it.
6. When it meets the string being held by the finger thread it through the loop as shown.

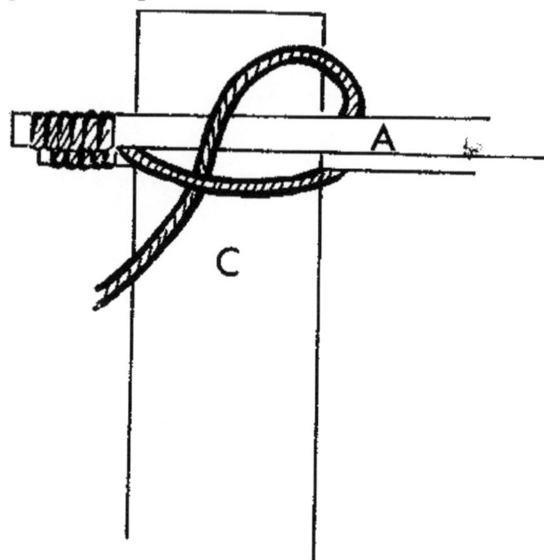

7. Pull down and then up to tighten the loop. Knot should be on the side of the meter length.
8. Repeat Steps 1 through 7 with the other two (2) pieces of A, attaching them to the bottom of piece C.

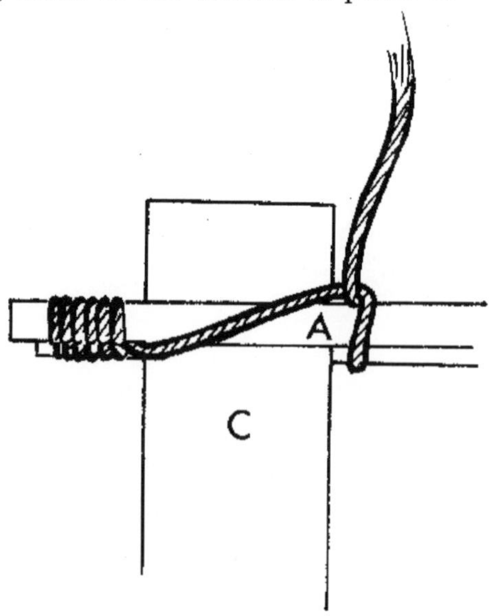

9. Place one of the slivers of reed between the two sticks. Loop the string around as diagramed.
10. There should be a space of about 0.1cm to 0.2cm created by the string. If there is no space, or if the space is too small for your warp, either start over using the string doubled, or make a second loop as done in Step 9.
11. Repeat Step 9 at bottom, fastening the reed in place at both ends.
12. Place another sliver of reed in position. Repeat the knot as shown in Steps 9 through 11.

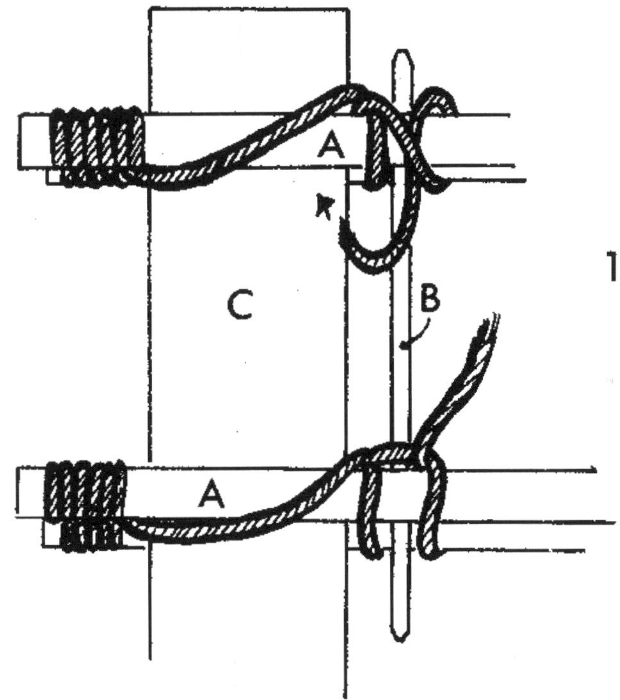

13. Continue, doing both top and bottom, until you are 3cm from the end. You may not be able to fit all the reed because of variation in the spacing, or for the same reason you may need a few more pieces to complete the length.
14. Place the remaining piece C at the end and tie off the string as You did in Step 3 with a figure eight, and a secure knot. At this point the string should hold all of the reeds securely enough so that they do not slip out.

The Comb is Now Complete.

V. The Heddles

A. Materials Needed for two (2) Heddles.

Note: Both looms may use up to eight (8) heddles each.

1. Four (4) rods of strong wood 2-4cm in diameter, 130cm long.
2. One (1) kilo of strong cotton string divided into four equal balls.
3. A board similar to the rod in width, 15cm high and 60cm long, to serve as a form.

B. Construction

1. Cut a groove 3cm from the end of each rod.
2. Cut a piece of string 140cm long and tie it in the notch at one end.
3. Tie one end of a ball of string to the same notch.
4. Place the rod on top of the board.
5. Hold the shorter string taut along the top length of the rod. (This string is shown as black in the illustrations).

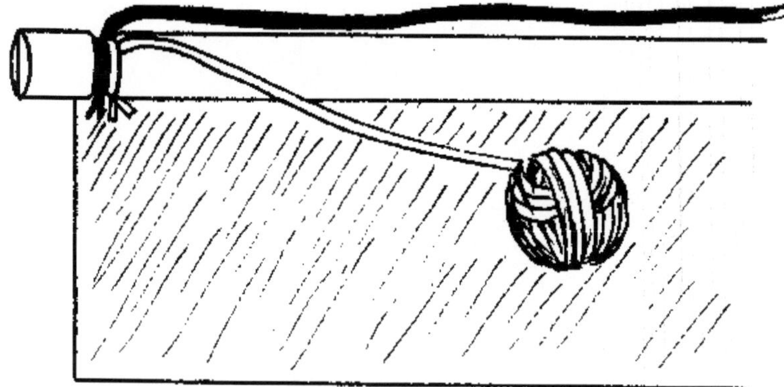

6. Steps a thru f show the "looping" process. Pass the ball of string under the board as shown in Step f.

Every ten loops pass the ball between the rod and the board to fasten it to the rod.

Note: The total number of loops made should be even and they should be double the number of spaces in your comb.

7. As the loops are made they are slipped off the board and the board is moved forward.
8. When the desired number of loops is reached, tie both strings in the groove at the other end.

9. Using the second rod, repeat the above except this time when each loop is passed under the board pick up a loop from the first rod and pass the ball of string through that as well.
10. When all the loops are picked up, one heddle is complete. Tie off in the grooved end.
11. Repeat all of the above directions for the second heddle.

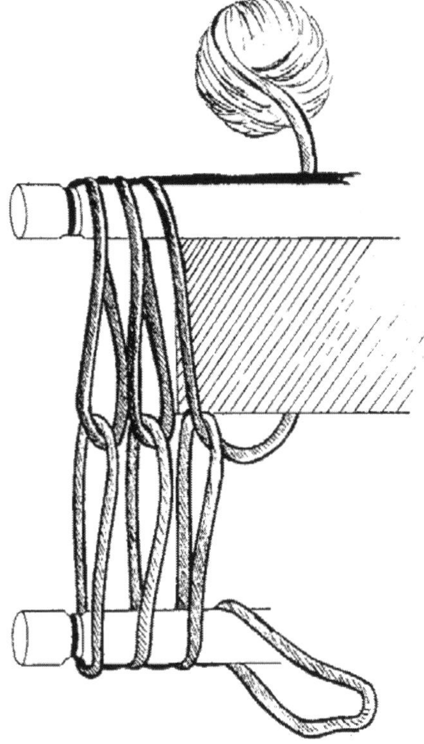

The Heddles Are Now Complete.

VI. Machinery for the Harnesses

A. Materials Needed:

1. Two (2) small pulleys.
2. Light rope, 1cm in diameter.
3. Four (4) hooks, either of heavy wire or appropriately shaped twigs.
4. Two (2) pieces of wood about 3cm x 8cm x 20cm.
5. Heavy rope, 2cm in diameter.
6. A piece of pipe, metal tubing or strong wood 30cm long, and about 1.5 - 2cm in diameter.

B. Foot Pedal Construction

1. Drill holes 2cm in diameter in the top of the two wooden pieces as shown.

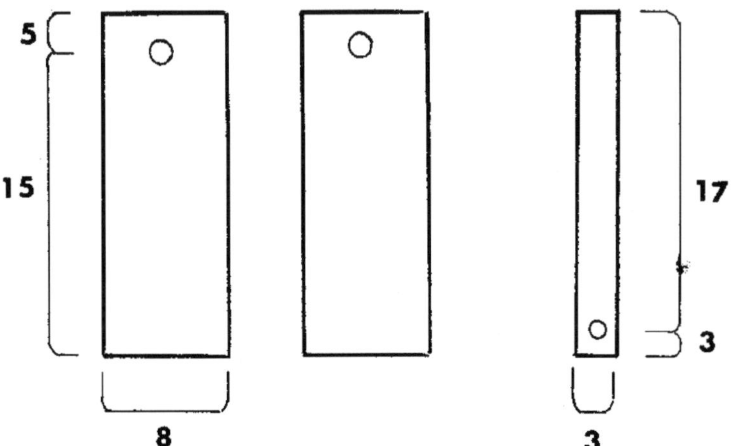

2. Drill holes 2cm in diameter in the side of the same wooden pieces as shown.

C. Machinery Set Up

1. Tie a loop of light rope to each end of the heddles about 10cm in from the end on the top rod.
2. Tie a similar loop in the center of the heddle from the bottom rod.
3. Hang pulleys from the same rod the beater is attached to on the pit loom and to a separate rod laid across pieces N on the self-supporting loom.
4. Cut two pieces of light rope, Tie one end to a hook, thread it over the pulley wheel and tie the other end to another hook.
5. Hang heddles by loop from the hooks.

   They should hang evenly and at the same height or slightly higher than the beater and the comb. Adjust lengths of ropes if necessary.
6. Put a secure knot in the ends of two short pieces of heavy rope. Thread them through holes in drilled blocks of wood so that the knots are on the bottom.
7. Thread metal pipe, tube or stick through holes in the side of wooden blocks.
8. Tie two pieces of rope to the ends of the pipe.

9. Tie rope at front of the blocks to the loop in the bottom of the heddles.
10. Tie rope at back of blocks to the cloth beam supports.

The Harness Is Now Functional

Note: During warping, the heddles are removed from the machinery for threading.

Machinery in place on frame loom side view

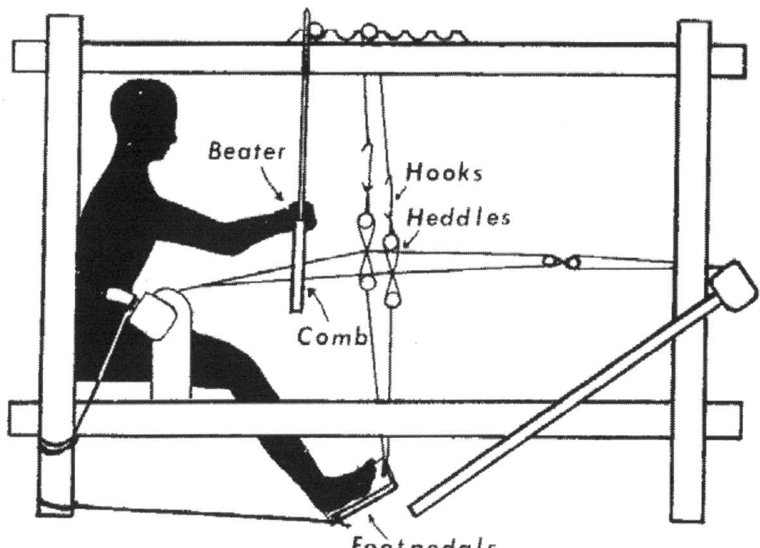

Machinery in place on ceiling-supported loom

Warp the Foot-Powered Loom

Note: Before warping the loom, read Chapter 7: Weaves Patterns and Finishing Touches for help with selecting a weave and/or pattern for a first project. Plain weave, basket weave and/or a striped or plaid pattern are recommended for the first weaving. It is also necessary to have the raddle (p. 115) ready before beginning.

I. Measuring the Warp

A. Equipment Needed:

Four wooden or metal stakes about 30cm high

B. Measuring Procedure:

1. Place two stakes in the ground: the total distance apart desired for the piece of weaving (2 to 36 meters).
2. Place two more stakes about 30cm inside the two stakes. 3. Tie the beginning of the warp (wound in a ball) to one of the

outer stakes. Walk between the stakes wrapping the warp in the pattern illustrated.

4. Count each length. It helps to tie warp threads in groups of tens when working with a large number of threads. When desired number is reached, untie the beginning of the warp and tie it to the end.
5. Tie a string around the warp where it crosses between the stakes.

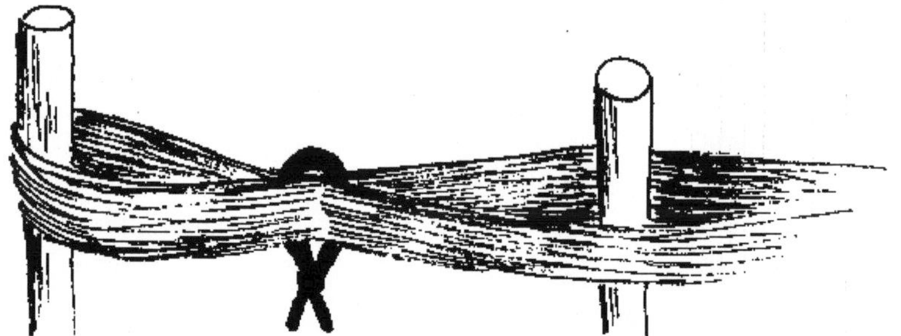

6. Ending: when the desired number of warp threads have been counted, untie the beginning end and tie in a weaver's knot to the other end.
7. Changing colour: Warp colours can be changed as was cribed for the frame loom (page 38, Steps a-h).

C. Gather up Warp in a Warp Chain

1. Slide the loop off at one end of the stakes.
2. Open the loop and put your hand through. Draw up a section of warp and bring it through the first loop to make a second loop.
3. Continue until end is reached. Pull the end through and pull snugly, but not tight.
4. To undo: Take the end out of the last loop and pull; chain will release.

II. Wind the Warp

A. Equipment Needed:

One (1) stick cut to fit the groove in the warp beam. One (1) stick that fits the hole in the end of the warp beam. Several thin sticks - 90cm long.

B. Procedure:

1. Place one of the open loops over the end of the warp beam. Slide to center.

2. Place warp beam on either of the beam supports of the loom. It does not matter which support or which direction the warp is going as long as it can be extended full length. This, of course, will depend on the location of the loom.

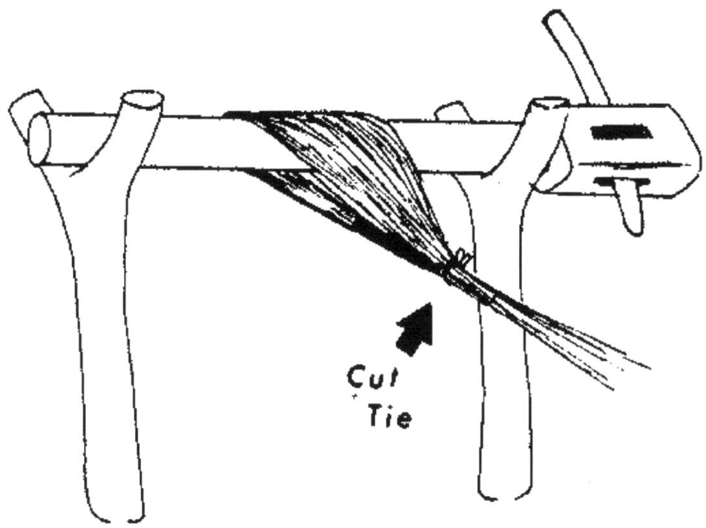

(If it is impossible to use the loom supports because of inadequate space, you can set up two forked posts similar to the beam supports on the pit loom in an open space. These can then be left in place permanently for future warping.

3. Prevent the warp from slipping as it is wound by: a) Cutting a stick to fit into the groove in the warp beam. b) Pushing the stick against the warp and into the groove. c) Turning the warp beam in a clockwise direction so that the stick is locked into place by the covering warp.
4. The following steps require two or three people:
   a) One person inserts a stick in the hole in the warp beam and slowly turns the beam in a clockwise direction winding on the warp. Every turn or so, he or she inserts a thin stick between the layers of the warp.
   b) Another person holds the end of the warp extended at full length, keeping it taut and straight as it is wound.
   c) A third person opens the raddle and lays groups of warp threads between the nails. The raddle is closed and tied shut. Then, holding the raddle, he or she guides the warp as it is wound, making sure it is evenly spread. If no other person is available to assist, the raddle can be tied to the other beam.

5. Place the lease sticks (two (2), one meter-lengths of reed or bamboo) in the positions shown just before winding the end of the warp on to the beam. Tie together as shown.

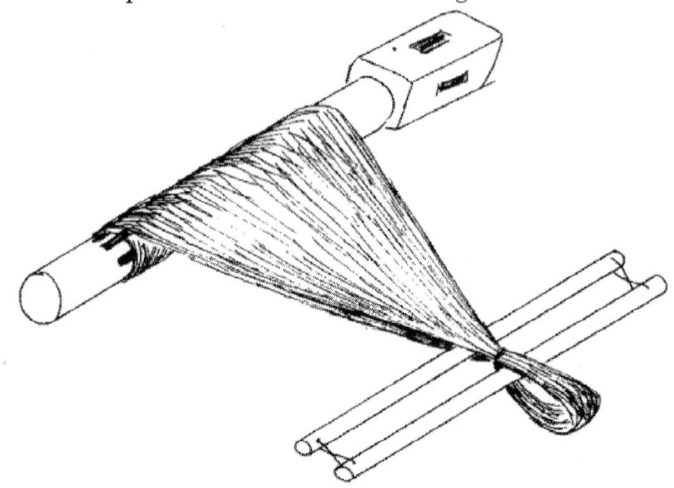

III. Thread the Heddles and Comb

The following process requires two people if it is to be done quickly and efficiently. (It is possible for one person to perform the task if he or she threads small sections of the warp - - first through the heddle and, then, reversing his or her position, threading the warp through the comb.)

A. Equipment Needed:

Small size crochet hook or bent piece of wire or sharp knife.

B. Threading Procedure:

1. Two people sit facing one another with the two heddles (removed from the loom) and with the comb suspended between them from the backs of two chairs or from the beam supports.
2. One person holds the warp beam, warp and lease sticks in his or her lap, and faces the heddles. The other person faces the comb.
3. Cut the end loop of the warp after sliding the two lease sticks back to free about 30cm of warp.
4. Take one piece of warp at a time in order check order against lease sticks and thread it through the heddles.
5. In Plain Weave, every other thread is inserted through a twist in the near heddle. The alternate thread is inserted in a twist in the far heddle.

6. Insert (second person) a crochet hook, needle or sharp knife edge through one of the dents of the comb after the thread is inserted.

   Loop the thread over and pull it through. Take care not to miss any threads or spaces, nor should threads cross.
7. Tie every group of ten threads in an overhand knot to prevent them from slipping out of the comb.
8. Put two warp threads through the same heddle at both ends.

IV. Place the Warp on the Loom

1. Place the warp beam on its supports so that the warp extends out to the cloth beam, and unrolls from the top of the beam.

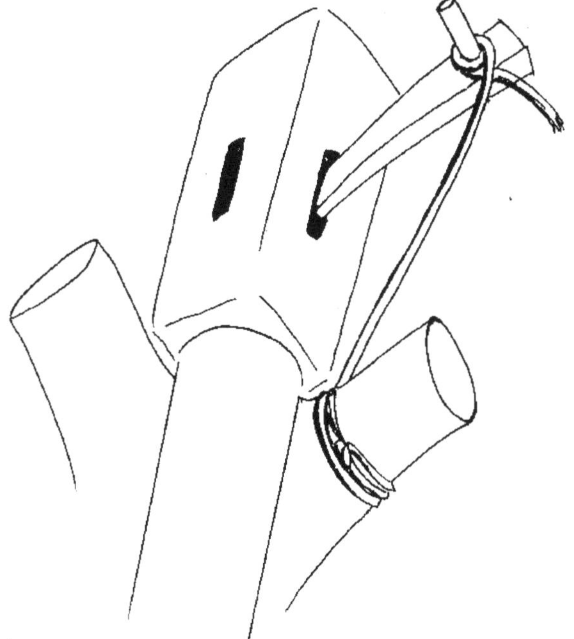

2. Use a pole such as a broomstick to wedge between the hole in the warp beam and the floor, to prevent it from turning.
3. Replace the heddles on the pulleys and attach the footpedals.
4. Open beater and insert the comb in the grooves. Close it snugly so that the comb is firmly caught and does not bend or move when the warp is pulled.
5. Place the cloth beam in position. Find a stick that fits the hole in the beam. Drill a small hole in the end of it and insert a strong piece of wood. Tie the beam in position as shown above.

V. Attach the Warp to the Cloth Beam

1. Tie a piece of cord to one end of the beam. Wrap it loosely around the beam twenty to thirty times.

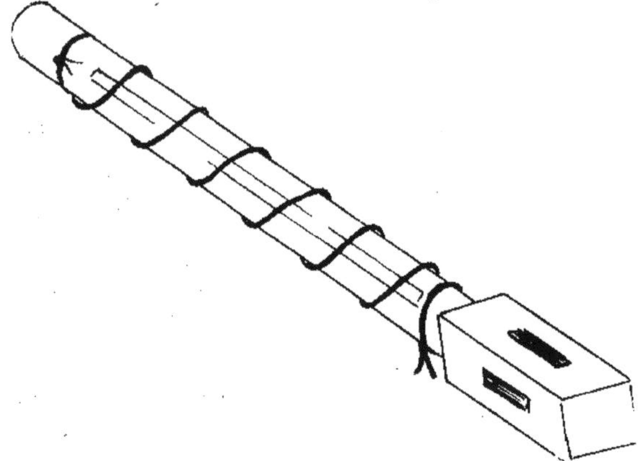

2. Sit down at the loom. Tie each group of ten (10) warp threads to the looped cord on the beam (do not undo the knots made during threading). Use the following knot to tie them.

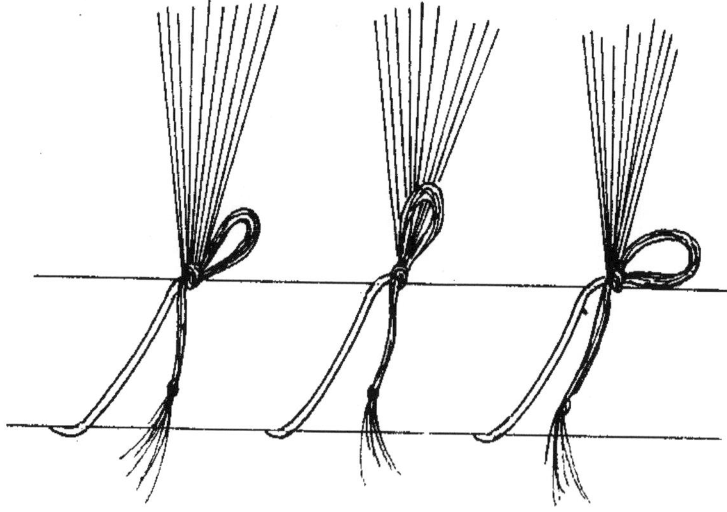

3. Tighten the tension on the warp when all have been tied on by removing the cloth beam counter clockwise and tying in place.
4. Test the tension of the warp by running your finger across the warp threads.
5. If necessary, release the tension on the warp slightly and retie any loose bunches of warp.

6. Tighten the warp as much as possible.

You Are Now Ready to Weave.

How to Weave on a Foot Powered Loom

You will need a shuttle and stretcher for weaving. Consult Chapter 6 The Weaver's Tools, for directions for making these and other helpful tools.

Steps in Weaving on Both Looms

1. To start or end weft: take end and bring through several opposing warps. After weaving several more rows cut off end even with weaving.

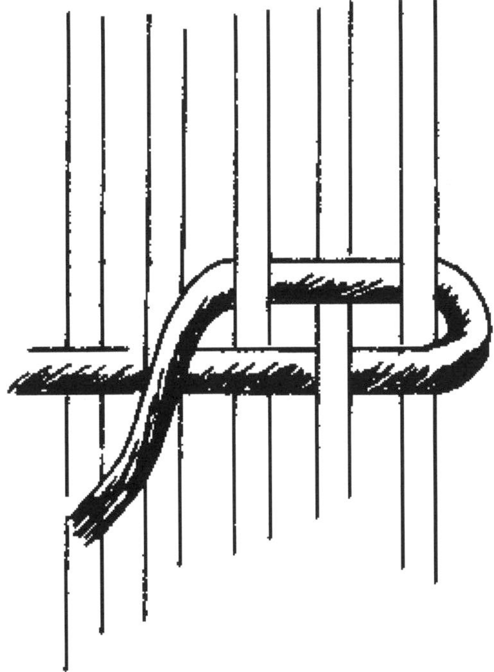

2. Wrap weft on the shuttle.
3. Depress right footpedal and feed weft through shed.
4. Place weft at oblique angle to the warp.
5. Depress left footpedal.
6. Push weft firmly into place using the beater.
7. Feed weft through from opposite side with left foot still depressed.
8. Depress right footpedal. Beat weft into place.

9. Release tension on warp and adjust.
10. Repeat steps 2 to 7 until there is about 10cm of woven fabric.
11. Put the stretcher into place and continue weaving.
12. Release the warp beam and cloth beams and turn them forward one hole when there is no more space between the fabric and the beater. Refasten and continue weaving.
13. Untie the warp from the beam and thread the cloth through the slot in the beam as shown after 1/2 meter of cloth or more has been woven.

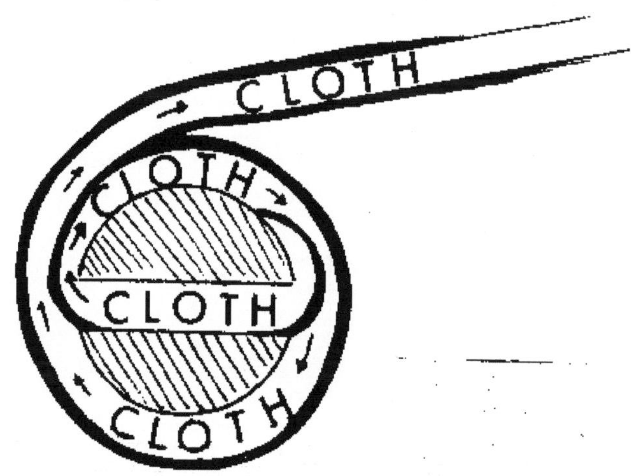

Cross section of cloth beam showing cloth wrapped around.

14. As the warp shifts to the cloth beam on the free-standing loom, it may be necessary to balance the weight of the weaver and the cloth by placing a rock on a board at the back of the loom.

4

Free-Standing Rug Loom

Free-standing looms are used to weave a variety of products from rugs to clothes. Manufactured free-standing rug looms are very expensive. Making your own rug loom will cost only a fraction of the price of a manufactured loom and can be made in less than 2 hours.

Pegged Loom

Peg Looms are simple wooden weaving frames that can produce lovely rugs and bags.

A peg loom is a very simple tool used for weaving. A key feature of the looms are the pegs that jut out from them. Some looms are four-sided, while others consist of a single row of pegs. The size of the peg loom depends on the size of the project being made. Small, square looms are commonly used by children to make pot holders, while professional weavers may use large, single-row looms to produce beautiful tapestries.

One common style of peg loom consists of a straight piece of wood with a row of dowels, or pegs, jutting out of the top. The pegs stretch from one end of the wood to the other and are spaced equally apart. Usually, the pegs fit into holes drilled into the wood and should be easy to remove as a person weaves on the loom. The pegs also have holes drilled through them at the bottom.

To use this type of peg loom, the weaver pulls one piece of warp thread through the hole at the bottom of each peg. The warp thread should be at least three times the length of the finished rug or tapestry. The weaver should line up the loose ends of the threads so that they are even and arrange the threads so that they hang neatly away from the loom. If the weaver wants tassels on the end of the tapestry, she should tie the threads together at the loose ends.

To weave on the peg loom, a weaver should take the weft thread and weave it in and out of the pegs, starting a few pegs in from the end of the loom. When the weaver reaches the opposite end, he should wrap the weft around the final peg and weave his way back, repeating the process until he has woven the weft up the vertical length of the pegs. Once the pegs are covered in weft threads, the weaver should slowly pull the pegs out of the loom one by one so that the warp thread is pulled up through the weft thread and she can continue to weave the rug.

Another type of peg loom is commonly used by children to create pot holders from fabric loops. This peg loom is a plastic or metal square with little pegs sticking up on all four sides. The child stretches loops from one peg to another across the width of the loom. The child then weaves another loop from one peg to the other, over and under the stretch loops, and across the length of the loom.

Power Looms

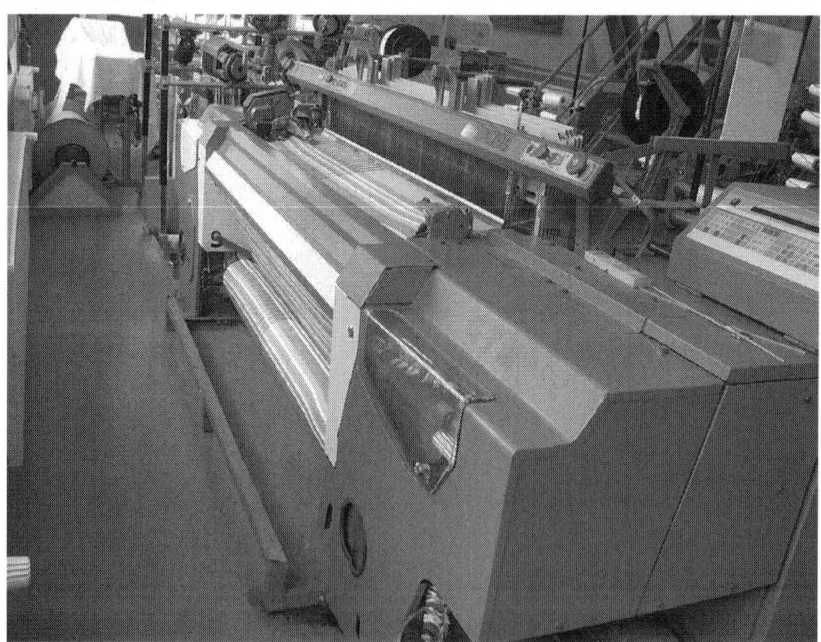

Figure: *A Picanol rapier loom*

A power loom is a mechanised loom powered by a line shaft. The first power loom was designed in 1784 by Edmund Cartwright and first built in 1785. It was refined over the next 47 years until a design by Kenworthy and Bullough made the operation completely automatic. This was known as the Lancashire Loom. By 1850 there were 260,000 in operation in England. Fifty years later came the Northrop Loom that would replenish the shuttle when it was empty and this replaced the Lancashire loom.

Edmund Cartwright built and patented a power loom in 1785, and it was this that was adopted by the nascent cotton industry in England. The silk loom made by Jacques Vaucanson in 1745 operated on the same principles but wasn't developed further. The invention of the flying shuttle by John Kay was critical to the development of a commercially successful power loom. Cartwright's loom was impractical but the ideas behind it were developed by numerous inventors in the Manchester area of England; where by 1818 there were 32 factories containing 5732 looms.

Horrocks loom was viable, but it was the Roberts Loom in 1830 that marked the turning point. Incremental changes to the three motions continued to be made. The problems of sizing, stop-motions, consistent take-up, and a temple to maintain the width remained. In 1841, Kenworthy and Bullough produced the Lancashire Loom which was self-acting or semi-automatic. This enables a youngster to run six looms at the same time. Thus, for simple calicos, the power loom became more economical to run than the hand loom- with complex patterning that used a dobby or Jacquard head, jobs were still put out to handloom weavers until the 1870s. Incremental changes were made such as the Dickinson Loom, culminating in the Keighley-born inventor Northrop, who was working for the Draper Corporation in Hopedale producing the fully automatic Northrop Loom. This loom recharged the shuttle when the pirn was empty. The Draper E and X models became the leading products from 1909. They were challenged by synthetic fibres such as rayon.

From 1942 the faster and more efficient shuttleless Sulzer looms and the rapier looms were introduced. Modern industrial looms can weave at 2000 weft insertions per minute.

Shuttle Looms

The huge components of the loom are the warp beam, heddles, harnesses, shuttle, reed and takeup roll. In the loom, yarn processing includes shedding, picking, battening and taking-up operations.

- *Shedding.* Shedding is the raising of the warp yarns to form a loop through which the filling yarn, carried by the shuttle, can be inserted. The shed is the vertical space between the raised and unraised warp yarns. On the modern loom, simple and intricate shedding operations are performed automatically by the heddle or heald frame, also known as a harness. This is a rectangular frame to which a series of wires, called heddles or healds, are attached. The yarns are passed through the eye holes of the heddles, which hang vertically from the harnesses. The weave pattern determines which harness controls which warp yarns, and the number of harnesses used depends on the complexity of the weave. Two common methods of controlling the heddles are dobbies and a Jacquard Head.

- *Picking.* As the harnesses raise the heddles or healds, which raise the warp yarns, the shed is created. The filling yarn is inserted through the shed by a small carrier device called a shuttle. The shuttle is normally pointed at each end to allow passage through the shed. In a traditional shuttle loom, the filling yarn is wound onto a quill, which in turn is mounted in the shuttle. The filling yarn emerges through a hole in the shuttle as it moves across the loom. A single crossing of the shuttle from one side of the loom to the other is known as a pick. As the shuttle moves back and forth across the shed, it weaves an edge, or selvage, on each side of the fabric to prevent the fabric from raveling.
- *Battening.* As the shuttle moves across the loom laying down the fill yarn, it also passes through openings in another frame called a reed (which resembles a comb). With each picking operation, the reed presses or battens each filling yarn against the portion of the fabric that has already been formed. The point where the fabric is formed is called the fell. Conventional shuttle looms can operate at speeds of about 150 to 160 picks per minute.

With each weaving operation, the newly constructed fabric must be wound on a cloth beam. This process is called taking up. At the same time, the warp yarns must be let off or released from the warp beams. To become fully automatic, a loom needs a filling stop motion which will brake the loom, if the weft thread breaks.

History

Edmund Cartwright patented a power loom in 1785. This used water as power instead of steam power which sped up the weaving process. Weavers were able to use all the thread that spinners could produce. It was to be forty years before his ideas were modified into a reliable automatic loom. Cartwright was not the first man to design an automatic loom, this had been done in 1678 by M. de Gennes in Paris, and again by Vaucanson In 1745, but these never developed and were forgotten. Those designs preceded John Kay's invention of the flying shuttle and they passed the shuttle through the shed using levers.

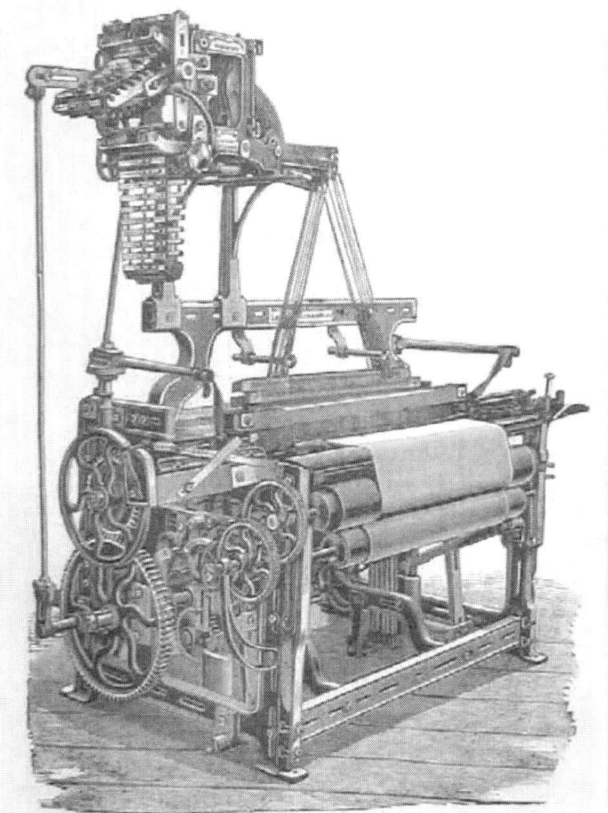

Figure: *A loom from the 1890s with a dobby head. Illustration from the Textile Mercury.*

It was not a commercially successful machine. His ideas were licensed first by Grimshaw, of Manchester who built a small steam-powered weaving factory in Manchester in 1790. The looms had to be stopped to dress the warp, but the factory burnt down before anything could be learned.

Series of Initial Inventors

A series of inventors incrementally improved all aspects of the three principle processes and the ancillary processes.

- Grimshaw 1790 Manchester- dressing the warp
- Austin 1789, 1790 -dressing the warp, 200 looms produced for Monteith of Pollockshaws 1800
- Thomas Johnson, 1803, Bredbury- dressing frame: Factory for 200 Steam Looms on Manchester 1806, and two factories at Stockport 1809. One at Westhoughton, Lancashire 1809.
- William Radcliffe of Stockport 1802- improved take up mechanism
- John Todd of Burnley 1803- a heald roller and new shedding arrangements, the healds were corded to treadles actuated by cams on the second shaft.
- William Horrocks of Stockport 1803- The frame was still wooden but the lathe was pendant from the frame and operated by cams on the first shaft, the shedding was operated by cams on the second shaft, the take up motion was copied from Radcliffe.
- Peter Marsland 1806- improvements to the lathe motion to counteract poor picking
- William Cotton 1810- improvements to the letting off motion
- William Horrocks 1813 -Horrocks Loom Modifications to the lathe motion- improving on Marsland
- Peter Ewart 1813 -a use of pneumatics
- Joseph and Peter Taylor 1815 -double beat foot lathe for heavy cloths
- Paul Moody 1815- produces the first power loom in North America. Exporting a UK loom would have been illegal.
- John Capron and Sons 1820- installed the first power looms for woolens in North America at Uxbridge, Massachusetts.
- William Horrocks 1821 -a system to wet the warp and weft during use, improving the effectiveness of the sizing
- Richard Roberts 1830, Roberts Loom, These improvements were a geared take up wheel and tappets to operate multiple heddles
- Stanford, Pritchard and Wilkinson- patented a method to stop on the break of weft or warp. It was not used.
- William Dickinson of Blackburn Loom the modern overpick loom

There now appear a series of useful improvements that are contained in patents for useless devices

- Hornby, Kenworthy and Bullough of Blackburn 1834- the vibrating or fly reed
- John Ramsden and Richard Holt of Todmorden 1834- a new automatic weft stopping motion
- James Bullough of Blackburn 1835- improved automatic weft stopping motion and taking up and letting off arrangements
- Andrew Parkinson 1836- improved stretcher (temple).
- William Kenworthy and James Bullough 1841- trough and roller temple (became the standard), A simple stop-motion.

At this point the loom has become fully automatic. The Cartwight loom weaver could work one loom at 120-130 picks per minute- with a Kenworthy and Bullough's Lancashire Loom, a weaver can run up to six looms working at 220-260 picks per minute- thus giving 12 times more through put.

Looms and the Manchester Context

The development of the power loom in and around Manchester was not a coincidence. Manchester has been a centre for Fustians by 1620 and acted as a hub for other Lancashire towns, so developing a communication network with them. It was an established point of export using the meandering River Mersey, and by 1800 it had a thriving canal network, with links to the Ashton Canal, Rochdale Canal the Peak Forest Canal and Manchester Bolton & Bury Canal. The fustian trade gave the towns a skilled workforce that was used to the complicated Dutch looms, and was perhaps accustomed to industrial discipline.

While Manchester became a spinning town, the towns around were weaving towns producing cloth by the *putting out* system. The business was dominated by a few families who had the capital needed for the investment in new mills, and buy hundreds of looms.

The mills were built along the new canals so immediately had access to their markets. Spinning developed first, and until 1830 the handloom was still more important economically than the power loom when the roles reversed. Because of the economic growth of Manchester, a new industry of precision machine tool engineering was born and here were the skills needed to build the precision mechanisms of a loom.

Adoption

Number of Looms in UK					
Year	1803	1820	1829	1833	1857
Looms	2400	14650	55500	100000	250000

Draper's strategy was to standardise on a couple of models which it mass produced. The lighter E-model of 1909 was joined in the 1930 by the heavier X-model. Continuous fibre machines, say for rayon, which was more break-prone, needed a specialist loom. This was provided by the purchase of the Stafford Loom Co. in 1932, and using their patents a third loom the XD, was added to the range. Because of their mass production techniques they were reluctant and slow to retool for new technologies such as shuttleless looms.

Decline and Reinvention

Originally, power looms used a shuttle to throw the weft across, but in 1927 the faster and more efficient shuttleless loom came into use. Sulzer Brothers, a Swiss company had the exclusive rights to shuttleless looms in 1942, and licensed the American production to Warner & Swasey. Draper licensed the slower rapier loom. Today, advances in technology have produced a variety of looms designed to maximise production for specific types of material. The most common of these are Sulzer shuttleless weaving machines, rapier looms, air-jet looms and water-jet looms.

Social and Economic Implications

The power loom reduced demand for skilled handweavers, initially causing reduced wages and unemployment. Protests followed its introduction. For example, in 1816 two thousand rioting Calton weavers tried to destroy power loom mills and stoned the workers. In the longer term, by making cloth more affordable the power loom increased demand and stimulated exports, causing a growth in industrial employment, albeit low-paid. The power loom also opened up opportunities for women mill workers. A darker side of the power loom's impact was the growth of employment of children in power loom mills.

Jacquard Looms

The Jacquard loom is a mechanical loom, invented by Joseph Marie Jacquard, first demonstrated in 1801, that simplifies the process of manufacturing textiles with complex patterns such as brocade, damask and matelasse. The loom was controlled by a "chain of cards", a number of punched cards, laced together into a continuous sequence. Multiple rows of holes were punched on each card, with one complete card corresponding to one row of the design. Several such paper cards, generally white in color, can be seen in the images below. Chains, like the much later paper tape, allowed sequences of any length to be constructed, not limited by the size of a card.

It is based on earlier inventions by the Frenchmen Basile Bouchon (1725), Jean Baptiste Falcon (1728) and Jacques Vaucanson (1740) A static display of a Jacquard loom is the centrepiece of the Musée des Tissus et des Arts Décoratifs in Lyon. Live displays of a Jacquard loom are available at a few private museums around Lyon.

Principles of Operation

This portrait of Jacquard was woven in silk on a Jacquard loom and required 24,000 punched cards to create (1839). It was only produced to order. Charles Babbage owned one of these portraits; it inspired him in using perforated cards in his analytical engine. It is in the collection of the Science Museum in London, England.

Each position in the card corresponds to a "Bolus" hook, which can either be raised or stopped dependent on whether the hole is punched out of the card or the card is solid. The hook raises or lowers the harness, which carries and guides the warp thread so that the weft will either lie above or below it. The sequence of raised and lowered threads is what creates the pattern. Each hook can be connected to a number of threads, allowing more than one repeat of a pattern. A loom with a 400 hook head might have four threads connected to each hook, resulting in a fabric that is 1600 warp ends wide with four repeats of the weave going across.

The term "Jacquard loom" is a misnomer. It is the "Jacquard head" that adapts to a great many dobby looms such as the "Dornier" brand that allow the weaving machine to then create the intricate patterns often seen in Jacquard weaving.

Jacquard looms, whilst relatively common in the textile industry, are not as ubiquitous as dobby looms which are usually faster and much cheaper to operate. However, unlike jacquard looms, they are not capable of producing so many different weaves from one warp. Modern jacquard looms are controlled by computers in place of the original punched cards, and can have thousands of hooks.

The threading of a Jacquard loom is so labor-intensive that many looms are threaded only once. Subsequent warps are then tied in to the existing warp with the help of a knotting robot which ties each new thread on individually. Even for a small loom with only a few thousand warp ends the process of re-threading can take days.

Importance in Computing

The Jacquard loom was the first machine to use punched cards to control a sequence of operations. Although it did no computation based on them, it is considered an important step in the history of computing hardware. The ability to change the pattern of the loom's weave by simply changing cards was an important conceptual precursor to the development of computer programming. Specifically, Charles Babbage planned to use cards to store programs in his Analytical engine. In the late 19th century, Herman Hollerith took the idea of using punched cards to store information a step further when he created a punched card tabulating machine which was used in the 1890 U.S. Census.

Circular Looms

A circular loom is used to create a seamless tube of fabric for products such as hosiery, sacks, clothing, fabric hose (such as fire hose) and the like. Circular looms can be small jigs used for hand knitting or large high speed machines for modern garments. A good example of the circular loom's work is the new seamless women's stockings, which no longer require a seam running up the back of the leg.

Dobby Looms

A Dobby loom is a type of floor loom that controls all the warp threads using a device called a dobby. (The word *dobby* is a corruption of "draw boy" which refers to the weaver's helpers who used to control the warp thread by pulling on draw threads.) A dobby loom is an alternative to a treadle loom. Both are floor looms in which every warp thread on the loom is attached to a single shaft using a device called a heddle. A shaft is sometimes known as a harness. Each shaft controls a set of threads. Raising or lowering several shafts at the same time gives a huge variety of possible sheds (gaps) through which the shuttle containing the weft thread can be thrown.

Dobby looms first appeared around 1843, roughly 40 years after Joseph Marie Jacquard invented the Jacquard device that can be mounted atop a loom to lift the individual heddles and warp threads.

A manual dobby uses a chain of bars or lags each of which has pegs inserted to select the shafts to be moved. A computer-assisted dobby loom uses a set of solenoids or other electric devices to select the shafts. Activation of these solenoids is under the control of a computer program. In either case the selected shafts are raised or lowered by either leg power on a dobby pedal or electric or other power sources.

On a treadle loom, each foot-operated treadle is connected by a linkage called a tie-up to one or more shafts. More than one treadle can operate a single shaft. The tie-up consists of cords or similar mechanical linkages tying the treadles to the lams that actually lift or lower the shaft.

On treadle operated looms, the number of sheds is limited by the number of treadles available. An eight-shaft loom can create 254 different sheds. There are actually 256 possibilities which is 2 to the eighth power, but having all threads up or all threads down is not very useful. Most eight-shaft floor looms have only ten to twelve treadles due to space limitations. This limits the weaver to ten to twelve distinct sheds. It is possible to use both feet to get more sheds, but this is rarely done in practice. It is even possible to change tie-ups in the middle of weaving a cloth but this is a tedious process, so this too is rarely done.

With a dobby loom, all 254 possibilities are available at any time. This vastly increases the number of cloth designs available to the weaver. The advantage of a dobby loom becomes even more pronounced on looms with 12 shafts (4094 possible sheds), 16 shafts (65,534 possible sheds), or more. It reaches its peak on a Jacquard loom in which each thread is individually controlled.

Another advantage to a dobby loom is the ability to handle much longer sequences in the pattern. A weaver working on a treadled loom must remember the entire sequence of treadlings that make up the pattern, and must keep track of where they are in the sequence at all times. Getting lost or making a mistake can ruin the cloth being woven. On a manual dobby the sequence that makes up the pattern is represented by the chain of dobby bars. The length of the sequence is limited by the length of the dobby chain. This can easily be several hundred dobby bars, although an average dobby chain will have approximately fifty bars.

A computer controlled dobby loom takes this one step further by replacing the mechanical dobby chain with computer controlled shaft selection. In addition to being able to handle sequences that are virtually unlimited, the construction of the shaft sequences is done on the computer screen rather than by building a mechanical dobby chain. This allows the weaver to load and switch weave drafts in seconds without even getting up from the loom. In addition, the design process performed on the computer provides the weaver with a more intuitive way to design fabric; seeing the pattern on a computer screen is easier than trying to visualize it by looking at the dobby chain.

Dobby looms expand a weaver's capabilities and remove some of the tedious work involved in designing and producing fabric. Many newer cloth design techniques such as network drafting can only reach their full potential on a dobby loom.

Rapier Looms

In each pick, the weft is pulled half way across the fabric by a metal rapier, it is caught by a second rapier and pulled the rest of the throw. No shuttle is involved, removing the need for dropboxes and the pirning process. Sulzer is a major manufacturer.

A stationary package of yarn is used to supply the weft yarns in the rapier machine. One end of a rapier, a rod or steel tape, carries the weft yarn. The other end of the rapier is connected to the control system. The rapier moves across the width of the fabric, carrying the weft yarn across through the shed to the opposite side. The rapier is then retracted, leaving the new pick in place.

In some versions of the loom, two rapiers are used, each half the width of the fabric in size. One rapier carries the yarn to the centre of the shed, where the opposing rapier picks up the yarn and carries it the remainder of the way across the shed. The double rapier is used more frequently than the single rapier due to its increases pick insertion speed and ability to weave wider widths of fabric. The housing for the rapiers must take up as much space as the width of the machine. To overcome this problem, looms with flexible rapiers have been devised. The flexible rapier can be coiled as it is withdrawn, therefore requiring less storage space. If, however, the rapier is too stiff then it will not coil; If it is too flexible, it will buckle. Rigid and flexible rapier machines operate at speeds operating at speeds ranging from about 200 to 260 ppm, using up to 1300 meters of weft yarn every minute. They have a noise level similar to that of modern projectile looms. They can produce a wide variety of fabrics ranging from muslin to drapery and upholstery materials.

Newer rapier machines are built with two distinct weaving areas for two separate fabrics. On such machines, one rapier picks up the yarn from the center, between the two fabrics, and carries it across one weaving area; as it finishes laying that pick, the opposite end of the rapier picks up another yarn from the center, and the rapier moves in the other direction to lay a pick for the second weaving area, on the other half of the machine. The above figure shows the action on a single width of fabric for a single rigid rapier system, a double rigid rapier system, and a double flexible rapier system .

Rapier machines weave more rapidly than most shuttle machines but more slowly than most other projectile machines. An important advantage of rapier machines is their flexibility, which permits the laying of picks of different colors. They also weave yarns of any type of fiber and can weave fabrics up to 110 inches in width without modification.

Special Jacquards

Fabrics are manufactured through weaving process. Certain fabrics have special characteristics brought through different types of fabric weaves. One of these weaves is the jacquard which produces jacquard fabric. It is a fabric woven on a special loom called the jacquard loom. This loom allows individual control on interlacing of up to several hundred warp threads that can give birth to innumerable unique patterns.

What is Jacquard Fabric

Jacquard fabrics have complex patterns on them. These fabrics are made on the jacquard loom. Jacquard fabrics have floats and luster. They are more stable and stretchy than the fabrics made through basic weaves. Some of the examples of jacquard fabric include matelasse fabric, satin fabrics, brocade fabric, damask fabric etc. Jacquard fabrics are mainly used for upholstery and as drapery fabrics.

The Origin of Jacquard Loom

The Jacquard Loom was invented by Joseph Marie Jacquard in 1801 which explains why this loom is called Jacquard loom. This was a mechanical loom and was controlled by punchcards having punched holes. Many rows of holes were punched on each card. Each row of the punch cards corresponded to one row of the design. A number of such cards composed the design of the textile that were arranged in a continuous string. These mechanical Jacquards were often small and were able to control independently only a few warp ends. Therefore it needed many repeats across the loom width. Then came the larger capacity machines that allowed comparatively greater control and needed fewer repeats. Multiple machines were also used to reduce the required number of repeats. In this way, it got possible to weave larger designs across the loom width.

The Invention of Electronic Jacquard Loom

It took about two centuries to introduce the electronic jacquard looms. The first electronic Jacquard was launched at ITMA, Milan in 1983 by Bonas Machine Company Ltd. This was initially a small machine but had greater capacity where single end warp control extended to more than 10,000 warp ends. It eliminated the need for repeats and symmetrical designs. Now almost infinite versatility could be produced in the patterns of the jacquard fabrics. It was a computer-controlled machine and thus it significantly reduced the time wasted in changing punched paper designs. Now smaller batch sizes of jacquard fabrics were possible to be made. However, electronic Jacquards are costly. They are not viable for a factory weaving large batch sizes, and smaller designs. These larger machines are apt for a factory that produces jacquard fabric with great versatility having specialized designs. They are, in fact, great for manufacturing jacquard clothing and jacquard linen such as jacquard duvet covers or damask sofa throws.

Jacquard Weaving

Jacquard weaving uses all types of fibers and blends of fibers and is capable of creating complex patterns on fabrics. For making these complex patterns, the jacquard loom can be programmed to raise each warp thread independently of the others. In this way, jacquard weaving gives highest warp yarn control. In fact, the invention of Jacquard loom and jacquard weaving made possible the automatic production of innumerable varieties of pattern weaving.

With mechanical jacquard loom, the weaving process is much labor intensive. The heddles with warp ends to be pulled up have to be manually selected by an operator, who assists the main weaver. In earlier times, it was known as a drawloom which is a very slow process and placed limitations on the complexity of patterns.

As mentioned earlier, the mechanical jacquard loom works on the basis of punched cards strung together. Every hole in the card corresponds to a "Bolus" hook. This hook can either be up or down raising or lowering the harness. In this way, it carries and guides the warp thread in a manner that the weft yarn either lies above or below it. The sequence of raised and lowered threads only creates the pattern. Each hook can be joined through the harness to a number of threads.

This allows more than one repeat of a pattern. A loom having a 400 hook head might have four threads joined to each hook. Thus, it will result in a fabric which is 1600 warp ends wide with four repeats of the weave going across.

Computerized Jacquard Weaving

The modern computer controlled jacquard looms don't have punched cards, and can have thousands of hooks. The threading of a Jacquard loom is very labor intensive process. As such, many looms are threaded for only once. Subsequent warps are tied in to the existing warp using a knotting robot that ties every new thread on individually. It can take several days for the process of re-threading even for a small loom having only a few thousand warp ends. In this context, it can be said that the term "Jacquard" is not confined to any particular loom but refers to the added control mechanism that automates the patterning of a fabric.

Types of Jacquard Fabrics

Apart from the woven fabric made with the help of jacquard loom, jacquard fabric also refers to a rib-based, double jersey weft-knit fabric on which a figure or design appears in a different color or texture. Jacquard fabrics are further sub-divided into flat-jacquard and blister fabrics. The flat jacquard patterns have equal number of loops in each wale of the pattern knitting. It is not so with blister fabrics. Commonly found jacquard fabrics are brocade, damask and tapestries etc.

Brocade fabric: It is a patterned fabric woven with the help of multi-colored threads. It shows a raised pattern in relief against the background and may or may not use metallic threads as part of the pattern. It is usually a heavier fabric mostly used in upholstery and decorative clothing.

Damask fabric: Although it looks like brocade but is much finer and sheer than it. It is also a patterned fabric woven mostly with single color. The fibers that are generally used for making such fabric include silk fiber, linen fiber, cotton fiber, rayon fiber or blends of other synthetic fibers.

Matelasse fabric: This fabric made with Jacquard weave has a quilted effect. It is generally made with silk, cotton, rayon or wool fiber. It can be made a little stretchy but that depends on the weave.

5

Woven Design Fundamentals

Woven fabric is a cloth formed by weaving. It only stretches diagonally on the bias directions (between the warp and weft directions), unless the threads are elastic. Woven cloth usually frays at the edges, unless measures are taken to counter this, such as the use of pinking shears or hemming.

Woven fabrics are worked on a big loom and made of many threads woven on a warp and a weft.

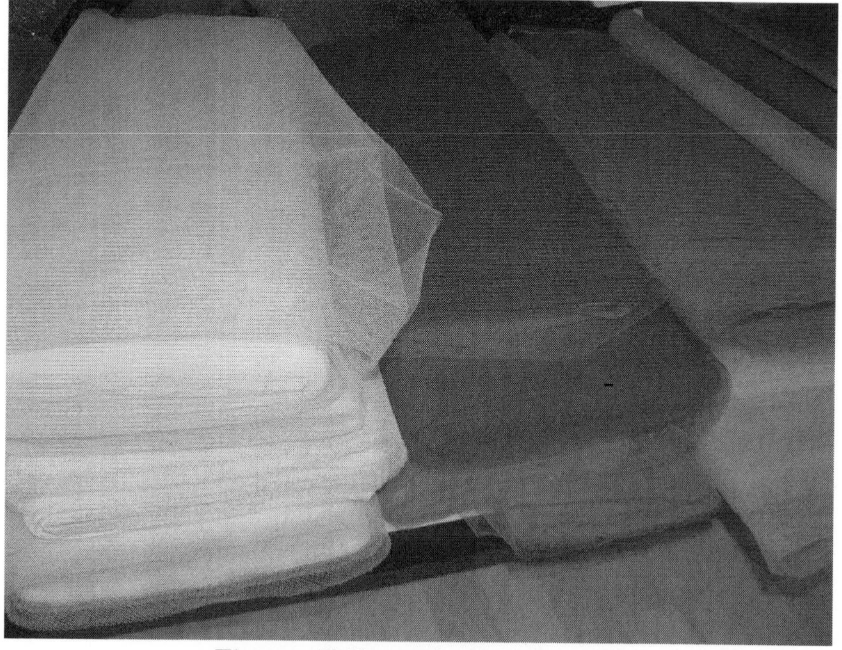

Figure: *Tulle netting woven cloth*

A woven cloth is formed by the interlacement of two sets of threads, namely, warp and weft threads. These threads are interlaced with one another according to the type of weave or design.

The warp threads are those that run longitudinally along the length of the fabric and the weft threads are those that run transversely across the fabric. For the sake of convenience the warp threads are termed as ends and the weft as picks or fillings.

Classification of Woven Structures

Woven structures are classified into the following categories:

- Simple structures
- Compound structures

In case of simple structures, there is only one series of warp and weft threads. These threads interlace with one another perpendicularly. All the neighbouring warp and weft threads are parallel to one another and play an equally important role in determining the properties of the fabric. In case of compound structures, there may be more than one series threads, of which one set forms the body or ground and the other forms the figuring or ornamentation. Unlike the simple structures, the neighbouring threads need not be parallel to one another.

Methods of Weave Representation

A weave is the interlacing pattern of the warp and weft. Two kinds of interlacing are possible :

- Warp overlap in which warp is above weft
- Weft overlap in which weft is above warp

When the warp is lifted above the inserted weft, a warp overlap is obtained. When the warp thread is lowered, the weft thread is inserted above the warp thread and the weft overlap is obtained.

There are two practical methods of weave representation:

- Linear
- Canvas

In the linear method each warp thread is represented by a vertical line and each weft thread by a horizontal line. The point of intersection of lines corresponding to a warp overlap is marked by the dot, and the point of intersection corresponding to weft overlap remains unmarked..

Though this is a simple method, it is seldom used because the designer has to draw plenty of horizontal and vertical lines, which is time consuming.

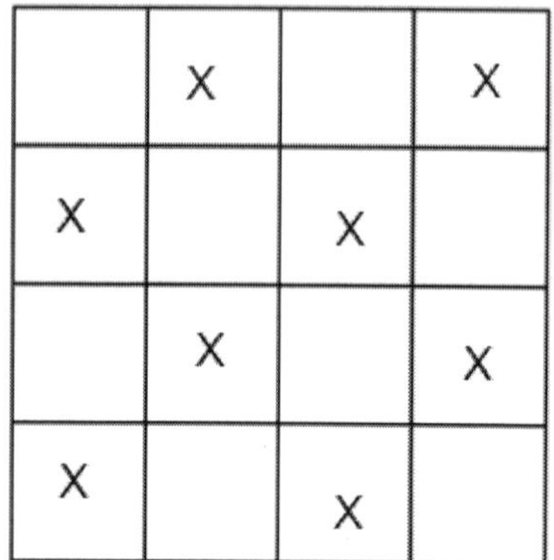

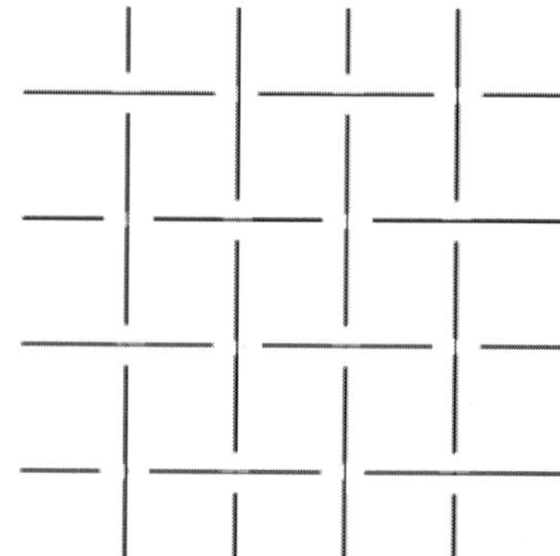

In the canvas method, a squared paper is employed, on which each vertical space represents a warp thread and each horizontal space represents a weft thread. Each square therefore indicates an intersection of warp and weft thread. To show the warp overlap, a square is filled in or shaded. The blank square indicates that the weft thread is placed over the warp i.e. weft overlap. Several types of marks may be used to indicate the warp overlap. The 'x' mark is most commonly used.

Weave Repeat

The repeat of a weave is a quantitative expression of any given weave. It indicates the minimum number of warp and weft threads for a given weave. It comprises of warp and weft repeat. The size of the repeat may be even or uneven depending upon the nature of the weave. In elementary weaves such as plain, twill, satin etc. the repeat size is normally even. However in weaves such as honey comb, huck a back the repeat size may be even or uneven. For any weave the repeat size is the sum of the warp and weft floats. Thus in case of a 2/1 twill the repeat size is 3 x 3. It is common practice to denote one repeat of a weave on design paper.

Basic Elements of a Woven Design

The three basic elements in a woven design are :

- Design
- Draft or drawing plan
- Peg or lifting plan

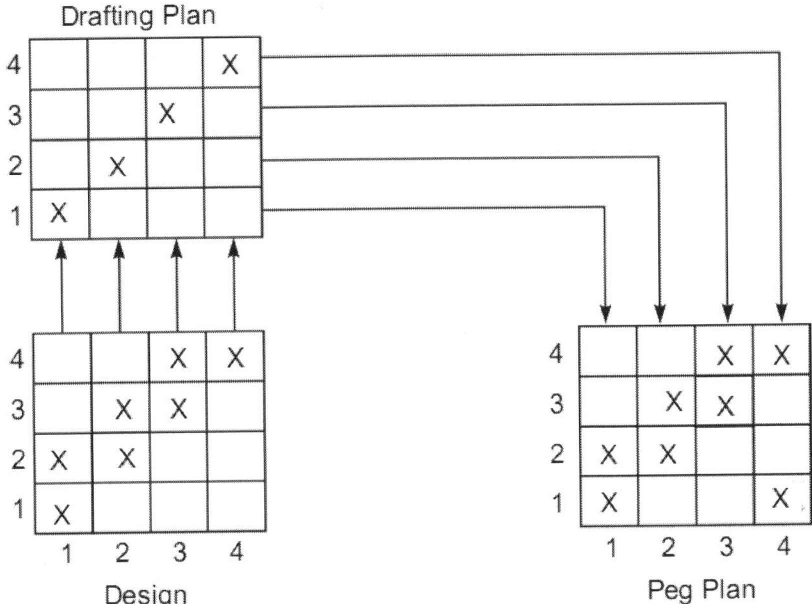

The design indicates the interlacement of warp and weft threads in the repeat of the design. It is made up of a number of squares, which constitute the repeat size of a design. The vertical direction of the squares indicate the picks and the horizontal direction indicates the ends. A blank in a square indicates that a warp goes below the corresponding weft and 'X' mark in the square indicates that the warp floats above the weft.

The draft or drawing plan indicates the manner of drawing the ends through the heald eyes and it also denotes the number of heald shaft required for a given weave repeat. The choice of the type of drafting plan depends upon the type of fabric woven.

The peg or lifting plan provides useful information to the weaver. It denotes the order of lifting of heald shafts. In a peg plan the vertical spaces indicate the heald shafts and the horizontal spaces indicate the picks. The peg plan depends upon the drafting plan. In the case of a straight draft, the peg plan will be the same as the design. Hence no peg plan is necessary in the case of a straight draft.

Plain Weaves

Plain weave (also called tabby weave, linen weave or taffeta weave) is the most basic of three fundamental types of textile weaves (along with satin weave and twill). It is strong and hard-wearing, used for fashion and furnishing fabrics.

A balanced plain weave can be identified by its checkerboard-like appearance. It is also known as one-up-one-down weave or over and under pattern. Some examples of fabric with plain weave are chiffon, organza, and taffeta.

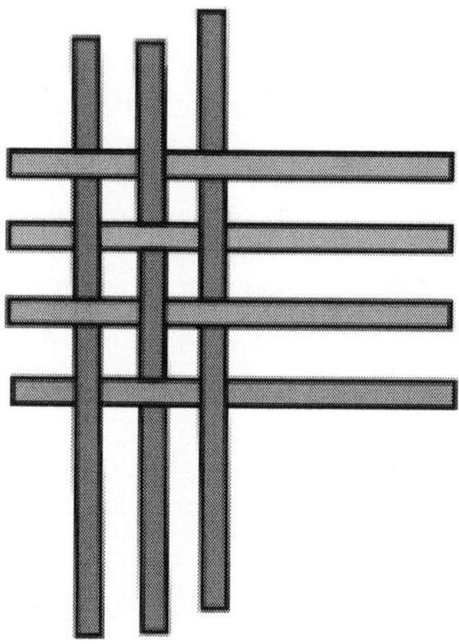

Figure: *An example of the thread crossing pattern in a plain weave fabric.*

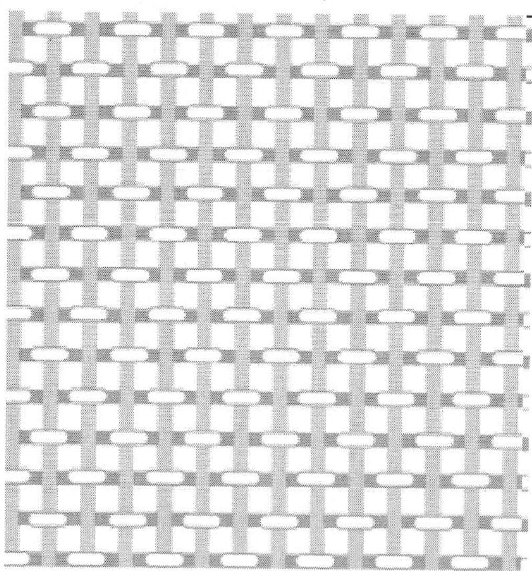

Figure: *Structure of plain-woven fabric*

In plain weave, the warp and weft are aligned so they form a simple criss-cross pattern. Each weft thread crosses the warp threads by going over one, then under the next, and so on. The next weft thread goes under the warp threads that its neighbour went over, and vice versa.

- Balanced plain weaves are fabrics in which the warp and weft are made of threads of the same weight (size) and the same number of ends per inch as picks per inch.
- Basketweave is a variation of plain weave in which two or more threads are bundled and then woven as one in the warp or weft, or both.

Figure: *Structure of basketweave fabric*

Designation

According to the 12th-century geographer al-Idrîsî, the city of Almería in Andalusia manufactured imitations of Iraqi and Persian silks called *'attâbî*, which David Jacoby identifies as "a taffeta fabric made of silk and cotton originally produced in Attabiya, a district of Baghdad."

Warp (Weaving)

In weaving cloth, the warp is the set of lengthwise yarns that are held in tension on a frame or loom. The yarn that is inserted over-and-under the warp threads is called the weft, woof, or filler. Each individual warp thread in a fabric is called a warp end or end. Warp means "that which is thrown across" (Old English *wearp*, from weorpan, to throw, cf. German *werfen*, Dutch *werpen*).

Very simple looms use a spiral warp, in which a single, very long yarn is wound around a pair of sticks or beams in a spiral pattern to make up the warp.

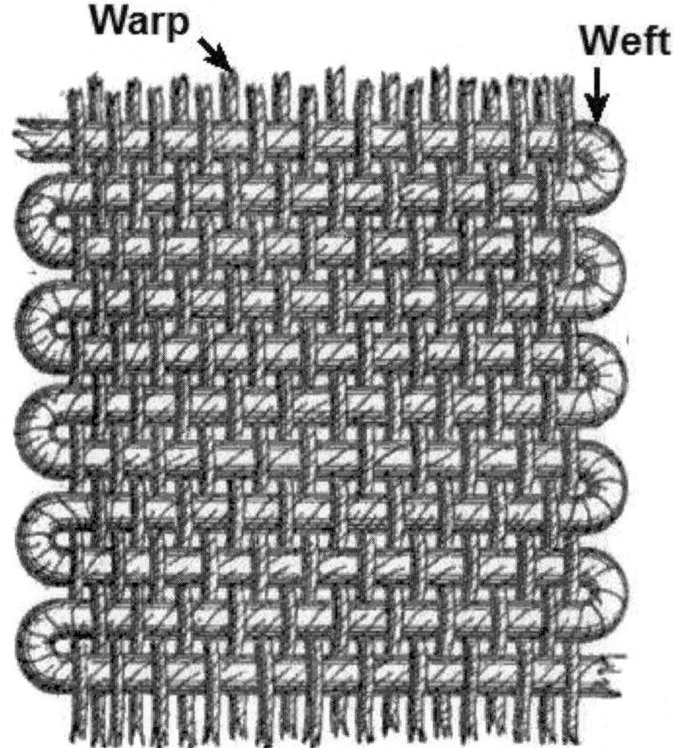

Figure: *Warp and weft in plain weaving*

Because the warp is held under high tension during the entire process of weaving and warp yarn must be strong, yarn for warp ends is usually spun and plied fibre. Traditional fibres for warping are wool, linen and silk. With the improvements in spinning technology during the Industrial Revolution, it became possible to make cotton yarn of sufficient strength to be used as the warp in mechanized weaving. Later, artificial or man-made fibres such as nylon or rayon were employed.

Warping machines have been invented to provide solutions for gauging yarn strength, length measurement and count measurement. Just like a sewing machine, warping machinery is manually operated for preparing leas yarn. Additionally, the machine is made available in two model options: the metric and the imperial system.

Weft

In weaving the weft (sometimes woof) is the term for the thread or yarn which is drawn through the warp yarns to create cloth. Warp is the lengthwise or longitudinal thread in a roll, while weft is the transverse thread. A single thread of the weft, crossing the warp, is called a *pick*. Terms do vary (for instance, in North America, the weft is sometimes referred to as the fill or the filling yarn).

The weft is a thread or yarn made of spun fibre. The original fibres used were wool, flax or cotton. Today, man-made fibres are often used in weaving. Because the weft does not have to be stretched on a loom in the way that the warp is, it can generally be less strong.

The weft is threaded through the warp using a "shuttle", air jets or "rapier grippers." Hand looms were the original weaver's tool, with the shuttle being threaded through alternately raised warps by hand. Inventions during the 18th century spurred the Industrial Revolution, with the "picking stick" and the "flying shuttle" (John Kay, 1733) speeding up production of cloth. The power loom patented by Edmund Cartwright in 1785 allowed sixty picks per minute.

The words *woof* and *weft* derive ultimately from the Old English word wefan, to weave.

Metaphorical Use

The expression "woof and warp" (also "warp and woof", "warp and weft") is sometimes used metaphorically as one might similarly use "fabric"; e.g., "the warp and woof of a student's life" means "the fabric of a student's life." The expression is used as a metaphor for the underlying structure on which something is built.

Other Cultures

In India, the weft is referred to as "baana", which is derived from another Hindi word "bun na" which means weaving with threads or strings, as is done in cane weaving and hand woven wool.

In Hairdressing

Weft is a hairdressing term for temporary hair extensions which are glued into a person's hair.

Plain Weaves

Plain weave is the most common and tightest of basic weave structures in which the filling threads pass over and under successive warp threads and repeat the same pattern with alternate threads in the following row, producing a chequered surface. They do not ravel easily but tend to wrinkle and have less absorbency than other weaves. The plain weave is variously known as ?calico? or ?tabby? weave. It is the simplest of all weaves having a repeat size of 2.

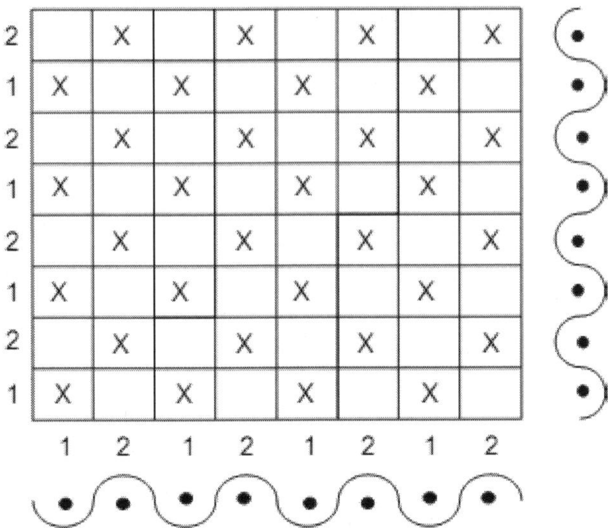

The plain weave is variously known as "calico" or "tabby" weave. It is the simplest of all weaves having a repeat size of 2. The range of application of this weave is wide. The plain weave has the following characteristics:

1. It has the maximum number of binding points
2. The threads interlace on alternate order of 1 up and 1 down.
3. The thread density is limited
4. Cloth thickness and mass per unit area are limited.
5. It produces a relatively stronger fabric that is obtained by any other simple combination of threads, excepting that of "gauze" or "cross weaving".

The principle involved in the construction of plain cloth is the interlacement of any two continuous threads either warp or weft in an exactly contrary manner to each other, with every thread in each series passing alternately under and over consecutive threads of other series interlaces uniformly throughout the fabric.

By this plan of interlacement, every thread in each series interlaces with every thread in the other series to the maximum extent, thereby producing a comparatively firm and strong texture of cloth. A complete unit of the plain weave occupies only two warp threads and two picks of weft which is the design for that weave.

The plain weave is produced in a variety of forms and textures, possessing totally different characteristics, which adapt it for specific purposes. A variety of forms in textures are produced :

(i) By causing a differential tension between the warp threads during weaving.

(ii) By using various counts of yarn for weaving different types of fabrics,

(iii) By using warp and weft yarns of different counts in the same fabric.

The term 'texture' is related to type of material, counts of yarn, relative density of threads, weight, bulk, feel during handle, and other properties. The range of textures produced in plain cloth is wide. An ideal plain cloth is one which has identical or similar warp and weft constructional parameters.

End Uses

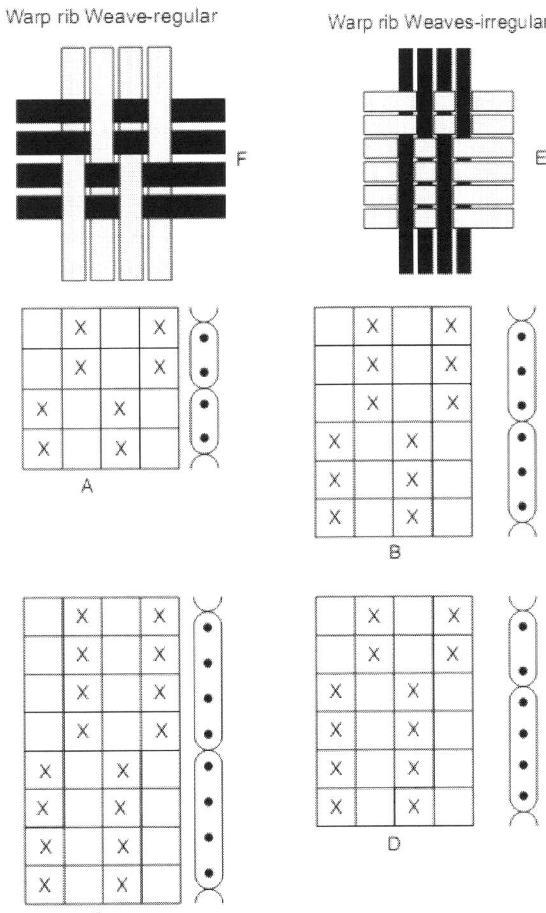

Figure: *These are constructed by extending the plain weave in weft direction*

Plain weave finds extensive uses. It is used in cambric, muslin, blanket, canvas, dhothi, saree, shirting, suiting, etc.

The plain weave may be modified by extending it warp or weft way or both. The extension of the plain weave thus produces a rib effect.

A warp rib results from extending the plain weave in the warp direction and a weft rib structure results from extending the plain weave in the weft direction. A matt rib results from extending the plain weave in both directions.

These are produced by extending the plain weave in warp wary direction. Figure shows the warp rib weaves constructed on regular and irregular basis.

At A, B and C are seen regular warp rib weaves and at D, is shown the irregular warp rib weave. E and F show the interlacing of D and A respectively.

In both the warp and weft rib weaves, the appearance of the cloth depends on the respective thread settings, and to achieve good effects, it is necessary to weave a weft rib with a high number of picks per inch and a comparatively low number of ends per inch.

Similarly the warp rib effect can be enhanced with a high number of ends per inch and a comparatively low number of picks per inch. The prominence of the rib can be increased by suitable use of coarse and fine yarns.

The dependence of all rib constructions upon the correct thread settings is marked.

The typical constructional particulars for a weft rib structure is given below:

- Warp - 2/14s & 36s
- Ends/inch - 56
- Weft - 18s
- Picks/inch - 100

The typical constructional particulars for a warp rib structure is given below:

- Warp - 30s cotton
- Ends/inch - 126
- Weft - 15s cotton
- Picks/inch - 38

Uses

Rib weaves are used in gross grain cloths, matelasse fabrics, repp cloth which is extensively employed for window blinds in railway carriages and other vehicles, upholstering furniture, and cambric picket handkerchief.

These weaves are also variously known as hopsack or basket weaves. The matt rib structures result from extending the plain weave in both directions.

In case of regular matt weave, the plain weaves are extended equally in the warp and weft directions, where as in case of irregular matt weaves, the plain weave is extended unevenly or irregularly in the warp and weft directions.

Uses

Matt weave finds extensive uses for a great variety of fabrics such as dress materials, shirtings, sail cloth, duck cloth etc.

Twill Weaves

Twill is a type of textile weave with a pattern of diagonal parallel ribs (in contrast with a satin and plain weave). This is done by passing the weft thread over one or more warp threads and then under two or more warp threads and so on, with a "step" or offset between rows to create the characteristic diagonal pattern. Because of this structure, twills generally drape well.

Examples of twill fabric are denim, tweed, chino, gabardine, drill, covert, and serge.

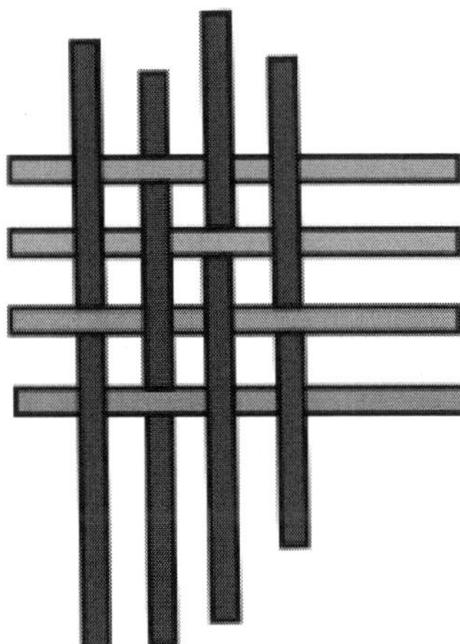

Figure: *A diagram of the thread crossing pattern in a twill weave fabric*

Structure

In a twill weave, each weft or filling yarn floats across the warp yarns in a progression of interlacings to the right or left, forming a distinct diagonal line. This diagonal line is also known as a wale. A float is the portion of a yarn that crosses over two or more yarns from the opposite direction.

A twill weave requires three or more harnesses, depending on its complexity. A twill weave is the second most basic weave that can be made on a fairly simple loom.

Twill weave is often designated as a fraction—such as 2/1—in which the numerator indicates the number of harnesses that are raised (and, thus, threads crossed – in this example, two), and the denominator indicates the number of harnesses that are lowered when a filling yarn is inserted (in this example, one).

The fraction 2/1 would be read as "two up, one down." The minimum number of harnesses needed to produce a twill can be determined by totalling the numbers in the fraction.

For the example described, the number of harnesses is three. (The fraction for plain weave is 1/1.)

Characteristics of Twill

Twill fabrics technically have a front and a back side, unlike plain weave, whose two sides are the same. The front side of the twill is the technical face; the back is called the technical back.

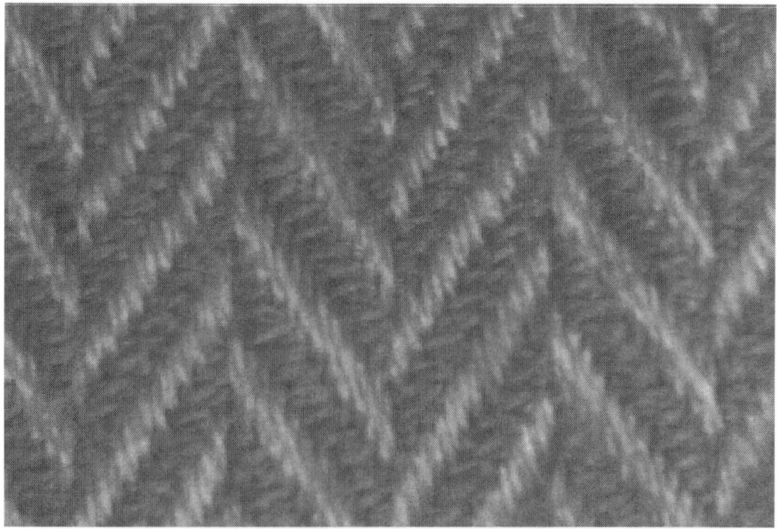

Figure: *A twill with ribs in both sides, called herringbone.*

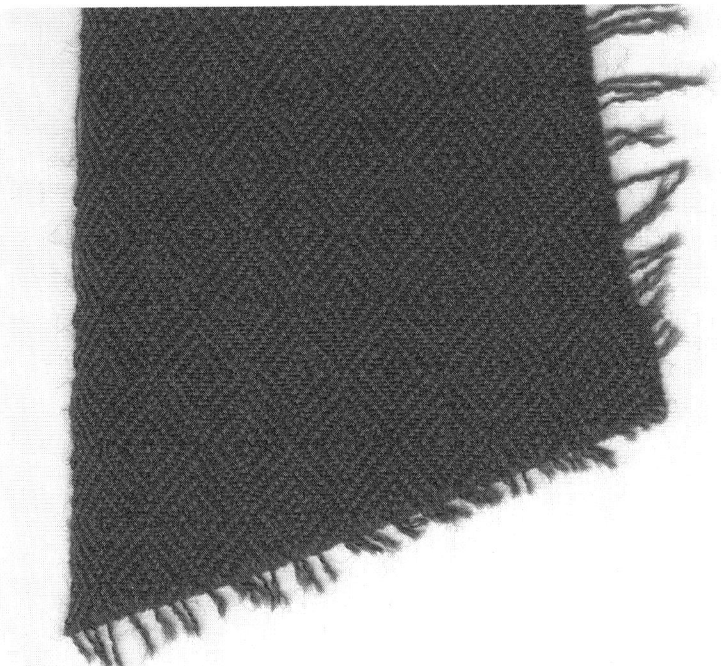

Figure: *Diamond twill, with weaving edge (left), blue warp, red weft.*

The technical face side of a twill weave fabric is the side with the most pronounced wale; it is usually more durable, more attractive, most often used as the fashion side of the fabric, and the side visible during weaving. If there are warp floats on the technical face (i.e., if the warp crosses over two or more wefts), there will be filling floats (the weft will cross over two or more warps) on the technical back. If the twill wale goes up to the right on one side, it will go up to the left on the other side. Twill fabrics have no up and down as they are woven.

Sheer fabrics are seldom made with a twill weave. Because a twill surface has interesting texture and design, printed twills (on which a design is printed on the cloth) are much less common than printed plain weaves. When twills are printed, they are typically done so on lightweight fabrics.

Soil and stains are less noticeable on the uneven surface of twills than on smooth surfaces, such as plain weaves. Thus, twills are often used for sturdy work clothing or durable upholstery. Denim, for example, is a twill.

The fewer interlacings in twills allow the yarns to move more freely, and thus they are softer, more pliable, and drape better than plain-weave textiles. Twills also recover from wrinkles better than plain-weave fabrics do.

When there are fewer interlacings, yarns can be packed closer together to produce high-count fabrics. In twills and higher counts, the fabric is more durable and air- and water-resistant.

There are even-sided twills and warp-faced twills. Even-sided twills include foulard or surah, herringbone, houndstooth, serge, sharkskin, and twill flannel. Warp-faced twills include cavalry twill, chino, covert, denim, drill, fancy twill, gabardine, and lining twill.

Characteristics of Twill Weave

Twill Weave is strong and hard-wearing, used for fashion and furnishing fabrics. In plain weave the warp and weftare aligned so that they form a simple criss-cross pattern.

Each weft thread crosses the warp threads by going over one, then under the next, and so on.

The next weft thread goes under the warp threads thatits neighbour went over, and vice versa. Plain weave is also known as “tabby weave” or “taffeta weave”. Twill is a type of fabric woven with a pattern of diagonal parallel ribs.

Common Characteristics of Twill Weaves

- May have face/back and up/down orientation
- Interesting surface and texture
- Seldom printed
- Soil less evident
- More pliable
- Better wrinkle recovery
- High counts possible (more durable)
- More expensive
- Wale may be prominent

Common twill fabrics

1. Even sided:
   - o Serge – Common worsted suiting fabric, 2/2 RH
   - o Herringbone – Alternating twill
   - o Checks – Colour effect weaves, usually 2/2 twill
   - o Houndstooth
   - o Surah- silk or silky yarns

2. warp faced
   - o Denim – (Serge de Nimes), Classically 3/1 LH
   - o Gabardine – Steep twill, slacks, uniform
3. Twills are not as strong as plain weaves with similar construction.
4. Twills show less dirt/stains because of their uneven surface as compared to plain weaves
5. Recover better from wrinkles

Denim

Denim (which gets its name from the French for "from Nîmes" (*de Nîmes*)) is a rugged cotton twill textile, in which the weft passes under two (*twi-* "double") or more warp threads. This twill weaving produces the familiar diagonal ribbing of the fabric, which distinguishes denim from cotton duck.

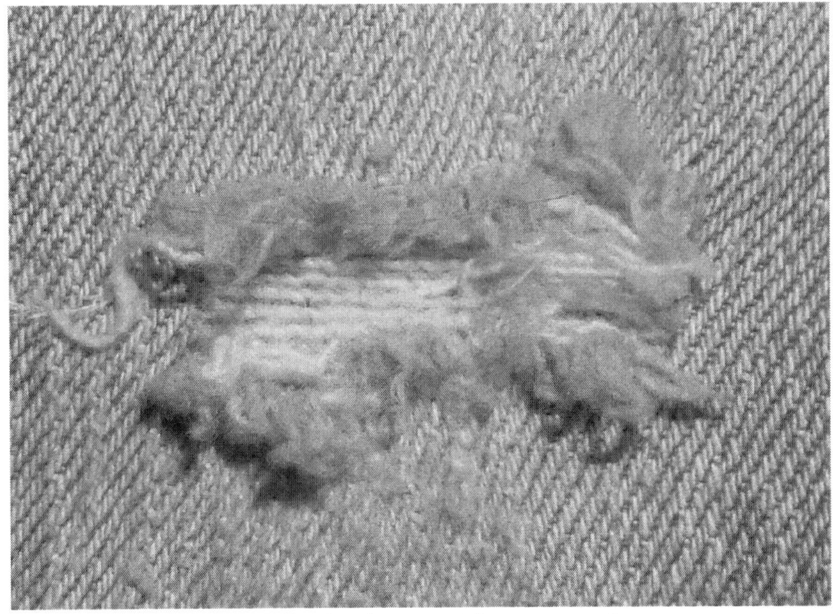

***Figure:** Denim jeans with wear and tear*

It is characteristic of any indigo denim that only the warp threads are dyed, whereas the weft threads remain plain white. As a result of the warp-faced twill weaving, one side of the fabric shows the blue warp threads, the other side shows the white weft threads. This is why jeans are white on the inside and what makes denim's fading characteristics unique compared to every other fabric. The word 'denim' comes from the name of a sturdy fabric called serge, originally made in Nîmes, France, by the André family. Originally called *Serge de Nîmes*, the name was soon shortened to denim. Denim has been used in America since the late 18th century.

Denim was traditionally coloured blue with indigo dye to make blue "jeans", though "jean" then denoted a different, lighter cotton textile; the contemporary use of jean comes from the French word for Genoa, Italy (Gênes), where the first denim trousers were made.

Worldwide Market

In 2007, the worldwide denim market equalled USD 51.6 billion, with demand growing by 5% and supply growing by 8% annually. Over 50% of denim is produced in Asia, specifically China, India, and Bangladesh. The following table shows where the world's denim mills are located.

Region	*No. of Denim Mills*
China	297
Asia (excluding China)	104
North America	9
Europe	41
Latin America	46
Africa	15
Australia	1
Total Denim Mills (World-wide)	513

Dry or raw denim

Dry or raw denim, as opposed to washed denim, is a denim fabric that is not washed after being dyed during its production. Over time, denim will generally fade, which is often considered desirable. During the process of wear, it is typical to see fading on areas that generally receive the most stress, which includes the upper thighs (whiskers), the ankles (stacks) and behind the knees (honey combs).

After being crafted into an article of clothing, most denim is washed to make it softer and to reduce or eliminate shrinkage, which could cause an item to not fit after the owner washes it. In addition to being washed, non-dry denim is sometimes artificially "distressed" to produce a worn look.

Much of the appeal of factory distressed denim is that it looks similar to dry denim that has, with time, faded. With dry denim, however, such fading is affected by the body of the person who wears the jeans and the activities of his/her daily life. This creates what many enthusiasts feel to be a more natural, unique look than distressed denim.

To facilitate the natural distressing process, some wearers of dry denim will often abstain from washing their jeans for more than six months, though it is not a necessity for fading.

Selvage Denim

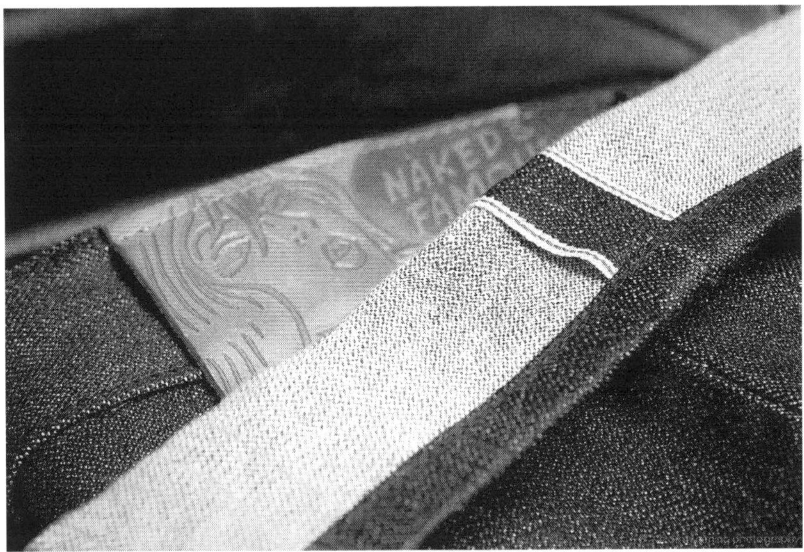

Figure: *Raw selvage denim*

All fabric has a selvedge (a portmanteau derived from the joining of "self" & "edge"), this is the natural edge of the cloth and contrary to some sources does not unravel or fray regardless of which weaving method or machinery is used.

"Selvage denim" refers to a unique type of closed selvage (derived from the Latin Salvare, meaning "to secure, to make safe") that is created using one continuous cross yarn (the weft) that is passed back and forth through the vertical warp beams.

This is traditionally finished at both edge with a contrast warp, most commonly red which is why sometimes this type of denim is referred to as "Red Selvage". This process is only possible using a Shuttle loom.

Shuttle looms weave a narrower 30 inch fabric, which is on average half the width of the more modern shuttleless Sulzer looms (invented in 1927 by the Sulzer brothers) and thus a longer piece of fabric is required to make a pair of jeans (approximately 3 yards).

To maximize yield, jean were traditionally made with a straight outseam that utilised the full width of the fabric including this edge. This became not only desirable but since the production of wider width denim, a mark of premium quality as when worn with a turn up the two selvages where visible rather than an unattractive overlocked edge.

Dying

Originally Indigo was produced using dye from plant Indigofera tinctoria but most denim today is dyed with synthetic indigo. In both cases the yarn will undergo a repetitive sequence of dipping and oxidization, the more dips, the stronger the indigo shade.

Rope dye is considered the best yarn dyeing method as it eliminated shading across the fabric width, although the alternative slasher process is cheaper as only one beaming process is needed (in rope dyeing, beaming is done twice).

Patterns of Fading

Fades caused by prolonged periods of wear, without washing, have become the main allure for raw denim. The fading patterns are a way of personalizing the garment for each customer. These fades are categorized by certain names:

- Whiskers – Faded streaks that surround the crotch area of the denim.
- Combs – Also known, as "honey combs" are the streaks of faded lines that are found behind the knee.
- Stacks – Produced by having the inseam of the denim hemmed a few inches longer than actual leg length. The extra fabric stacks on top of the shoe causing a fade to form around the ankle to calf area of the denim.
- Train Tracks – appears on the outseams of the denim. This fade showcases the selvedge by forming two sets of fades that resemble train tracks.

Stretch Denim

Stretch denim usually incorporates an elastic component (such as elastane) into the fabric to allow a degree of give in garments. Only a small percentage is required within the fabric (approximately 3%)

to allow a significant stretch capacity of around 15 percent. But this will reduce the life span of the product.

Colour Denim

Denim fabric dyeing is divided into two categories; indigo dyeing and sulphur dyeing. Indigo dyeing produces traditional blue colours or shades similar to blue colours.

Sulphur dyeing (also called colour denim) is used to create speciality black colours and other colours like pink, grey, rust, mustard, green, and also improve the quality.

Foulard

A foulard is a lightweight fabric, either twill or plain-woven, made of silk or a mix of silk and cotton. Foulards usually have a small printed design of various colours. *Foulard* can also refer by metonymy to articles of clothing, such as scarves and neckties, made from this fabric.

Foulard is believed to have originated in the Far East. The word comes from the French word *foulard*, with the same proper and metonymic meanings.

In modern French, *foulard* is the usual word for a scarf or neckerchief.

Home decor use of foulard fabric: "Wall coverings are check, tattersalls, and foulards."

Honey Comb Weaves

The honey comb weaves derive their name from their partial resemblance to the hexagonal honey comb cells of wax in which bees store their honey.

The high and low parts of Honey comb weaved fabrics are formed by different intersections of the warp and filling. Where the warp filling threads float the farthest they lie on the face of the fabric causing a raised effect. These weaves require a certain grouping of loosely and tightly intersecting threads.

Huck a Back Weaves

This surface embroidery form has several different versions and is known by many names: Huck Embroidery, Huckaback darning, Punto Oitinho (Brazilian), Yugoslavian Weaving, and Swedish weaving. (There is a form of loom weaving called Swedish weaving also.)

History

The style we are talking about today is best known as Huck Embroidery or Swedish weaving. The name Huck Embroidery comes from the specialty fabric, huck, which it is stitched on. It was difficult to find the reason why the technique is called Swedish Weaving. Phyllis Maurer from Ethnic Fibre Arts researches ethnic needlework. She says this technique has been found in linens dating back to the 16002s.

Sweden may have gotten the credit because many of the surviving linens and clothes came from this country. Swedish weaving was at its height of popularity in the 1930s and 1940s in the United States where the stitching was done on huck kitchen towels and linens. Phyllis suggests the usage of automatic dishwashers in homes created a decline in the need for dish towels, and therefore, the technique began to die off.

Thankfully there has been a resurgence in the popularity of Huck Embroidery. Designers are creating new exciting patterns which use today's wide range of fabrics and fibres. Today one of the most popular projects is making Monk's cloth afghans.

What distinguishes huck weaving from other similar styles is the design is worked completely on the top of the fabric, so the thread never appears on the back. That is great news for those of us who hold our breath when someone picks up our work and turns it over to see how neat it is!

This is a very easy technique to learn working with basically two stitches. It works well for both right- and left-hand stitchers. Designers combine the stitches in a repeating pattern that is easy to follow and relaxing to stitch. Let me show you just how easy this technique is to learn.

Work Basket

Fabrics: There are several specialty fabrics which make your stitching a breeze.

- Huck fabric is a descendant of a linen weave called huckaback. It is usually 14 count (7 floats) per inch, 100% cotton and 553 wide. This fabric has a smooth and rough side. Sometimes it is hard to tell them apart by feel. The easiest method is to check the floats. One side will have 1 thread per float, while the other will have 2 threads per float. You want to stitch on the side with two threads per float. This fabric does not have to be prewashed. The way you finish your edges will depend on the project. To stitch the design you will want to use a size #8 or #12 pearl cotton or equivalent, or 3-6 strands of embroidery floss. Metallic threads look great on this fabric, if you are not going to use or wash it often. With huck fabric you can make tablecloths, runners, place mats, wall hangings, box lids, or card inserts. The possibilities are almost endless.

- Huck towelling is approximately 143 wide. The stitch and float counts can vary, so check your fabric if your pattern needs to be a specific size. A majority of the fabric is 16 count (7-8 floats per inch), 100% cotton. The selvages have been pre-finished. It is milled in such a way that one side is more textured with one float thread running vertically. The smoother side has two float threads running vertically. You can use either side, but most people prefer the side with two floats. You do not need to prewash this fabric. You will need to decide how long you want your towel to be and what type of finished edge you want, hemmed or fringed, for example. I would recommend buying 18" – 24" for one towel. For stitching use a 6-strand embroidery floss or #5 size pearl cotton. You can use this fabric for runners, placemats, and hand towels.
- Monk's cloth is an even weave fabric, 100% cotton, 603 wide, 7 count (4 floats per inch) Monks' cloth has floats going in both directions, so you can work your design either way. Monk's cloth has to be pre-shrunk before you start to stitch. I cannot stress that enough, because there is significant shrinkage. Zigzag the edges of the fabric to keep it from unraveling. Machine wash the prepared fabric with detergent in warm water. You can use fabric softener. Dry the fabric in the dryer. Sources can't agree on the temperature setting. Some say hot, others say medium or low heat. My recommendation is you dry it on the setting you would normally dry it on when you when you wash it later. Depending on the manufacturer, you will see a 4-6" shrinkage per yard. We recommend you purchase 2 1/2 yards for an afghan and 1 2/3 yards for a baby blanket. Monk's cloth is great for afghans, lap robes, runners, and placemats. It is also an alternative for folks who want to continue to stitch, but their eye sight has declined significantly. There are many ways to finish an afghan, such as hemming and fringing. Monk's cloth now comes in quite a variety of colours including radical new colours:

- o Monk's cloth – Turquoise – 603 wide – 7 count ct. – 8900
- o Monk's cloth – Lime Green – 603 wide – 7 count ct. – 8903
- o Monk's cloth – Hot Pink – 603 wide – 7 count ct. – 8902

Because of the size of floats, you can experiment with lots of fibres. Many folks use size #3 pearl cotton, multiple strands of #5 pearl cotton, 4-ply worsted yarn, ribbon, or Rainbow Gallery Plastic Canvas 7 or Overture.

- Popcorn fabric, is also known as popkorn or Stockholm, and is 7-count (3 floats per inch) fabric with floats going both vertically and horizontally. The fabric is 70" wide and 100% cotton. You do not need to prewash this fabric. Stitch with size #3 pearl cotton, 1-2 strands of #5 pearl cotton, or 6-12 strands of embroidery floss. This fabric has a nice look and feel to it, and it would be great to use for pillows, placemats, napkins, box lids, and wall hangings.
- Waffle cloth is 100% cotton, 45" wide and has 5 rows per inch. This cloth is woven so it has little "boxes" on the top of the fabric. You stitch through the longer threads on the edge of the boxes. Waffle cloth must be prewashed. Zigzag the edges of the fabric to keep it from unraveling. Machine wash with detergent in warm water on the delicate cycle. Dry in the dryer on low heat. This fabric has a unique look and works great for pillows box lids, and wall hangings. You can use size #3 or #5 pearl cotton, ribbon, or 6-12 strands of embroidery floss.
- Aida cloth can be used in place of a huck fabric by running the needle under the loose top threads, but not through the back of the fabric. Designers may recommend whether to pick up all four or just the two center threads when stitching. Aida is 100% cotton. You do not need to prewash. A good size to use is 14 count (7 floats) per inch. You do not need to prewash. Stitch with #5 pearl cotton or 6 strands of embroidery floss. You can make ornaments, placemats, napkin rings, card inserts, and wall hangings.

Threads: Floss and pearl cottons were the threads of choice for earlier hand towels. Today the possibilities are almost endless with over-dyed, variegated, silk, metallic, and synthetic fibres. When you choose your threads, keep in mind what the project is. Will it be handled and washed often, or will it be displayed with little cleaning? For those items that will be used, you will probably want to stick to strong fibres such as cotton and silk. Silks have been found in costumes and household linens dating back centuries, so don't be afraid to use this fibre in your projects. Ornaments and samplers can be accented with metallic and specialty threads.

For the larger float sizes, such as Monk's cloth, you can use a 4-ply worsted weight yarn. Check the content so you don't get something with special washing instructions or that won't take heat well.

The ribbon mentioned above is not the silk ribbon type. Silk ribbon can tend to stretch or separate with a lot of use. Use the ribbon you can get in the craft department that comes on the rolls.

Needles: You need a blunt needle so you don't split the floats as you stitch. For huck towelling, fabric, and Aida, you should use a tapestry needle that works well with your thread, such as size 24 tapestry needles. Clover makes a Huck Embroidery needle set with 3 needles (2.25", 2.62", and 3".) The 3" needle has a bent end to help get under the floats.

- Huck Embroidery Needles – pkg/3 – 7123

For Monk's cloth, a bodkin or weaving needle is preferred. Here are a few of the choices we carry:

- John James Bodkin Set – 7083
- John James Raffia and Bodkin Set (3-one has a slightly bent (cranked) tip for easier stitching) – 7082
- John James Weaving Needles (1 flat raffia needle, a bent weaving needle and a flat bent raffia needle) – 7065

Other handy accessories would include safety pins to mark your center on Monk's cloth projects. Many people do not use a hoop when doing Huck Embroidery. stitch in hand, not using a hoop.

For small projects or specialty fibres, you may want to use a hoop (click for embroidery hoops & frames) to help maintain an even tension. The choice is yours. Experiment and do what works best for you for each project. Some stitchers have found stitch counters and lighted-magnifiers (click for lights & magnifiers) a big help.

Reading the Pattern

Sometimes it is hard to get used to the diagrams and terminology that designers use to lay out their pattern. You need to know how the code works to decipher some of the patterns, especially older ones that come with no additional instructions or photographs.

Here are some common things to look for in Huck Embroidery patterns:

- The order of stitching may be marked. On the edge of the pattern you may see "1", "A", or "row 1". This tells you the order in which to stitch the rows.
- Sometimes the designer gives you the length of thread for each row. The code for 3 times the length of the design or fabric might appear as "3W", "3L", "3T", or "2 times length plus 8". There will be times you find a pattern and it doesn't give you the thread length. Here is a general rule of thumb:
- For a straight stitch, width of the fabric or design plus three inches
- For a straight looped stitch, one and a half times the width of the fabric or design plus three inches
- For a stitch that goes up or down several rows, use two times the width of the fabric.
- For a stitch that goes up or down more than 4 rows, use three times the width of the fabric or design

Often you will get a pattern charted with the fabric diagrams showing the floats and a dark line showing the path. Some designers print their patterns in colour, which is a wonderful help if you have multiple threads in one space. This is the road map for your needle.

Tips and Tricks

To start a row, leave about 3" of thread. When you are done with the row or project, your choice, work the ends under three or four floats that you worked on that row, making sure that you loop around the edge float (otherwise it would just pull through). Cut the thread close to the fabric. You can wiggle it around with your blunt needle so the end doesn't show.

How you end your threads will depend on how you plan on finishing the edges. If you want a fringe all the way around, you will want to leave them long. (Be sure to add more to your thread length to allow for the fringe length.) You can hide the ends in the hem if you are hemming or binding the edge. If you are working on a towel that has a pre-finished edge, you will want to loop around the last float and weave your thread back through several floats. Cut the thread close to the fabric.

Where do you start? Read the designer's instructions to see if there is a suggestion. Most patterns will have you start the first thread in the middle of the fabric and stitch out to the ends. This helps center your work and reduces wear on the thread. For items such as afghans and lap quilts you should start in the middle of the row and the fabric length. This will ensure that your stitching will be centered, and you can treat the ends equally. Safety pins will help you mark the center points.

For the remaining rows, it will depend on your piece whether you start in the center or on an edge. For large pieces you may want to always begin in the center and work out to reduce the length of thread you are stitching with and reduces the wear on your thread. If you are using specialty threads such as metallic, you may want to work from the center out for each row to reduce the wear on your thread.

You should calculate the amount of thread you need for each row so that you don't run out in the middle of the row. However, there are a few patterns that have you stitch back and forth and you may run out in the middle of the row.

To join a new thread you want to work your stitching thread following the pattern and when you get to the end of the thread, cut it as close to fabric as possible. Begin your new thread about four or five floats back from where you ended. You will have double thread for those four or five floats.

You want to be sure to stitch with an even tension. If your tension is too loose, your design may lose its shape. If your tension is too tight, your fabric will pucker or your stitches will pull tight creating harsh edges.

Finishing the Edges

How you plan to finish your huck weaving project plays a big part in preparing to do the pattern. Here are some suggestions:

- For projects such as box tops, card inserts, or stool covers the edges will be hidden. When you are done stitching, you can machine zigzag or fray check (6622) the edges to reduce fraying.
- For towels, linens, and wall hangings you may want a finished edge, perhaps hemmed, fringed, bound, or lace.
- For larger items such as afghans and lap robes you may want an edge that is hemmed, fringed, bound, or finished with a blanket stitch or crocheting.

Hemmed Edge: You turn the edges over twice and hem stitch, either by hand or by machine.

Self Fringing: Decide how long you want your fringe to be and machine stitch just above that point. For example, if you want a 1" fringe, machine stitch 1.25" up from the edge. A zigzag stitch is best. Remove the cross threads below the stitched line and trim your ends.

Fibre Fringe: You can have fringe along the edges of your piece by leaving a length of your fibre at the beginning and end of each row. The fibres should be secured when you finish the project.

You can hem the fabric so only the fibre fringe will show, or you can zigzag above the point you want to fringe, then pull the cross threads from the fabric giving you fabric and fibre threads in the fringe. Trim your fringe to a uniform length when completely done.

Blanket Stitch: Hem the edges and do a regular blanket stitch around the outside. Keep the distance between your stitches even.

Single crochet: Hem the edges. Crochet a single crochet through the fabric so the crochet loop is on the edge.

Bound: Zigzag the fabric close to the edge, then stitch seam binding around the project.

Lace: Add a prepared lace or trim to your project. You will probably want to hem the edges or zigzag close to the edge of the fabric to secure your threads Add lace or trim to the top of your finished edge.

Techniques to Try

There are basically two stitches (straight and looped) which are worked in differing ways to create wonderful patterns.

Straight Stitches (click the stitch names for visual guides to those stitches)

- Straight Stitch, Darning Stitch or Stitch a Float
- Skip Straight Stitch, Darning Skip Stitch
- Zigzag Straight Stitch – one and two row examples

Loop Stitches (click the stitch names for visual guides to those stitches)

- Open Loop
- Offset Open Loop
- Step Stitch using Open Loops
- Single Closed Loop
- Large Closed Loop
- Figure Eight, Twisted Loop

Crepe Weave

Crape or crepe (Anglicized versions of the Fr. *crêpe*) is a silk, wool, or polyester fabric of a gauzy texture, having a peculiar crisp or crimpy appearance. (The word *crape* is also used as an Anglicized spelling of crêpe (pancake).)

Silk crape is woven of hard spun silk yarn in the gum or natural condition. There are two distinct varieties of the textile: soft, Canton, or Oriental crape, and hard or crisped crape. Thin crêpe is called crêpe de Chine ("Chinese crêpe").

The wavy appearance of Canton crape results from the peculiar manner in which the weft is prepared, the yarn from two bobbins being twisted together in the reverse way. The fabric when woven is smooth and even, having no crape appearance, but when the gum is subsequently extracted by boiling, it at once becomes soft, and the weft, losing its twist, gives the fabric the waved structure which constitutes its distinguishing feature. Canton crapes are used, either white or coloured, for scarves and shawls, bonnet trimmings, etc.

The crisp and elastic structure of hard crape is not produced either in the spinning or in the weaving, but is due to processes through which the gauze passes after it is woven. In 1911, the details of these processes were known to only a few manufacturers, who so jealously guarded their secrets that, in some cases, the different stages in the manufacture were conducted in towns far removed from each other. Commercially they are distinguished as single, double, three-ply and four-ply crapes, according to the nature of the yarn used in their manufacture. They are almost exclusively dyed black and used in mourning dress.

In Great Britain, hard crapes are made at Braintree in Essex, Norwich, Yarmouth, Manchester and Glasgow. The crape formerly made at Norwich was made with a silk warp and worsted weft and is said to have afterwards degenerated into bombazine. A very successful imitation of real crape is made in Manchester of cotton yarn and sold under the name of Victoria crape.

Types of Crepe Fabric

Crepe is a supple fabric with a twisted, pebbled or puckered appearance. The distinctive crepe surface can be the result of tight weaving, twisting or knotting the fibres prior to weaving, using irregular patterns during the weaving process or by embossing a finished fabric with rollers engraved with a crepe pattern. The pattern is permanently embedded into the fibres using a combination of heat and pressure. Several types of fibres can be used to produce crepe fabrics, notably silk, silk-like fabrics and cotton. There is a wide variety of types of crepe, including crepe de chine, plisse crepe, Moroccan crepe, wool crepe and crepe georgette.

Crepe de Chine

- Crepe de chine is a lightweight fabric, usually made of silk, without a pronounced crepe finish. It tends to have a smooth, pebbled, matte finish and is used to make luxury garments and evening wear. The fabric is made with highly twisted, worsted yarns in the weft and silk yarns in the warp, or of just silk warps and wefts. It weakens when exposed to perspiration or sunlight.

Crepe Georgette

- Crepe georgette is a thin, matte silk or silk-like fabric that drapes well and is very elastic. It is sheer and flat with a grainy texture and is sometimes referred to as chiffon. Its fluidity and easy draping makes it ideal for women's clothing. It is used to make evening wear, gowns, blouses, dresses and skirts.

Moroccan Crepe

- Moroccan crepe, also known as crepe marocain, is a heavy textured, woven, ribbed crepe fabric made of silk, rayon or wool. It is made using heavily twisted yarns in the weft, resulting in the characteristic wavy, ribbed texture. It is used to make dresses and suits.

Plisse Crepe

- Plisse crepe is made by using heavy rollers to impress a crepe pattern into fabric or by chemically treating the fabric to give it a characteristic crepe-like appearance. The fabric, often cotton, is covered in wax in a striped or pebbled pattern and dipped into an alkaline solution. The uncovered portions of the fabric shrink, resulting in a striping or puckering when the wax is removed. The resulting plisse crepe fabric is very strong and does not need ironing.

Wool Crepe

- Wool crepe, also known as crepon, is a wiry crepe fabric made from mixtures of silk and cotton fibres. The crepe effect on the surface of the fabric comes about through the treatment of the yarn during the weaving process.

The fabric can be woven with a combination of left- and right-hand twists in the same fabric or by having different degrees of slackness in the warp yarns or in the tightness of the twists. Wool crepe is used to make lingerie and dresses.

Scarf

A scarf, also known as a muffler, or neck-wrap is a piece of fabric worn around the neck, or near the head or around the waist for warmth, cleanliness, fashion or for religious reasons. They can come in a variety of different colours.

History

Ancient Rome is one of the first origins of the scarf, where it was not used to keep warm, but to keep clean. It was called the *sudarium*, which translates from Latin to English as "sweat cloth", and was used to wipe the sweat from the neck and face in hot weather.

They were originally worn by men around their neck or tied to their belt. Soon women started using the scarves, which were made of cloth and not made of wool, pashmina, or silk, and ever since the scarf has been fashionable among women.

Scarves were used to hide the face of ugly people.

Historians believe that during the reign of the Chinese Emperor Cheng, scarves made of cloth were used to identify officers or the rank of Chinese warriors.

In later times scarves were also worn by soldiers of all ranks in Croatia around the 17th century.

The only difference in the soldiers' scarves that designated a difference in rank was that the officers had silk scarves whilst the other ranks were issued with cotton scarves. The men's scarves were sometimes referred to as "cravats" (from the French *cravate*, meaning "Croat"), and were the precursor of the necktie.

The scarf became a real fashion accessory by the early 19th century for both men and women. By the middle of the 20th century scarves became one of the most essential and versatile clothing accessories for both men and women.

In recent years, scarves have experienced a revival.

Uses and Types

In cold climates, a thick knitted scarf, often of wool, is tied around the neck to keep warm. This is usually accompanied by a warm hat and heavy coat.

In drier, dustier warm climates, or in environments where there are many airborne contaminants, a thin headscarf, kerchief, or bandanna is often worn over the head to keep the hair clean. Over time, this custom has evolved into a fashionable item in many cultures, particularly among women. The cravat, an ancestor of the necktie and bow tie, evolved from scarves of this sort in Croatia.

Religions such as Judaism under Halakhah (Jewish Law) promote modest dress code among women. Married Jewish women wear a tichel to cover their hair. The Tallit is commonly worn by Jewish men especially for prayers, which they wrap around their head to recite the blessing of the Tallit.

Young Sikh boys, and sometimes girls often wear a bandanna to cover their hair, before moving on to the turban. Older Sikhs may wear them as an under-turban.

Islam promotes modest dress among men and women; many Muslim women wear a headscarf often known as a hijab, and in Quranic Arabic as the khimar. The Keffiyeh is commonly used by Muslim men.

Several Christian denominations include a scarf known as a Stole as part of their liturgical vestments.

Silk scarfs were used by pilots of early aircraft in order to keep oily smoke from the exhaust out of their mouths while flying. Silk Scarfs were worn by pilots of closed cockpit aircraft to prevent neck chafing, especially fighter pilots, who were constantly turning their heads from side to side watching for enemy aircraft.

Today, military flight crews wear scarfs imprinted with unit insignia and emblems not for functional reasons but instead for esprit-de-corps and heritage.

Wollen scarfs with Bandhani work are becoming very popular. Bandhani or Bandhej is the name of the tie and dye technique used commonly in Bhuj and Mandvi of Kutch District of Gujarat State in India.

An absurdly long scarf that is striped is heavily associated with the Fourth Doctor from the television series Doctor Who. His iconic scarf is sometimes known as a "Whovian scarf."

Scarfs can be tied in many ways including the pussy-cat bow, the square knot, the cowboy bib, the ascot knot, the loop, the necktie, and the gypsy kerchief.

Uniforms

Students in the United Kingdom traditionally wear academic scarves with distinctive combinations of striped colours identifying their individual university or college.

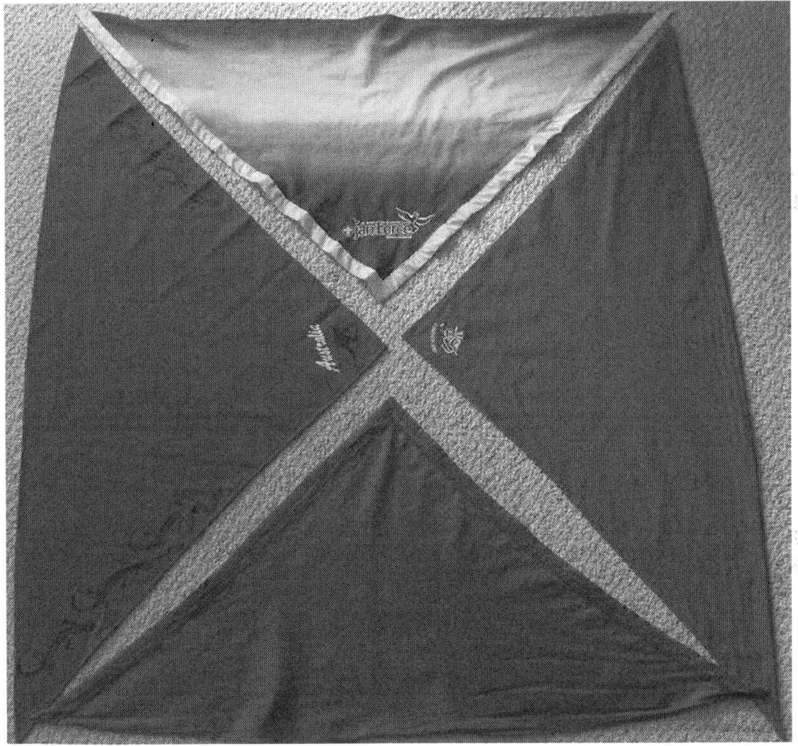

Figure: *Four Scout scarves. They are (clockwise from top) the 21st World Scout Jamboree scarf, a Gang Show scarf from Cumberland Gang Show, the troop and group scarf from 1st Cherrybrook Scout Group, and the national scarf for Australia.*

Members of the Scouting Movement wear scarfs as part of their uniform, with different colours and logos to represent their scout group. They are also used at camps to represent units, subcamps or the camp as a whole.

Fun scarves are also used as memorabilia at Scout events and country scarves are often traded at international gatherings. In some Socialist countries Young pioneers wore a red scarf.

Bib Scarf

The US Army and other American military units often wore branch of service colour or camouflage bib scarves with various uniforms.

Sport

Since at least the early 1900s, when the phenomenon began in Britain, coloured scarves have been traditional supporter wear for fans of association football teams across the world, even those in warmer climates. These scarves come in a wide variety of sizes and are made in a club's particular colours and may contain the club crest, pictures of renowned players, and various slogans relating to the history of the club and its rivalry with others.

At some clubs supporters will sometimes perform a 'scarf wall' in which all supporters in a section of the stadium will stretch out their scarves above their heads with both hands, creating an impressive 'wall' of colour. This is usually accompanied by the singing of a club anthem such as "You'll Never Walk Alone" at Liverpool F.C. or "Grazie Roma" at A.S. Roma.

This was initially solely a British phenomenon, but has since spread to the rest of Europe, North and South America. Some clubs supporters will perform a scarf 'twirl' or 'twirly' in which a group of supporters hold the scarves above their heads with one hand, and twirl the scarf, creating a 'blizzard' of colour. This is usually accompanied by a club anthem such as "Hey Jude" at Heart of Midlothian F.C.

Scarf wearing is also a noted feature of support for Australian rules football clubs in the Australian Football League. The scarves are in the form of alternating bars of colour, usually with the team name or mascot written on each second bar.

Manufacturing of Scarves

The craft of knitting garments such as scarves is an important trade in some countries. Hand-knitted scarves are still common as gifts as well.

Printed scarves are additionally offered internationally through high fashion design houses. Among the latter are Burberry, Missoni, Alexander McQueen, Cole Haan, Chanel, Etro, Lanvin, Hermès, Nicole Miller, Ferragamo, Emilio Pucci, Dior, Fendi, Louis Vuitton and Prada.

There are three basic scarf shapes: square, triangular and rectangular.

The leading manufacturer of fashion scarves used today is China, with India, Hong Kong and Indonesia close behind. The most common materials used to make fashion scarves are silk, fleece, pashmina and cashmere.

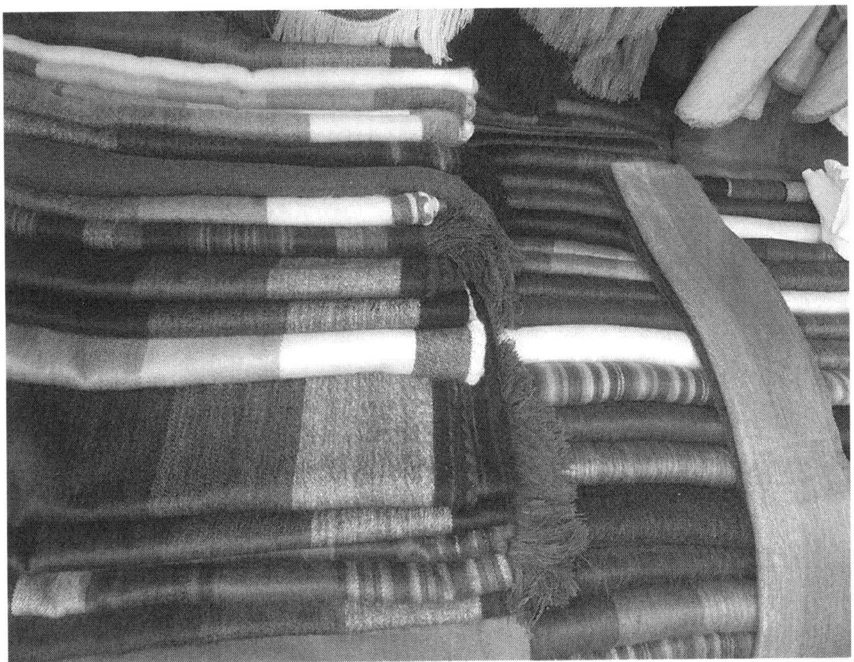

***Figure:** Alpaca scarves at the Otavalo Artisan Market in the Andes Mountains of Ecuador.*

Headscarf

Headscarves or head scarves are scarves covering most or all of the top of a woman's hair and her head. Headscarves may be worn for a variety of purposes, such as for warmth, for sanitation, for fashion or social distinction; with religious significance, to hide baldness, out of modesty, or other forms of social convention.

Types

Headscarves may have specific religious significance. Observant married Jewish women, for example, are required to cover their hair, often employing scarves, known as tichels or snoods, in compliance with the code of modesty known as tzniut.

Headscarves were also worn by married Christian women in medieval Europe, and even by some of the unmarried. This headcovering habit is better known as a wimple in English.

Headscarves and veils are most commonly used by Observant Muslim women. The Muslim religious dress include *burqa, chador, niqab, dupatta,* and others.

The Arabic word *hijab,* which refers to modest behaviour or dress in general, is often used to describe the headscarf worn by Muslim women. A "head dress" could also be worn by men.

The most common, keffiyeh, is worn by men (most commonly Middle Eastern) for cultural purposes rather than religious.

Headscarves were once used by Christian women as well. Mainly in the Eastern Orthodox Church, Oriental Orthodox Church, Assyrian Church of the East, and some traditionalist Roman Catholics. Some Anabaptist Protestants make use of veils also.

Some English speakers use the word "babushka" (the word for 'grandma' into indicate the headscarf tied below the chin, as commonly worn in Europe, especially by elderly women in Russia. In many parts of Europe and the Balkan region, headscarves are used mainly by elderly women and this led to the use of the term "babushka", a Slavic word meaning 'grandmother'. In Chile, Mapuche women wear headscarves tied behind the head.

A plain red or scarlet headscarf was worn by female commissars and other women aligning themselves with Bolshevism in times of Russian revolution and civil war.

A head tie is an elaborate ornamental head covering worn by women of western and southern Africa.

Many women with medical hair loss, due to chemotherapy, alopecia or other causes, use scarves as protective head coverings.

Shawl

A shawl is a simple item of clothing, loosely worn over the shoulders, upper body and arms, and sometimes also over the head. It is usually a rectangular or square piece of cloth, that is often folded to make a triangle but can also be triangular in shape. Other shapes include oblong shawls.

History

Kashmir Textiles-Shawls, Namdas, Gubbas: Kashmir, a disputed region between India and Pakistan, was a pivotal point through which the wealth, knowledge, and products of ancient India passed to the world. Perhaps the most widely known woven textiles are the famed Kashmir shawls. The *Kanikar*, for instance, has intricately woven designs that are formalized imitations of Nature.

The *Chenar* leaf (plane tree leaf), *apple and cherry blossoms*, the *rose and tulip*, the *almond and pear*, the *nightingale*—these are done in deep mellow tones of maroon, dark red, gold yellow and browns. Yet another type of Kashmir shawl is the *Jamiavr*, which is a brocaded woolen fabric sometimes in pure wool and sometimes with a little cotton added.

The floral designing appears like heavy close embroidery-like weave in dull silk or soft *pashmina* wool, and usually comprises small or large flowers delicately sprayed and combined; some shawls have net-like patterns with floral ensemble motifs in them. Still another type of Kashmir shawl is the *Dourukha*, a woven shawl that is so done as to produce the same effect on both sides.

This is a unique piece of craftsmanship, in which a multi-coloured pattern scheme is woven all over the surface, and after the shawl is completed, the *rafugar* (expert embroiderer) works the outlines of the motifs in darker shades to bring into relief the beauty of design. This attractive mode of craftsmanship not only produces a shawl which is reversible because of the perfect workmanship on both sides, but it combines the crafts of both weaving and embroidery and religious beliefs believe in different shawls.

The most expensive shawls, called *Shatoosh*, are made from the beard hairs of the wild ibex and are so fine that a whole shawl can be pulled through a small finger ring.

The *naksha*, a Persian device like the Jacquard loom invented centuries later, enabled Indian weavers to create sinuous floral patterns and creeper designs in brocade to rival any painted by a brush. The Kashmir shawl that evolved from this expertise in its heyday had greater fame than any other Indian textile. Always a luxury commodity, the intricate, tapestry-woven, fine wool shawl had become a fashionable wrap for the ladies of the English and French elite by the 1700s.

The supply fell short of demand and manufacturers pressed to produce more, created convincing embroidered versions of the woven shawls that could be produced in half the time. As early as 1803, Kashmiri needlework production was established to increase and hasten output of these shawls, which had been imitated in England since 1784 and even in France.

By 1870, the advent of the *Jacquard* loom in Europe destroyed the exclusivity of the original Kashmir shawl, which began to be produced in Paisley, Scotland. Even the characteristic Kashmiri motif, the *mango-shape*, began to be known simply as the *paisley*.

The paisley motif is so ubiquitous to Indian fabrics that it is hard to realize that it is only about 250 years old. It evolved from 1600's floral and tree-of-life designs that were created in expensive, tapestry-woven Mughal textiles. Early designs depicted single plants with large flowers and thin wavy stems, small leaves and roots. As the designs became denser over time, more flowers and leaves were compacted within the shape of the tree, or issuing from vases or a pair of leaves.

By the late 1700s, the archetypal curved point at the top of an elliptical outline had evolved. The elaborate paisley created on Kashmir shawls became the vogue in Europe for over a century, and it was imitations of these shawls woven in factories at Paisley, Scotland, that gave it the name *paisley* still commonly used in the United States and Europe. In the late 1700s and 1800s, the paisley became an important motif in a wide range of Indian textiles, perhaps because it was associated with the Mughal court. It also caught the attention of poorer and non-Muslim Indians because it resembles a mango. "Rural Indians called an *aam* or mango a symbol of fertility".

The first shawls, or "shals", were used in Assyrian times; later they went into widespread use in the Middle East. Shawls were also part of the traditional male costume in Kashmir, which was probably introduced via assimilation to Persian culture. They were woven in extremely fine woollen twill, some such as the Orenburg shawl, were even said to be as fine as the Shatoosh. They could be in one colour only, woven in different colours (called *tilikar*), ornately woven or embroidered (called *ameli*).

Kashmiri shawls were high-fashion garments in Western Europe in the early- to mid-1800s. Imitation Kashmiri shawls woven in Paisley, Renfrewshire are the origin of the name of the traditional paisley pattern. Shawls were also manufactured in the city of Norwich, Norfolk from the late 1700s (and some two decades before Paisley) until about the 1870s.

Silk shawls with fringes, made in China, were available by the first decade of the 1800s. Ones with embroidery and fringes were available in Europe and the Americas by 1820. These were called China crêpe shawls, China shawls, and in Spain *mantones de Manila* because they were shipped to Spain from China via the port of Manila.

The importance of these shawls in fashionable women's wardrobes declined between 1865 and 1870 in Western culture. However, they became part of folk dress in a number of places including Germany, the Near East, various parts of Latin America, and Spain where they became a part of Romani (*gitana*) dress especially in Andalusia and Madrid.

These embroidered items were revived in the 1920s under the name of Spanish shawls. Their use as part of the costume of the lead in the opera *Carmen* contributed to the association of the shawls with Spain rather than China.

Some cultures incorporate shawls of various types into their national folk dress, mainly because shawls were much more commonly used in earlier times.

Uses

Shawls are used in order to keep warm, to complement a costume, and for symbolic reasons. One famous type of shawl is the tallit, worn by Jewish men during prayers and ceremonies. Today, shawls are worn for added warmth (and fashion) at outdoor or indoor evening affairs, where the temperature is warm enough for men in suits but not for women in dresses and where a jacket might be inappropriate.

The Kashmir Shawls

Kashmir is India's northernmost state and was the point through which ancient India passed to the world. The Kashmir shawl that evolved from a local expertise had greater fame than any other Indian textile.

Pashmina or Amlikar

The majority of the woollen fabrics of Kashmir, and particularly the best quality shawls, were and are still made of *Pashm* or *Pashmina*, which is the wool of *Capra hircus*, a species of the wild Asian mountain goat. Hence the shawls came to be called Pashmina. The fine fleece used for the shawls is that which grows under the rough, woolly, outer coat of the animal; that from the under-belly, which is shed on the approach of hot weather. Materials of an inferior grade were of the wool of the wild Himalayan mountain sheep or the Himalayan Ibex.

However, the best fleece wool is soft, silky and warm is of the wild goats, and painstakingly gathered from shrubs and rough rocks against which the animals rub off their fleece on the approach of summer.

This was undoubtedly the soft fleece wool from which were made the famous and much coveted 'ring shawls' in Mughal times. Unfortunately very inferior and second rate wool taken from domesticated sheep and goats provide most of the wool used today on the looms of Kashmir.

The needle-worked *Amlikar* or *Amli,* made from Pashmina wool is a shawl embroidered almost all over with the needle on a plain woven ground.

The colours most commonly seen on pashmina shawls are yellow, white, black, blue, green, purple, crimson and scarlet. The design motifs are usually formalised imitations of nature like the leaf, flower and tree designs mentioned above; they are always done in rich colours.

The embroidery stitch employed is rather like the parallel darning stitch and is rarely allowed to penetrate the entire fabric.

The outlines of the design are further touched up and emphasized with silk or woollen thread of different colours run round the finer details; the stitch used for this is at an angle overlapping darn stitch, all the stitches used are so minute and fine that individually they can be seen with the unaided eye only with difficulty.

When Pashmina wool is used for the embroidery work, it is made to blend so intimately with the texture of the basic shawl material that it would be difficult to insert even a fine needle between the embroidery stitches and the basic fabric.

Do-Shalla

The Emperor Akbar was a great admirer of the shawls of Kashmir. It was he who began the fashion of wearing them in duplicate, sewn back to back, so that the under surfaces of the shawls were never seen. During that time the most desired shawls were those worked in gold and silver thread or shawls with border ornamented with fringes of gold, silver and silk thread.

The *Do-shala,* as the name designates ("two-shawl"), are always sold in pairs, there being many varieties of them. In the *Khali-matan* the central field is quite plain and without any ornamentation. The

Char-bagan is made up of four pieces in different colours neatly joined together; the central fluid of the shawl is embellished with a medallion of flowers. However, when the field is ornamented with flowers in the four corners we have the Kunj.

Perhaps the most characteristic of the Kashmir shawls is the one made like patchwork. The patterns are woven on the looms in long strips, about twelve to eighteen inches in length and from one half to two inches in width.

These design strips, made on very simple and primitive looms, are then cut to the required lengths and very neatly and expertly hand sewn together with almost invisible stitches and finally joined by sewing to a plain central field piece. As a variation, pieces may be separately woven, cut up in various shapes of differing sizes and expertly sewn together and then further elaborated with embroidery. But there is a difference between these two types:

while the patchwork loom shawls are made up from separate narrow strips, the patchwork embroidered shawls consists of a certain number of irregularly shaped pieces joined together, each one balancing the predominant colour scheme of the shawl.

Namda and Gubba

The basic material for a *gubba* is milled blanket dyed in plain colour. Embroidery is bold and vivid in designing and done with woollen or cotton threads. Gubbas have more of a folk flavour blankets cut and patched into geometric patterns, with limited, embroidery on joining and open space. It is more like appliqué work. Colours are bright and attractive. They are cheap and used for *dewan* covering or as floor covering—*namdas.*

Costumes of Kashmir

Female costume: Salwar is the main lower garment for the women; it may be fitted or gathered which may be embroidered. The embroidered design is based on the natural beauty of the area. The most widely used pattern is the leaf of the Chinar tree.

The upper garment called a pheran is like a gown which hangs in loose folds and has sleeves. A sleeveless jacket of embroidered velvet of a dark shade is occasionally worn over the gown.

The word pheran comes from the Persian word *paithar* meaning shirt. The pheran has an open collar down the neck with heavy folds. The outfit is completed with a scarf similar to the *ordhnai* of Rajasthan and Punjab but different in quality and design. However, it is customary for a bride to wear a veil at her wedding which is elaborately embroidered and adorned with lace. Dresses for Muslim and Hindu brides are the same but head dress shows a slight difference.

The women usually wear the traditional costume of Kashmir with slight variations to distinguish themselves form the Brahmins. The Hindu women use a girdle whereas a Muslim woman does not.

The Hindu woman wears a round white head dress having embroidery only on the sleeves and around the collar, the Muslim woman wears a high red head dress and a heavily embroidered tunic.

Male costume

Salwar is the lower garment. It is similar to that used by the women. The upper garment is a loose shirt called *pheran.*

In Kashmir the Hindu and the Muslim man could be easily distinguished by their dress. Hindus wear the tuck of the turban on his right and the Muslim on the left. Hindus fasten their gown on the left and Muslims on the right. Hindus have long narrow sleeves and Muslim have short sleeves. In olden days, the costume of males consisted of a lower garment and turban called *sirasheta.*

The shawls made in Kashmir occupy a pre-eminent place among textile products; and it is to them and to their imitations from Western looms that specific importance attaches.

The Kashmir shawl is characterized by the elaboration of its design, in which the "cone" pattern is a prominent feature, and by the glowing harmony, brilliance, depth, and enduring qualities of its colours. The basis of these excellences is found in the very fine, soft, short, flossy under-wool, called pashm or pashmina, found on the shawl-goat, a variety of *Capra hircus* inhabiting the elevated regions of Tibet. There are several varieties of pashm, but the finest is a strict monopoly of the maharaja of Kashmir.

Inferior pashm and Kerman wool — a fine soft Persian sheep's wool — are used for shawl weaving at Amritsar and other places in the Punjab, where colonies of Kashmiri weavers are established. Of shawls, apart from shape and pattern, there are only two principal classes:

(1) loom-woven shawls called tiliwalla, tilikar or kani kar — sometimes woven in one piece, but more often in small segments

which are sewn together with such precision that the sewing is quite imperceptible; and

(2) embroidered shawls — amlikar — in which over a ground of plain pashmina is worked by needle a minute and elaborate pattern.

Knit Shawls

Triangular knit lace shawls are usually knitted from the neck down and may or may not be shaped. In contrast, Faroese lace shawls are knitted bottom up and contain a centre back gusset. Each shawl consists of two triangular side panels, a trapezoid-shaped back gusset, an edge treatment, and usually shoulder shaping.

Bedford Cords

Bedford cord, named after the town of Bedford in England, is a durable fabric that resembles corduroy. The weave has faint lengthwise ridges, but without the filling yarns that make the distinct wales characteristic of corduroy. Trousers made with Bedford cord are sometimes called “Bedford cords”.

A water-repellent cotton version of Bedford cord called Jungle Cloth was used by the U.S. Navy for flight clothing during the 1920s-1940s era.

Bedford cord is a specific variety of durable, woven fabric. It is similar to corduroy in that the weave has raised ridges running in a lengthwise direction. The fibres that make up Bedford cord typically are wool or worsted, but the cloth also is sometimes made of cotton, rayon or silk. The ridges occasionally are made more pronounced with stuffing.

Sources disagree about whether Bedford cord was first named for the town of Bedford, England, or for New Bedford, Massachusetts. Bedford which has been in the cotton textile industry since 1846, and New Bedford also has a textile history that dates to the 19th century. Both cities have produced corded fabrics known as Bedford cord, and both claim the name as their own.

The ridges in Bedford cord and other corded fabrics are called cords or wale, and the size or thickness of the ridge is measured in wale numbers. Higher wale numbers indicate the thinnest cords, and lower wale numbers signify a broader cord width. Particularly broad cording is usually referred to as wide wale.

It is a particularly durable fabric, so Bedford cord's use in the fashion industry predominantly is in the construction of outerwear, winter trousers or garments that do not require a fabric with draping ability. Blazers, heavy jackets, coats and suits are typical uses of this somewhat inflexible cloth, and trousers of Bedford cord are ubiquitous enough that the slacks themselves often are referred to as Bedford cords. Bedford cord also is used in the construction of jodhpurs or riding breeches and can be used to upholster furniture that requires a hard-wearing cloth surface.

Bedford cord can be woven from pure wool, cotton pique, silk, rayon or blends of fibre. Its name sometimes is used interchangeably with other corded fabrics, such as corduroy, Manchester cloth or corded velveteen, though there are slight variations between the various corded fabrics that are of little consequence to those outside the textile industry. In terms of clothing and fashion, the term "cord" generally is specific enough to be understood.

6

Pile Fabrics

In textiles, pile is the raised surface or nap of a fabric, which is made of upright loops or strands of yarn.

Examples of pile textiles are carpets, corduroy, velvet, plush, and Turkish towels. The word is derived from Latin *pilus* for "hair".

The surface and the yarn in these fabrics also called "pile". In particular "pile length" or "pile depth" refer to the length of the yarn strands (half-length of the loops).

The types of pile include

- loop pile
- uncut pile
- cut pile
- knotted pile
- tufted pile
- woven pile
- cord pile
- twist pile

Carpet Pile

A carpet is a textile floor covering consisting of an upper layer of "pile" attached to a backing.

The pile is generally either made from wool or a manmade fibre such as polypropylene, nylon or polyester and usually consists of twisted tufts which are often heat-treated to maintain their structure.

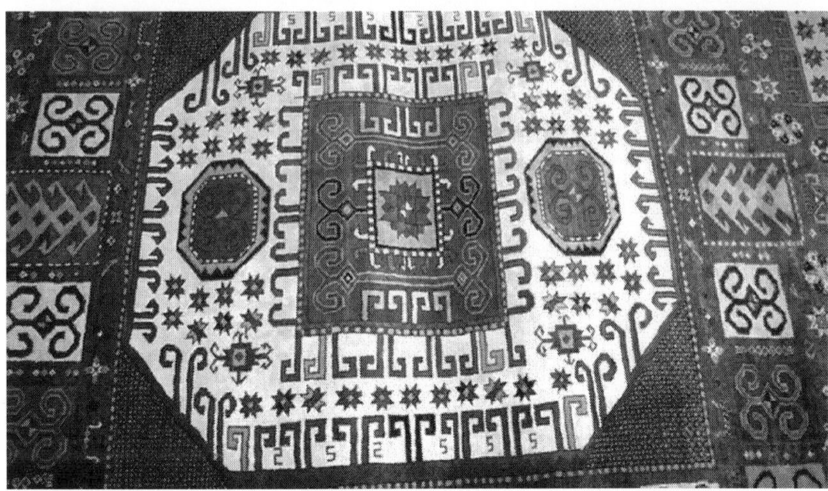

Figure: *The Azerbaijani carpet, a UNESCO Masterpiece of Intangible Heritage of Humanity*

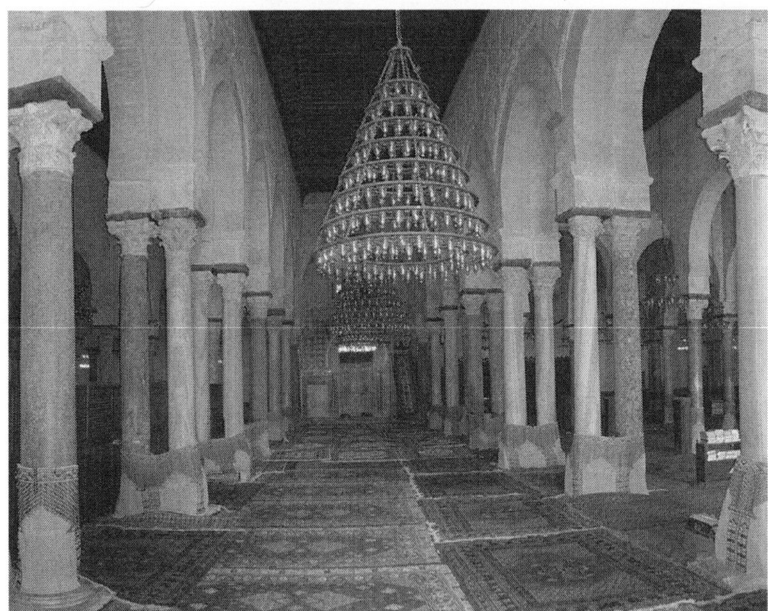

Figure: *Carpets covering the floor of the prayer hall of the Great Mosque of Kairouan (also called the Mosque of Uqba), in Tunisia.*

The term "carpet" comes from Old Italian *carpita*, "carpire" meaning *to pluck*. The term "carpet" is often used interchangeably with the term "rug". Some define a carpet as stretching from wall to wall. Another definition treats rugs as of lower quality or of smaller size, with carpets quite often having finished ends.

Historically the word was also used for table and wall coverings, as carpets were not commonly used on the floor in European interiors until the 18th century, with the opening of trade routes between Persia and Western Europe.

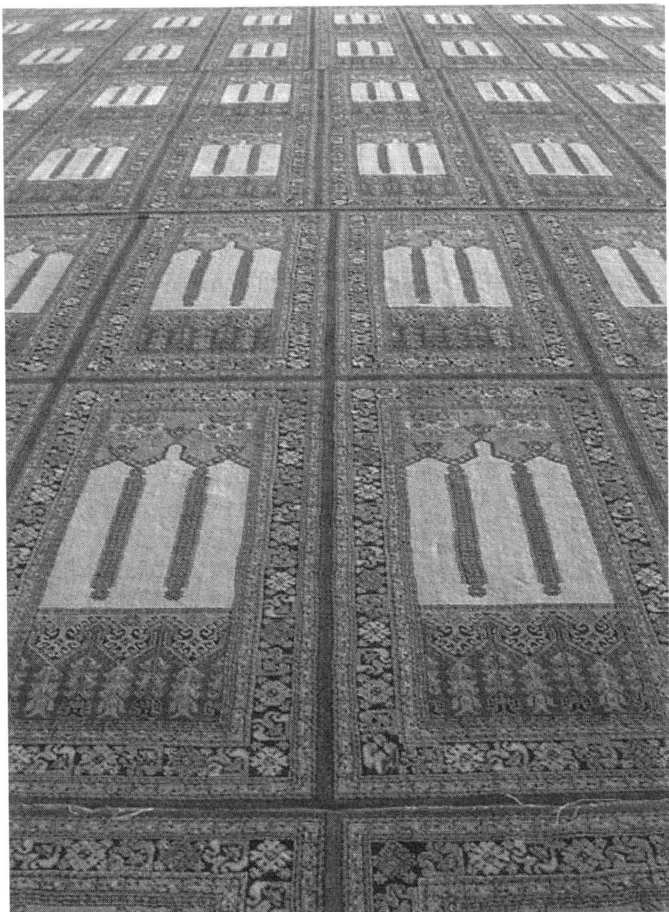

Figure: *The Sultan Ahmet Camii Prayer Carpet Saph. "The Blue Mosque", Istanbul, Turkey 2006*

Carpet Types

Woven

The carpet is produced on a loom quite similar to woven fabric. The pile can be plush or berber. Plush carpet is a cut pile and Berber carpet is a loop pile. There are new styles of carpet combining the two styles called cut and loop carpeting. Normally many coloured yarns are used and this process is capable of producing intricate patterns from pre-determined designs (although some limitations apply to certain weaving methods with regard to accuracy of pattern within the carpet). These carpets are usually the most expensive due to the relatively slow speed of the manufacturing process. These are very famous in India, Pakistan and Arabia

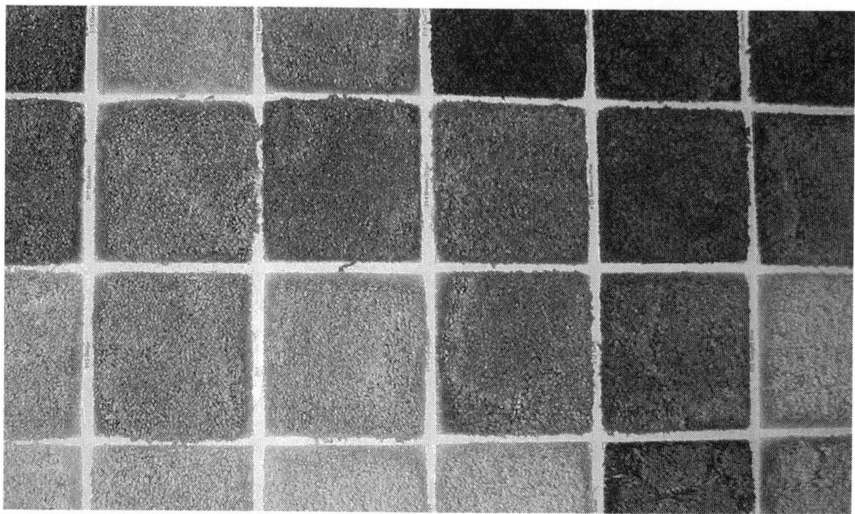

Figure: *Swatches of carpet of tufted construction*

Needlefelt

These carpets are more technologically advanced. Needle felts are produced by intermingling and felting individual synthetic fibres using barbed and forked needles forming an extremely durable carpet. These carpets are normally found in the contract market such as hotels etc. Where there is a lot of traffic and are extensively found in isstanbul and other islamian countries

Knotted

On a knotted pile carpet (formally, a supplementary weft cut-loop pile carpet), the structural weft threads alternate with a supplementary weft that rises at right angles to the surface of the weave. This supplementary weft is attached to the warp by one of three knot types, such as shag carpet which was popular in the 1970s, to form the pile or nap of the carpet. Knotting by hand is most prevalent in oriental rugs and carpets. Kashmir carpets are also hand-knotted.

Tufted

These are carpets that have their pile injected into a backing material, which is itself then bonded to a secondary backing made of a woven hessian weave or a man made alternative to provide stability. This is the most common method of manufacturing of domestic carpets for floor covering purposes in the world.

Others

A flatweave carpet is created by interlocking warp (vertical) and weft (horizontal) threads. Types of oriental flatwoven carpet include kilim, soumak, plain weave, and tapestry weave. Types of European flatwoven carpets include Venetian, Dutch, damask, list, haircloth, and ingrain (aka double cloth, two-ply, triple cloth, or three-ply).

A hooked rug is a simple type of rug handmade by pulling strips of cloth such as wool or cotton through the meshes of a sturdy fabric such as burlap. This type of rug is now generally made as a handicraft.

Embroidery

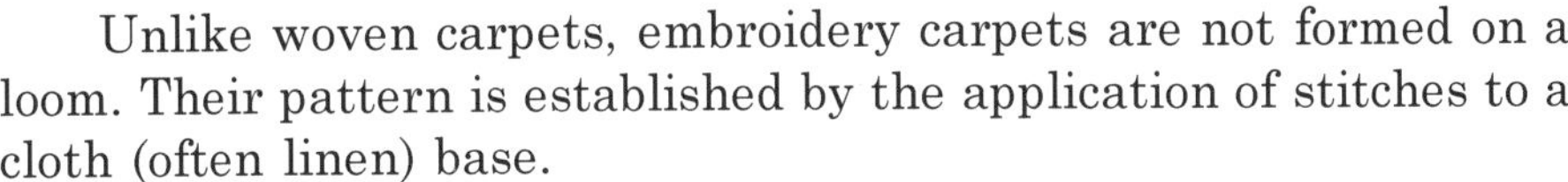

Unlike woven carpets, embroidery carpets are not formed on a loom. Their pattern is established by the application of stitches to a cloth (often linen) base.

The tent stitch and the cross stitch are two of the most common. Embroidered carpets were traditionally made by royal and aristocratic women in the home, but there has been some commercial manufacture since steel needles were introduced (earlier needles were made of bone) and linen weaving improved in the 16th century.

Mary, Queen of Scots, is known to have been an avid embroiderer. 16th century designs usually involve scrolling vines and regional flowers (for example, the Bradford carpet). They often incorporate animal heraldry and the coat of arms of the maker. Production continued through the 19th century.

Victorian embroidered carpet compositions include highly illusionistic, 3-dimensional flowers.

Patterns for tiled carpets made of a number of squares, called Berlin wool work, were introduced in Germany in 1804, and became extremely popular in England in the 1830s. Embroidered carpets can also include other features such as a pattern of shapes, or they can even tell a story.

Production of Knotted Pile Carpet

Both flat and pile carpets are woven on a loom. Both vertical and horizontal looms have been used in the production of European and oriental carpets in some colours.

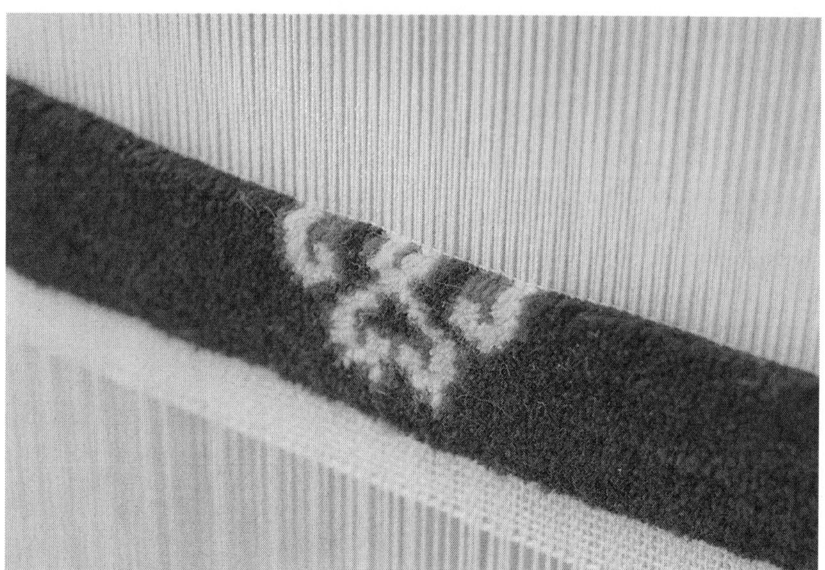

Figure: *A traditional carpet/rug design in preparation on a carpet loom.*

The warp threads are set up on the frame of the loom before weaving begins. A number of weavers may work together on the same carpet. A row of knots is completed and cut. The knots are secured with (usually one to four) rows of weft. The warp in woven carpet is usually cotton and the weft is jute.

There are several styles of knotting, but the two main types of knot are the symmetrical (also called Turkish or Ghiordes) and asymmetrical (also called Persian or Senna).

Contemporary centres of carpet production are: Lahore and Peshawar (Pakistan), Kashmir (India / Pakistan), Bhadohi, Tabriz (Iran), Afghanistan, Azerbaijan, Turkey, Northern Africa, Nepal, Spain, Turkmenistan, and Tibet.

The importance of carpets in the culture of Turkmenistan is such that the national flag features a vertical red stripe near the hoist side, containing five carpet guls (designs used in producing rugs).

Kashmir (India) is known for handknotted carpets. These are usually of silk and some woolen carpets are also woven.

Child labour has often been used in Asia. The GoodWeave labelling scheme used throughout Europe and North America assures that child labour has not been used: importers pay for the labels, and the revenue collected is used to monitor centres of production and educate previously exploited children.

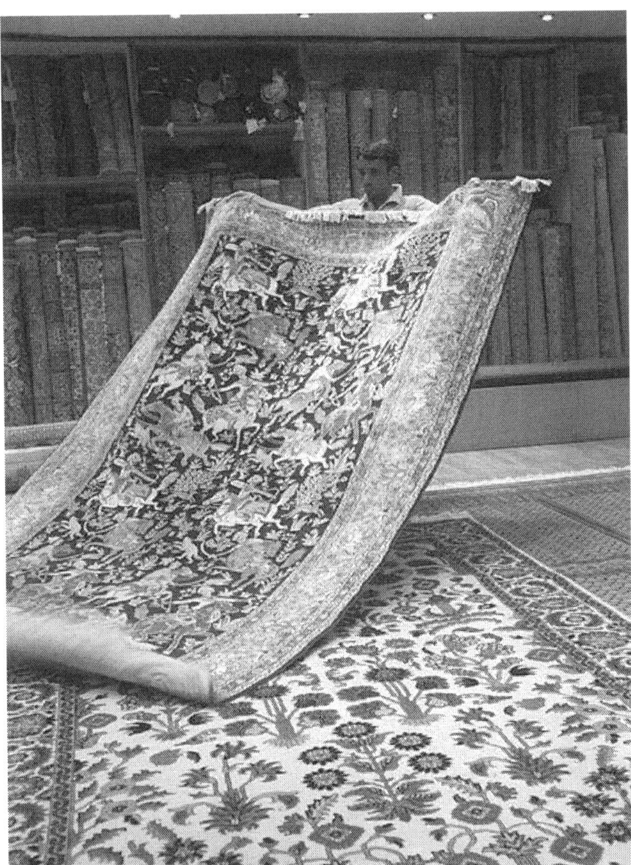

Figure: *A carpet seller in Jaipur, India*

Fibres and Yarns used in Carpet

Carpet can be made from many single or blended natural and synthetic fibres. Fibres are chosen for durability, appearance, ease of manufacture, and cost. In terms of scale of production, the dominant yarn constructions are polyamides (nylons) and polypropylene with an estimated 90% of the commercial market.

Nylon

Nylon is the most common material for construction of carpets. Both nylon 6 and nylon 6-6 are used. Nylon can be dyed topically or dyed in a molten state (solution dying). Nylon can be printed easily and has excellent wear characteristics. In carpets Nylon tends to stain easily because it possesses dye sites on the fibre. These dye sites need to be filled in order to give Nylon any type of stain resistance. As nylon is petroleum-based it varies in price with the price of oil.

Polypropylene

Polypropylene is used to produce carpet yarns because it is inexpensive. It is difficult to dye and does not wear as well as wool or nylon. Polypropylene is commonly used to construct Berber carpets. In this case, polypropylene is commonly referred to as olefin. Large looped olefin Berber carpets are usually only suited for light domestic use and tend to mat down quickly. Berber carpets with smaller loops tend to be more resilient and retain their new appearance longer than large looped Berber styles.

Commercial grade level-loop carpets have very small loops, and commercial grade cut-pile styles are well constructed. When made with polypropylene these styles wear very well, making them very suitable for areas with heavy foot traffic such as offices. Polypropylene carpets are known to have good stain resistance but not against oil based agents. If a stain does set, it can be difficult to clean. Commercial grade carpets can be glued directly to the floor or installed over a 1/4" thick, 8-pound density padding. Outdoor grass carpets are usually made from polypropylene.

Wool and Wool-blends

Wool has excellent durability, can be dyed easily and is fairly abundant. When blended with synthetic fibres such as nylon the durability of wool is increased. Blended wool yarns are extensively used in production of modern carpet, with the most common blend being 80% wool to 20% synthetic fibre, giving rise to the term "80/20". Wool is relatively expensive and consequently a small portion of the market.

Polyester

The polyester known as "PET" (polyethylene terephthalate) is used in carpet manufacturing in both spun and filament constructions. After the price of raw materials for many types of carpet rose in the early 2000s, polyester became more competitive. Polyester has good physical properties and is inherently stain-resistant because it is hydrophobic, and, unlike nylon, does not have dye sites. Colour is infused in a molten state (solution dyeing). Polyester has the disadvantage that it tends to crush or mat down easily. It is typically used in mid- to low-priced carpeting.

Another polyester, "PTT" (Polytrimethylene terephthalate), also called Sorona or 3GT (Dupont) or Corterra (Shell), is a variant of PET. Lurgi Zimmer PTT was first patented in 1941, but it was not produced until the 1990s, when Shell Chemicals developed the low-cost method of producing high-quality 1,3 propanediol (PDO), the starting raw material for PTT Corterra Polymers.

Acrylic

Acrylic is a synthetic material first created by the Dupont Corporation in 1941 but has gone through various changes since it was first introduced.

In the past Acrylic used to fuzz or pill easily, this happened when the fibres degraded over time and short strands broke away with contact or friction. Over the years Acrylics have been developed to alleviate some of these problems although the issues have not been completely removed. Acrylic is fairly difficult to dye but is colourfast, washable and has the feel and appearance of wool making it an ideal rug fabric.

Carpet Binding

Carpet binding is a term used for any material being applied to the edge of a carpet to make a rug. Carpet binding is usually cotton or nylon, but also comes in many other materials, such as leather. Non-synthetic binding is frequently used with bamboo, grass, and wool rugs, but is often used with carpet made from other materials.

History of Carpets

The knotted pile carpet probably originated in the 3rd or 2nd millennium BC in West Asia, perhaps the Caspian Sea area or the Armenian Highland, although there is evidence of goats and sheep being sheared for wool and hair which was spun and woven as far back at the 7th millennium.

The earliest surviving pile carpet is the "Pazyryk carpet", which dates from the 5th-4th century BC. It was excavated by Sergei Ivanovich Rudenko in 1949 from a Pazyryk burial mound in the Altai Mountains in Siberia. This richly coloured carpet is 200 x 183 cm (6'6" x 6'0") and framed by a border of griffins. Many experts in oriental carpets hypothesize that it is of Urartian workmanship.

Afghan Carpets

There has recently been a surge in demand for Afghan carpets, although many Afghan carpet manufacturers market their products under the name of a different country. The carpets are made in Afghanistan, as well as by Afghan refugees who reside in Pakistan and Iran. Afghan rugs are usually inexpensive. Famous Afghan rugs include the *Shindand* or *Adraskan* (named after local Afghan villages), woven in the Herat area, in western Afghanistan.

Armenian Carpets

Armenian carpets were renowned by foreigners who travelled to Artsakh; the Arab geographer and historian Al-Masudi noted that, among other works of art, he had never seen such carpets elsewhere in his life.

Art historian Hravard Hakobyan notes that "Artsakh carpets occupy a special place in the history of Armenian carpet-making." Common themes and patterns found on Armenian carpets were the depiction of dragons and eagles. They were diverse in style, rich in colour and ornamental motifs, and were even separated in categories depending on what sort of animals were depicted on them, such as *artsvagorgs* (eagle-carpets), *vishapagorgs* (dragon-carpets) and *otsagorgs* (serpent-carpets).

The rug mentioned in the Kaptavan inscriptions is composed of three arches, "covered with vegatative ornaments", and bears an artistic resemblance to the illuminated manuscripts produced in Artsakh.

The art of carpet weaving was in addition intimately connected to the making of curtains as evidenced in a passage by Kirakos Gandzaketsi, a 13th-century Armenian historian from Artsakh, who praised Arzu-Khatun, the wife of regional prince Vakhtang Khachenatsi, and her daughters for their expertise and skill in weaving.

Chinese Carpets

As opposed to most antique rug manufactory practices, Chinese carpets were woven almost exclusively for internal consumption. China has a long history of exporting traditional goods; however, it was not until the first half of the 19th century that the Chinese began to export their rugs. Once in contact with western influences, there was a large change in production: Chinese manufactories began to produce art-deco rugs with commercial look and price point.

The centuries old Chinese textile industry is rich in history. While most antique carpets are classified according to a specific region or manufactory, scholars attribute the age of any specific Chinese rug to the ruling emperor of the time. The earliest surviving examples of the craft were produced during the time of Ch'ung Chen, the last emperor of the Chen Dynasty.

Indian Carpets

Carpet weaving may have been introduced into the area as far back as the eleventh century with the coming of the first Muslim conquerors, the Ghaznavids and the Ghauris, from the West. It can with more certainty be traced to the beginning of the Mughal Dynasty in the early fifteenth century, when the last successor of Timur, Babar, extended his rule from Kabul to India to found the Mughal Empire. Under the patronage of the Mughals, Indian craftsmen adopted Persian techniques and designs. Carpets woven in the Punjab made use of motifs and decorative styles found in Mughal architecture.

Akbar, a Mogul emperor, is accredited to introducing the art of carpet weaving to India during his reign. The Mughal emperors patronized Persian carpets for their royal courts and palaces. During this period, he brought Persian craftsmen from their homeland and established them in India. Initially, the carpets woven showed the classic Persian style of fine knotting. Gradually it blended with Indian art. Thus the carpets produced became typical of the Indian origin and gradually the industry began to diversify and spread all over the subcontinent.

During the Mughal period, the carpets made on the Indian subcontinent became so famous that demand for them spread abroad. These carpets had distinctive designs and boasted a high density of knots. Carpets made for the Mughal emperors, including Jahangir and Shah Jahan, were of the finest quality. Under Shah Jahan's reign, Mughal carpet weaving took on a new aesthetic and entered its classical phase.

The Indian carpets are well known for their designs with attention to detail and presentation of realistic attributes. The carpet industry in India flourished more in its northern part with major centres found in Kashmir, Jaipur, Agra and Bhadohi.

Indian carpets are known for their high density of knotting. Hand-knotted carpets are a speciality and widely in demand in the West. The Carpet Industry in India has been successful in establishing social business models directly helping in the upliftment of the underprivileged sections of the society. Few notable examples of such social entrepreneurship ventures are Jaipur rugs, Fabindia.

Another category of Indian rugs which, though quite popular in most of the western countries, have not received much press is hand-woven rugs of Khairabad (Citapore rugs). Khairabad small town in

Citapore (now spelled as "Sitapur") district of India had been ruled by Raja Mehmoodabad. Khairabad (Mehmoodabad Estate) was part of Oudh province which had been ruled by shi'i Muslims having Persian linkages. Citapore rugs made in Khairabad and neighbouring areas are all hand-woven and distinct from tufted and knotted rugs.

Flat weave is the basic weaving technique of Citapore rugs and generally cotton is the main weaving material here but jute, rayon and chenille are also popular. *Ikea* and *Agocha* have been major buyers of rugs from this area.

Pakistani Carpets

The art of weaving developed in South Asia at a time when few other civilizations employed it. Excavations at Moenjodaro and Harappa – ancient cities of the Indus Valley civilization – have established that the inhabitants used spindles and spun a wide variety of weaving materials. Some historians consider that the Indus Valley civilization first developed the use of woven textiles.

At present, hand-knotted carpets are among Pakistan's leading export products and their manufacture is the second largest cottage and small industry. Pakistani craftsmen have the capacity to produce any type of carpet using all the popular motifs of gulls, medallions, paisleys, traceries, and geometric designs in various combinations.

Recently, at the time of independence, manufacturing of carpets was set up in Sangla Hill, a small Town of District Sheikhupura. Chaudary Mukhtar Ahmad Member son of Maher Janda introduced and taught this art to locals and immigrants. He is considered founder of this industry in Pakistan. Sangla Hill is now a focal point in Carpet Industry in Pakistan. Almost all the exporters and manufacturers who are running their business at Lahore, Faisalabad and Karachi have their area offices in Sangla Hill.

Persian Carpets

The Persian carpet is a part of Persian (Iranian) art and culture. Carpet-weaving in Persia dates back to the Bronze Age.

The earliest surviving corpus of Persian carpets come from the Safavid dynasty (1501–1736) in the 16th century. However, painted depictions prove a longer history of production. There is much variety among classical Persian carpets of the 16th and 17th century. Common motifs include scrolling vine networks, arabesques, palmettes, cloud bands, medallions, and overlapping geometric compartments rather than animals and humans. This is because Islam, the dominant religion in that part of the world, forbids their depiction. Still, some show figures engaged either in the hunt or feasting scenes. The majority of these carpets are wool, but several silk examples produced in Kashan survive.

Iranian carpets are the finest in the world and their designs are copied by weavers from other countries as well. Iran is also the world's largest producer and exporter of handmade carpets, producing three quarters of the world's total output and having a share of 30% of world's export markets. Iran is also the maker of the largest handmade carpet in history, measuring 60,546 square feet.

Scandinavian Carpets

Scandinavian rugs are among the most popular of all weaves in modern design. Preferred by influential modernist thinkers, designers, and advocates for a new aesthetic in the mid-twentieth century, Scandinavian rugs have become very widespread in many different avenues of contemporary interior design. With a long history of adaptation and evolution, the tradition of Scandinavian rug-making is among the most storied of all European rug-making traditions.

Turkish Carpets

Turkish carpets (also known as Anatolian), whether hand knotted or flat woven, are among the most well known and established hand crafted art works in the world. Historically: religious, cultural, environmental, sociopolitical and socioeconomic conditions created widespread utilitarian need and have provided artistic inspiration among the many tribal peoples and ethnic groups in Central Asia and Turkey.

Turks; nomadic or pastoral, agrarian or town dwellers, living in tents or in sumptuous houses in large cities, have protected themselves from the extremes of the cold weather by covering the floors, and sometimes walls and doorways, with carpets and rugs. The carpets are always hand made of wool or sometimes cotton, with occasional additions of silk.

These carpets are natural barriers against the cold. Turkish pile rugs and kilims are also frequently used as tent decorations, grain bags, camel and donkey bags, ground cushions, oven covers, sofa covers, bed and cushion covers, blankets, curtains, eating blankets, table top spreads, prayer rugs, and for ceremonial occasions.

The oldest records of flat woven kilims come from Çatalhöyük Neolithic pottery, circa 7000 B.C. One of the oldest settlements ever to have been discovered, Çatalhöyük is located south east of Konya in the middle of the Anatolian region. The excavations to date (only 3% of the town) not only found carbonized fabric but also fragments of kilims painted on the walls of some of the dwellings. The majority of them represent geometric and stylized forms that are similar or identical to other historical and contemporary designs.

The knotted rug is believed to have reached Asia Minor and the Middle East with the expansion of various nomadic tribes peoples during the latter period of the great Turkic migration of the 8th and 9th centuries.

Famously depicted in European paintings of The Renaissance, beautiful Anatolian rugs were often used from then until modern times, to indicate the high economic and social status of the owner.

Women learn their weaving skills at an early age, taking months or even years to complete the beautiful pile rugs and flat woven kilims that were created for their use in every aspect of daily life. As is true in most weaving cultures, traditionally and nearly exclusively, it is women and girls who are both artisan and weaver.

Turkmen ("Bukhara") Carpet

Azerbaijani rug: In November 2010 the Azerbaijani carpet was proclaimed a Masterpiece of Intangible Heritage by UNESCO.

Oriental Carpets in Europe

Oriental carpets began to appear in Europe after the Crusades in the 11th century. Until the mid-18th century they were mostly used on walls and tables. Except in royal or ecclesiastical settings they were considered too precious to cover the floor. Starting in the 13th century oriental carpets begin to appear in paintings (notably from Italy, Flanders, England, France, and the Netherlands). Carpets of Indo-Persian design were introduced to Europe via the Dutch, British, and French East India Companies of the 17th and 18th century.

Spanish Carpets

Although isolated instances of carpet production pre-date the Muslim invasion of Spain, the Hispano-Moresque examples are the earliest significant body of European-made carpets. Documentary evidence shows production beginning in Spain as early as the 10th century AD. The earliest extant Spanish carpet, the so-called Synagogue carpet in the Museum of Islamic Art, Berlin, is a unique survival dated to the 14th century. The earliest group of Hispano-Moresque carpets, Admiral carpets (also known as armorial carpets), has an all-over geometric, repeat pattern punctuated by blazons of noble, Christian Spanish families. The variety of this design was analyzed most thoroughly by May Beattie. Many of the 15th-century, Spanish carpets rely heavily on designs originally developed on the Anatolian Peninsula. Carpet production continued after the Reconquest of Spain and eventual expulsion of the Muslim population in the 15th century. 16th-century Renaissance Spanish carpet design is a derivative of silk textile design. Two of the most popular motifs are wreaths and pomegranates.

During the Moorish (Muslim) period production took place in Alcaraz in the province of Murcia, as well as being recorded in other towns. Carpet production after the Christian reconquest continued in Alcaraz while Cuenca, first recorded as a weaving centre in the 12th century, became increasingly important, and was dominant in the 17th and early 18th century. Carpets of completely different French based designs began to be woven in a royal workshop, the Royal Tapestry Factory *(Real Fábrica de Tapices de Santa Bárbara)* in Madrid in the 18th century. Cuenca was closed down by royal degree of Carlos IV in the late 18th century to stop it competing with the new workshop.

Madrid continued as a weaving centre through to the 20th century, producing brightly coloured carpets most of whose designs are strongly influenced by French carpet design, and which are frequently signed (on occasions with the monogram MD; also sometimes with the name Stuyck) and dated in the outer stripe. After the Spanish civil war General Franco revived the carpet weaving industry in workshops named after him, weaving designs that are influenced by earlier Spanish carpets, usually in a very limited range of colours.

Bulgarian carpets

The Chiprovtsi carpet is a type of handmade carpet with two absolutely identical sides, part of Bulgarian national heritage, traditions, arts and crafts. Its name is derived from the town of Chiprovtsi where their production started in the 17th century. The carpet weaving industry played a key role in the revival of Chiprovtsi in the 1720s after the devastation of the failed 1688 Chiprovtsi Uprising against Ottoman rule. The western traveller Ami Boué, who visited Chiprovtsi in 1836–1838, reported that "mainly young girls, under shelters or in corridors, engage in carpet weaving. They earn only five francs a month and the payment was even lower before". By 1868, the annual production of carpets in Chiprovtsi had surpassed 14,000 square metres. In 1896, almost 1,400 women from Chiprovtsi and the region were engaged in carpet weaving. In 1920, the locals founded the *Manual Labour* carpet-weaving cooperative society, the first of its kind in the country.

At present, the carpet (*kilim*) industry remains dominant in the town. Carpets have been crafted according to traditional designs, but in recent years it is up to the customers to decide the pattern of the carpet they have ordered. The production of a single 3 by 4 m (9.8 by 13 ft) carpet takes about 50 days; primarily women engage in carpet weaving. Work is entirely manual and all used materials are natural; the primary material is wool, coloured using plant or mineral dyes. The local carpets have been prized at exhibitions in London, Paris, Liège and Brussels. In recent decades, however, the Chiprovtsi carpet industry has been in decline as it had lost its firm foreign markets. As a result, the town and the municipality have been experiencing a demographic crisis.

French Carpets

In 1608 Henry IV initiated the French production of "Turkish style" carpets under the direction of Pierre DuPont. This production was soon moved to the Savonnerie factory in Chaillot just west of Paris. The earliest, well-known group produced by the Savonnerie, then under the direction of Simon Lourdet, are the carpets that were produced in the early years of Louis XIV's reign. They are densely ornamented with flowers, sometimes in vases or baskets, against dark blue or brown grounds in deep borders. The designs are based on Netherlandish and Flemish textiles and paintings. The most famous Savonnerie carpets are the series made for the Grande Galerie and the Galerie d'Apollon in the Palais du Louvre between c. 1665-1685. These 105 masterpieces, made under the artistic direction of Charles Le Brun, were never installed, as Louis XIV moved the court to Versailles in 1688. Their design combines rich acanthus leaves, architectural framing, and mythological scenes (inspired by Cesare Ripa's Iconologie) with emblems of Louis XIV's royal power.

Pierre-Josse Perrot is the best-known of the mid-eighteenth-century carpet designers. His many surviving works and drawings display graceful rococo s-scrolls, central rosettes, shells, acanthus leaves, and floral swags. The Savonnerie manufactory was moved to the Gobelins in Paris in 1826.

The Beauvais manufactory, better known for their tapestry, also made knotted pile carpets from 1780 to 1792. Carpet production in small, privately owned workshops in the town of Aubusson began in 1743. Carpets produced in France employ the symmetrical knot.

English Carpets

Knotted pile carpet weaving technology probably came to England in the early 16th century with Flemish Calvinists fleeing religious persecution. Because many of these weavers settled in South-eastern England in Norwich the 14 extant 16th and 17th century carpets are sometimes referred to as "Norwich carpets." These works are either adaptations of Anatolian or Indo-Persian designs or employ Elizabethan-Jacobean scrolling vines and blossoms. All but one are dated or bear a coat of arms. Like the French, English weavers used the symmetrical knot. There are documented and surviving examples of carpets from three 18th-century manufactories: Exeter (1756–1761, owned by Claude Passavant, 3 extant carpets),

Moorfields (1752–1806, owned by Thomas Moore, 5 extant carpets), and Axminster (1755–1835, owned by Thomas Whitty, numerous extant carpets). Exeter and Moorfields were both staffed with renegade weavers from the French Savonnerie and, therefore, employ the weaving structure of that factory and Perrot-inspired designs. Neoclassical designer Robert Adam supplied designs for both Moorfields and Axminster carpets based on Roman floor mosaics and coffered ceilings. Some of the most well-known rugs of his design were made for Syon House, Osterley House, Harewood House, Saltram House, and Newby Hall. Axminster carpet was a unique floor covering made originally in a factory founded at Axminster, Devon, England, in 1755 by the cloth weaver Thomas Whitty.

Resembling somewhat the Savonnerie carpets produced in France, Axminster carpets were symmetrically knotted by hand in wool on woolen warps and had a weft of flax or hemp. Like the French carpets, they often featured Renaissance architectural or floral patterns; others mimicked oriental patterns. Similar carpets were produced at the same time in Exeter and in the Moorfields section of London and, shortly before, at Fulham in Middlesex. The Whitty factory closed in 1835 with the advent of machine-made carpeting. The name Axminster, however, survived as a generic term for machine-made carpets whose pile is produced by techniques similar to those used in making velvet or chenille. Axminster carpet has three main types of broadloom carpet construction in use today (machine woven, tufted & hand knotted). Machine woven carpet is an investment that will last 20 or 30 years and woven Axminster and Wilton carpets are still extremely popular in areas where longevity and design flexibility are a big part of the purchasing decision. Hotels and leisure venues almost always choose these types and many homes use woven Axminsters as design statements. Machine woven carpets like Axminster and Wilton are made by massive looms that weave together 'bobbins' of carpet yarn and backing.

The finished result, which can be intricately patterned, creates a floor that provides supreme underfoot luxury with high performance. Tufted carpets are also popular in the home. They are relatively speedy to make - a pre-woven backing has yarns tufted into it. Needles push the yarn through the backing and which is then held in place with underlying "loopers". Tufted carpets can be twist pile, velvet, or loop pile. Twist pile carpets are produced when one or more fibres are twisted in the tufting process, so that in the finished carpet they appear to be bound together. Velvet pile carpets tend to have a shorter pile and a tighter construction, giving the finished article a smooth, velvety appearance.

Loop pile carpets are renowned for being hard wearing and lend carpets great texture. The traditional domain of rugs from far away continents, hand knotted squares and rugs use the expertise of weavers to produce work of the finest quality. Traditional rugs often feature a deliberate 'mistake' on behalf of the weaver to guarantee their authenticity. Six of Axminster carpets are known as the "Lansdowne" group. These have a tripartite design with reeded circles and baskets of flowers in the central panel flanked by diamond lozenges in the side panels. Axminster Rococo designs often have a brown ground and include birds copied from popular, contemporary engravings. Even now a large percentage of the 55,000 population town still seek employment in this industry. The town of Wilton, Wiltshire is also known for its carpet weaving, which dates back to the 18th century.

Modern Carpeting and Installation

Carpet is commonly made in widths of 12 feet (3.7 m) and 15 feet (4.6 m) in the USA, 4 m and 5 m in Europe. Where necessary different widths can be seamed together with a seaming iron and seam tape (formerly it was sewn together) and it is fixed to a floor over a cushioned underlay (pad) using nails, tack strips (known in the UK as gripper rods), adhesives, or occasionally decorative metal stair rods, thus distinguishing it from rugs or mats, which are loose-laid floor coverings. For environmental reasons, the use of wool, natural bindings, natural padding, and formaldehyde-free glues is becoming more common. These options are almost always at a premium cost, though with no sacrifice to performance.

In the UK some carpets are still manufactured for pubs and clubs in a narrow width of 27 inches (0.69 m) and then sewn to size. Carpeting which covers an entire room area is loosely referred to as 'wall-to-wall', but carpet can be installed over any portion thereof with use of appropriate transition moldings where the carpet meets other types of floor coverings. Carpeting is more than just a single item; it is, in fact, a system comprising the carpet itself, the carpet backing (often made of latex), the cushioning underlay, and a method of installation.

Carpet tiles are also available, typically 50 centimetres (20 in) square. These are usually only used in commercial settings and are affixed using a special pressure-sensitive glue, which holds them into place while allowing easy removal (in an office environment, for example) or to allow rearrangement in order to spread wear.

Pile Weave

Pile weave is a form of textile created by weaving. Pile fabrics used to be made on traditional hand weaving machines. The warp ends that are used for the formation of the pile are woven over metal rods or wires that are inserted in the shed (gap caused by raising alternate threads) during weaving. The pile ends lie in loops over the inserted rods. When a rod is extracted the pile ends remain as loops on top of the base fabric. The pile ends laying over the rod may be left as 'loop pile', or cut to form 'cut pile' or velvet.

On mechanical looms the technology of 'wire weaving' still exists, using modern technology and electronics. This weaving technique allows users to obtain both loop pile and cut pile in the same fabric. Other techniques involve the weaving of two layers of fabric on top of each other, whereby the warp ends used for the pile are inserted in such a way that they form a vertical connection between the two layers of fabric. By cutting the pile ends in between the two layers one obtains two separate pile fabrics. With this technique only the cut pile effect can be obtained. This is known as 'face-to-face weaving'. Both 'wire weaving' and 'face-to-face' weaving are used for the manufacturing of upholstery and furnishing fabrics as well as in rug making.

Pile weave or knotted weave is the method of weaving used in most rugs. In this technique the rug is woven by creation of knots. A short piece of yarn is tied by hand around two neighbouring warp strands creating a knot on the surface of the rug. After each row of knots is created, one or more strands of weft are passed through a complete set of warp strands. Then the knots and the weft strands are beaten with a comb securing the knots in place. A rug can consist of 25 to over 1,000 knots per square inch.

Warp Pile Weave

Velvet

Frieze: Terrycloth, a pile fabric (usually cotton) with uncut loops on both sides. The pile in terrycloth is formed by a special weaveing arrangement in which three picks or fillings are inserted and beaten up with one motion of the reed. Common varieties include two-pick and three-pick terries with three-pick one being the highest quality, it has two picks under the pile loop and one pick between loops. Each loop acts as a tiny sponge.

Terrycloth is used to make bath towels and bath robes due to its ability of absorbing large amounts of water

Filling Pile Weave: Corduroy, is a textile composed of twisted fibres that, when woven, lie parallel (similar to twill) to one another to form the cloth's distinct pattern, a "cord." Modern corduroy is most commonly composed of tufted cords, sometimes exhibiting a channel (bare to the base fabric) between the tufts. Corduroy is, in essence, a ridged form of velvet.

Velveteen: Another form of velvet distinguished by their fibre length and pile yarn position. A velveteen is made of staple fibres and the pile yarn is in filling direction, where velveteen is made of filament fibre and the pile yarn is in warp direction.

Polar Fleece

Polar fleece usually referred to simply as "fleece," is a soft napped insulating synthetic fabric made from Polyethylene terephthalate (PET) or other synthetic fibres. Other names for this fabric are "Polar Wool," "Vega Wool," or "Velo Wool." Despite names suggesting the composition is made up of organic materials, fleece is 100% Polyethylene Terephthalate. One of the first forms was Polar Fleece, created in 1979 by Malden Mills, now Polartec LLC. This was a new, light, and strong pile fabric meant to mimic—and in some ways surpass—wool.

Fleece has some of wool's finest qualities but weighs a fraction of the weight of the lightest available woolens.

Polar fleece is used in jackets, hats, sweaters, jogging bottoms/sweatpants, cloth diapers, gym clothes, hoodies, inexpensive throw blankets, and high-performance outdoor clothing, and can be used as a vegan alternative to wool. It can be made partially from recycled plastic bottles and is very light, soft and easy to wash.

Aaron Feuerstein intentionally declined to patent Polar fleece, allowing the material to be produced cheaply and widely by many vendors, leading to the material's quick and wide acceptance.

Fleece garments traditionally come in different thickness: micro, 100, 200, and 300, with 300 being the thickest and least flexible.

Advantages and Disadvantages

Fleece is a very soft, lightweight, warm and comfortable fabric. It is hydrophobic, holding less than 1% of its weight in water, it retains much of its insulating powers even when wet, and it is highly breathable. These qualities make it useful for making clothing intended to be used during strenuous physical activity; perspiration is able to readily pass through the fabric. It is machine washable and dries quickly. It is a good alternative to wool (of particular importance to those who are allergic or sensitive to wool). It can also be made out of recycled PET bottles, or even recycled fleece.

There are disadvantages to this fabric as well. If not treated with a flame retardant, fleece is quite flammable, in contrast to wool, which is relatively nonflammable. Non-recycled fleece is made from non-renewable petroleum derivatives. Regular fleece is not windproof and does not absorb moisture (although this is often seen as a benefit, per above).

Fleece also tends to generate a high amount of static electricity, which causes the accumulation of lint, dust, and pet hair. It is also susceptible to damage from high temperature washing, tumble drying or ironing. Lower-quality fleece material is also prone to pilling.

Extra Warp and Extra Weft Figured Fabrics

Weaving with more than one warp is something. We call it a "supplementary warp" when in theory, it could be removed and an intact cloth would remain.

"Red Square" was woven on 10 shafts–2 for the foundation warp and 8 for the red warp.

Double Cloths

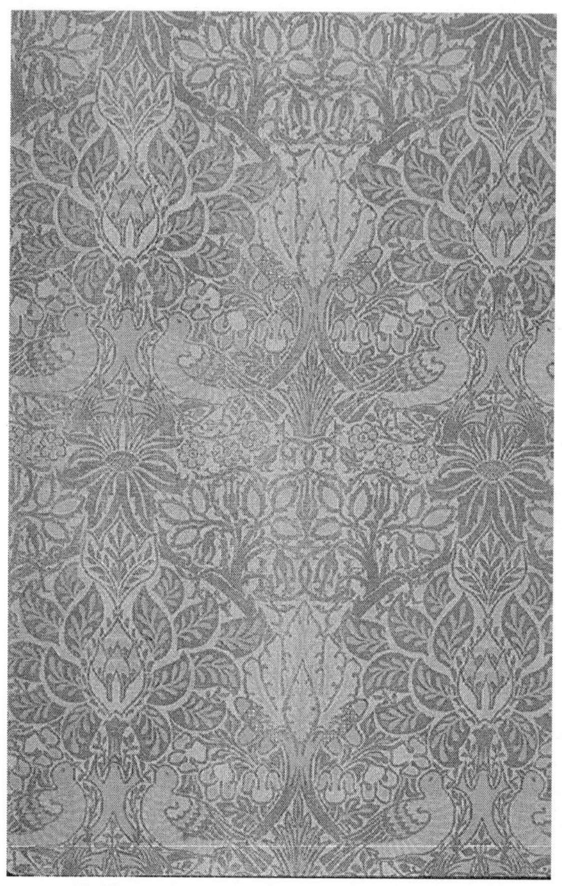

Figure: Dove and Rose *jacquard-woven silk and wool double cloth furnishing textile, designed by William Morris in 1879.*

Double cloth or double weave (also doublecloth, double-cloth) is a kind of woven textile in which two or more sets of warps and one or more sets of weft or filling yarns are interconnected to form a two-layered cloth.

The movement of threads between the layers allows complex patterns and surface textures to be created.

In contemporary textile manufacturing, the term "double cloth" or "true double cloth" is sometimes restricted to fabrics with two warps and three wefts, made up as two distinct fabrics lightly connected by the third or binding weft, but this distinction is not always made, and double-woven fabrics in which two warps and two wefts interlace to form geometric patterns are also called double cloths.

Double-faced fabrics are a form of double cloth made of one warp and two sets of wefts, or (less often) two warps and one weft. These fabrics have two right sides or faces and no wrong side, and include most blankets, satin ribbons, and interlinings.

Double weaving is an ancient technique. Surviving examples from the Paracas culture of Peru have been dated to before AD 700.

Modern applications of double cloth include haute couture coats, blankets, furnishing fabrics, and some brocades.

Uses

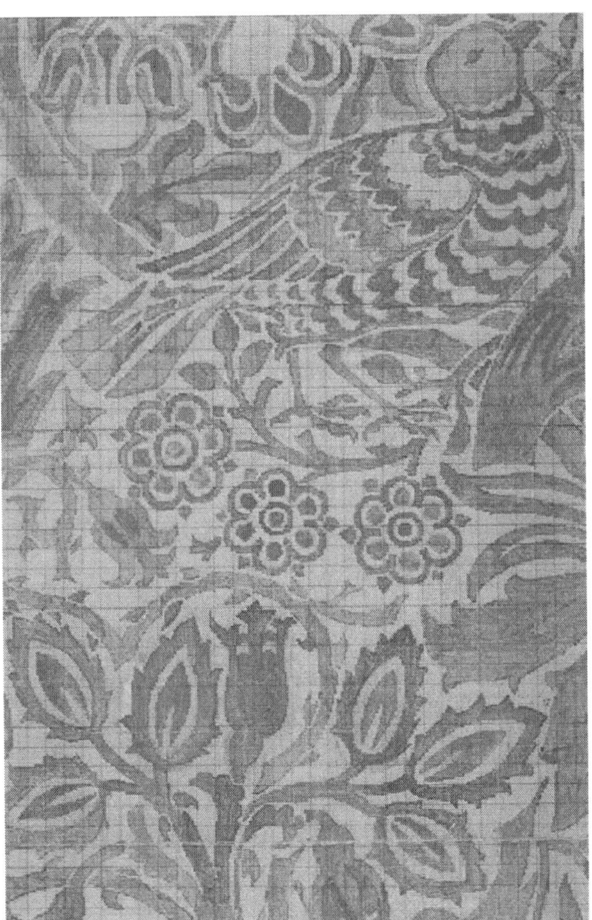

Figure: *"Point-paper" or weaving design for* Dove and Rose.

Double cloth textiles are a characteristic artifact of Pre-Columbian Peru, where they were woven of cotton and alpaca yarns in various combinations

In Medieval England, double weaves called *compound weft-faced twills* featured weft or filling yarns in multiple colours, with the design completely covering the face warp yarns and the unused colours for any particular section woven into a binding warp on the reverse side.

In early 19th century America, double cloth wool and cotton woven coverlets were made by professional weavers from wool that was spun (and often dyed) at home and then delivered to a local weaver who made up the coverlet.

In the later 19th century, craftsman and designer William Morris offered wool and silk double cloth fabrics for furnishing through his firm Morris, Marshall, Faulkner & Co. (later Morris & Co.). These double-woven fabrics had separate warps of wool and silk yarn and were woven by Alexander Morton & Co. of Darvel, Scotland, who would later weave similar fabrics from designs by C. F. A. Voysey and others.

Contemporary couture designers use "true" double cloth to make self-lined or reversible coats and jackets by using hand-finishing techniques such as separating the two layers at the hem and turning the raw edges under. Double cloth garments may also be made reversible by binding or overcasting edges.

Interchanging Double Cloths

Interchanging Double Cloths: Double Cloths can be joined together by interchanging fabric layers. The interchanging of threads means that the series which actually alternates between the face and back of the cloth can no longer be designated as the face or back yarns because it will occasionally be the one and occasionally be the other.

Thus in a cloth in which the ends and picks are arranged in an alternate 1 black, 1 white order, the black cloth will form the face when all the black ends are raised over white picks and vice versa.

Basic Aspects of Colours and its Effects

Colour is the visual perceptual property corresponding in humans to the categories called *red, blue, yellow, green* and others. Colour derives from the spectrum of light (distribution of light power versus wavelength) interacting in the eye with the spectral sensitivities of the light receptors. Colour categories and physical specifications of colour are also associated with objects, materials, light sources, etc., based on their physical properties such as light absorption, reflection, or emission spectra. By defining a colour space, colours can be identified numerically by their coordinates.

Because perception of colour stems from the varying spectral sensitivity of different types of cone cells in the retina to different parts of the spectrum, colours may be defined and quantified by the degree to which they stimulate these cells. These physical or physiological quantifications of colour, however, do not fully explain the psychophysical perception of colour appearance.

The science of colour is sometimes called *chromatics, chromatography, colourimetry,* or simply *colour science.* It includes the perception of colour by the human eye and brain, the origin of colour in materials, colour theory in art, and the physics of electromagnetic radiation in the visible range (that is, what we commonly refer to simply as *light*).

Physics of Colour

Continuous optical spectrum rendered into the sRGB colour space.

The colours of the visible light spectrum

Colour	*Wavelength interval*	*Frequency interval*
red	~ 700–635 nm	~ 430–480 THz
orange	~ 635–590 nm	~ 480–510 THz
yellow	~ 590–560 nm	~ 510–540 THz
green	~ 560–490 nm	~ 540–610 THz
blue	~ 490–450 nm	~ 610–670 THz
violet	~ 450–400 nm	~ 670–750 THz

Colour, Wavelength, Frequency and energy of light

Colour	*(nm)*	*(THz)*	*(μm^{-1})*	*(eV)*	*(kJ mol^{-1})*
Infrared	>1000	<300	<1.00	<1.24	<120
Red	700	428	1.43	1.77	171
Orange	620	484	1.61	2.00	193
Yellow	580	517	1.72	2.14	206
Green	530	566	1.89	2.34	226
Blue	470	638	2.13	2.64	254
Violet	420	714	2.38	2.95	285
Near ultraviolet	300	1000	3.33	4.15	400
Far ultraviolet	<200	>1500	>5.00	>6.20	>598

Electromagnetic radiation is characterized by its wavelength (or frequency) and its intensity. When the wavelength is within the visible spectrum (the range of wavelengths humans can perceive, approximately from 390 nm to 700 nm), it is known as "visible light".

Most light sources emit light at many different wavelengths; a source's *spectrum* is a distribution giving its intensity at each wavelength. Although the spectrum of light arriving at the eye from a given direction determines the colour sensation in that direction, there are many more possible spectral combinations than colour sensations.

In fact, one may formally define a colour as a class of spectra that give rise to the same colour sensation, although such classes would vary widely among different species, and to a lesser extent among individuals within the same species. In each such class the members are called *metamers* of the colour in question.

Spectral Colours

The familiar colours of the rainbow in the spectrum – named using the Latin word for *appearance* or *apparition* by Isaac Newton in 1671 – include all those colours that can be produced by visible light of a single wavelength only, the *pure spectral* or *monochromatic* colours.

The table at right shows approximate frequencies (in terahertz) and wavelengths (in nanometers) for various pure spectral colours. The wavelengths are measured in air or vacuum.

The colour table should not be interpreted as a definitive list – the pure spectral colours form a continuous spectrum, and how it is divided into distinct colours linguistically is a matter of culture and historical contingency (although people everywhere have been shown to *perceive* colours in the same way).

A common list identifies six main bands: red, orange, yellow, green, blue, and purple. Newton's conception included a seventh colour, indigo, between blue and purple. It is possible that what Newton referred to as blue is nearer to what today we call cyan, and that indigo was simply the dark blue of the indigo dye that was being imported at the time.

The *intensity* of a spectral colour, relative to the context in which it is viewed, may alter its perception considerably; for example, a low-intensity orange-yellow is brown, and a low-intensity yellow-green is olive-green.

Colour of Objects

The colour of an object depends on both the physics of the object in its environment and the characteristics of the perceiving eye and brain.

Physically, objects can be said to have the colour of the light leaving their surfaces, which normally depends on the spectrum of the incident illumination and the reflectance properties of the surface, as well as potentially on the angles of illumination and viewing. Some objects not only reflect light, but also transmit light or emit light themselves, which also contribute to the colour.

A viewer's perception of the object's colour depends not only on the spectrum of the light leaving its surface, but also on a host of contextual cues, so that colour differences between objects can be discerned mostly independent of the lighting spectrum, viewing angle, etc. This effect is known as colour constancy.

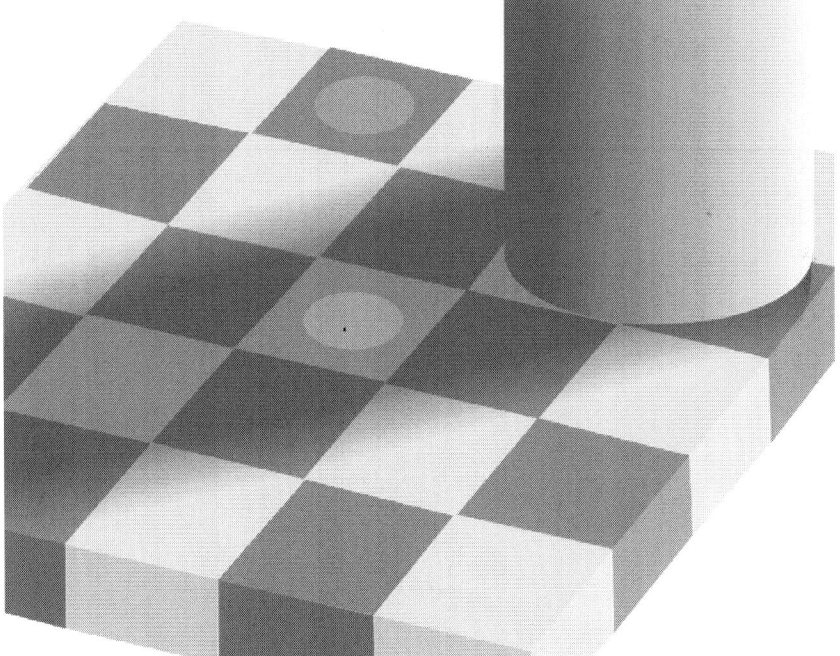

Figure: *The upper disk and the lower disk have exactly the same objective colour, and are in identical gray surroundings; based on context differences, humans perceive the squares as having different reflectances, and may interpret the colours as different colour categories.*

Some generalizations of the physics can be drawn, neglecting perceptual effects for now:

- Light arriving at an opaque surface is either reflected "specularly" (that is, in the manner of a mirror), scattered (that is, reflected with diffuse scattering), or absorbed – or some combination of these.
- Opaque objects that do not reflect specularly (which tend to have rough surfaces) have their colour determined by which wavelengths of light they scatter strongly (with the light that is not scattered being absorbed).

  If objects scatter all wavelengths with roughly equal strength, they appear white. If they absorb all wavelengths, they appear black.
- Opaque objects that specularly reflect light of different wavelengths with different efficiencies look like mirrors tinted with colours determined by those differences.

  An object that reflects some fraction of impinging light and absorbs the rest may look black but also be faintly reflective; examples are black objects coated with layers of enamel or lacquer.
- Objects that transmit light are either *translucent* (scattering the transmitted light) or *transparent* (not scattering the transmitted light). If they also absorb (or reflect) light of various wavelengths differentially, they appear tinted with a colour determined by the nature of that absorption (or that reflectance).
- Objects may emit light that they generate from having excited electrons, rather than merely reflecting or transmitting light. The electrons may be excited due to elevated temperature (*incandescence*), as a result of chemical reactions (*chemoluminescence*), after absorbing light of other frequencies ("fluorescence" or "phosphorescence") or from electrical contacts as in light emitting diodes, or other light sources.

To summarize, the colour of an object is a complex result of its surface properties, its transmission properties, and its emission properties, all of which contribute to the mix of wavelengths in the light leaving the surface of the object.

The perceived colour is then further conditioned by the nature of the ambient illumination, and by the colour properties of other objects nearby, and via other characteristics of the perceiving eye and brain.

Perception

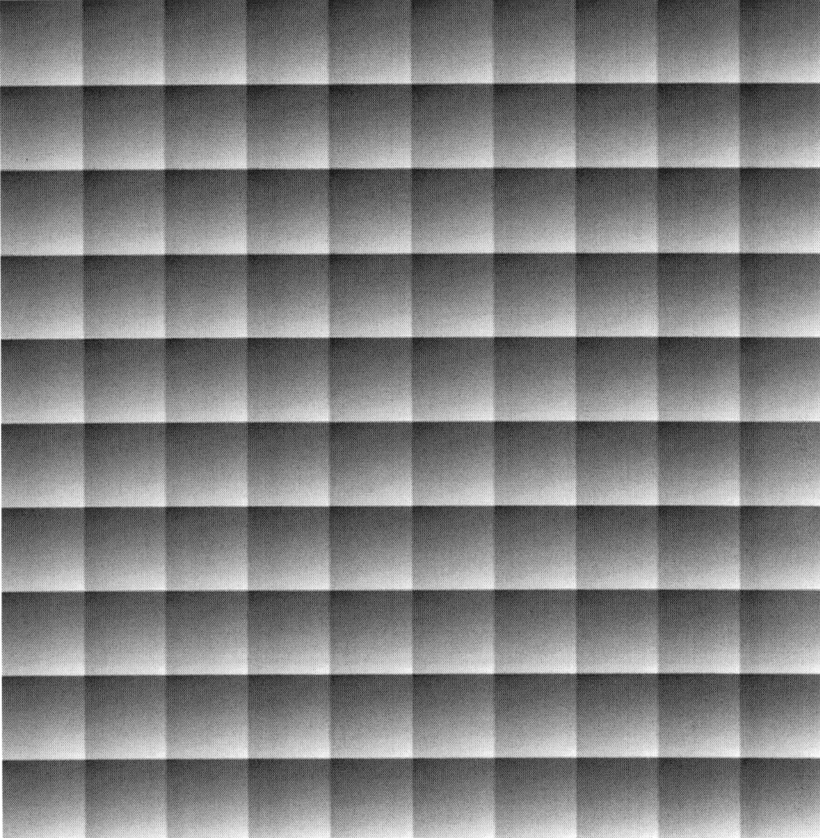

Figure: *This image (when viewed in full size, **1000** pixels wide) contains **1** million pixels, each of a different colour. The human eye can distinguish about **10** million different colours.*

Development of Theories of Colour Vision

Although Aristotle and other ancient scientists had already written on the nature of light and colour vision, it was not until Newton that light was identified as the source of the colour sensation. In 1810, Goethe published his comprehensive *Theory of Colours* in which he ascribed physiological effects to colour that are now understood as psychological.

In 1801 Thomas Young proposed his trichromatic theory, based on the observation that any colour could be matched with a combination of three lights. This theory was later refined by James Clerk Maxwell and Hermann von Helmholtz.

As Helmholtz puts it, "the principles of Newton's law of mixture were experimentally confirmed by Maxwell in 1856. Young's theory of colour sensations, like so much else that this marvelous investigator achieved in advance of his time, remained unnoticed until Maxwell directed attention to it."

At the same time as Helmholtz, Ewald Hering developed the opponent process theory of colour, noting that colour blindness and afterimages typically come in opponent pairs (red-green, blue-orange, yellow-purple, and black-white).

Ultimately these two theories were synthesized in 1957 by Hurvich and Jameson, who showed that retinal processing corresponds to the trichromatic theory, while processing at the level of the lateral geniculate nucleus corresponds to the opponent theory.

In 1931, an international group of experts known as the *Commission internationale de l'éclairage* (CIE) developed a mathematical colour model, which mapped out the space of observable colours and assigned a set of three numbers to each.

Colour in the Eye

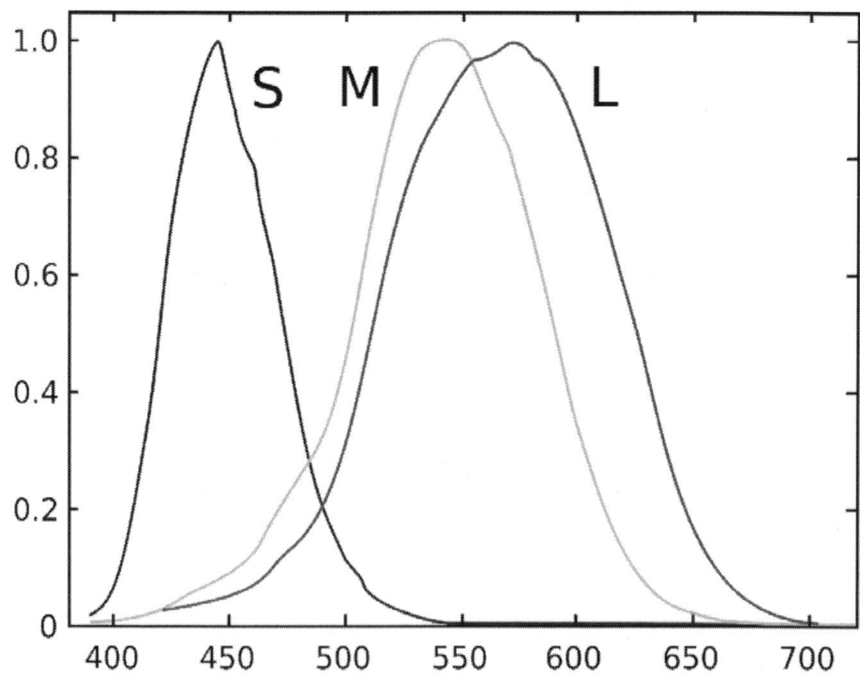

Figure: *Normalized typical human cone cell responses (S, M, and L types) to monochromatic spectral stimuli*

The ability of the human eye to distinguish colours is based upon the varying sensitivity of different cells in the retina to light of different wavelengths. Humans being trichromatic, the retina contains three types of colour receptor cells, or cones.

One type, relatively distinct from the other two, is most responsive to light that we perceive as blue or blue-violet, with wavelengths around 450 nm; cones of this type are sometimes called *short-wavelength cones*, *S cones*, or *blue cones*. The other two types are closely related genetically and chemically: *middle-wavelength cones*, *M cones*, or *green cones* are most sensitive to light perceived as green, with wavelengths around 540 nm, while the *long-wavelength cones*, *L cones*, or *red cones*, are most sensitive to light we perceive as greenish yellow, with wavelengths around 570 nm.

Light, no matter how complex its composition of wavelengths, is reduced to three colour components by the eye. For each location in the visual field, the three types of cones yield three signals based on the extent to which each is stimulated. These amounts of stimulation are sometimes called *tristimulus values*.

The response curve as a function of wavelength varies for each type of cone. Because the curves overlap, some tristimulus values do not occur for any incoming light combination. For example, it is not possible to stimulate *only* the mid-wavelength (so-called "green") cones; the other cones will inevitably be stimulated to some degree at the same time.

The set of all possible tristimulus values determines the human *colour space*. It has been estimated that humans can distinguish roughly 10 million different colours.

The other type of light-sensitive cell in the eye, the rod, has a different response curve. In normal situations, when light is bright enough to strongly stimulate the cones, rods play virtually no role in vision at all. On the other hand, in dim light, the cones are understimulated leaving only the signal from the rods, resulting in a colourless response. (Furthermore, the rods are barely sensitive to light in the "red" range.)

In certain conditions of intermediate illumination, the rod response and a weak cone response can together result in colour discriminations not accounted for by cone responses alone. These effects, combined, are summarized also in the Kruithof curve, that describes the change of colour perception and pleasingness of light as function of temperature and intensity.

Colour in the Brain

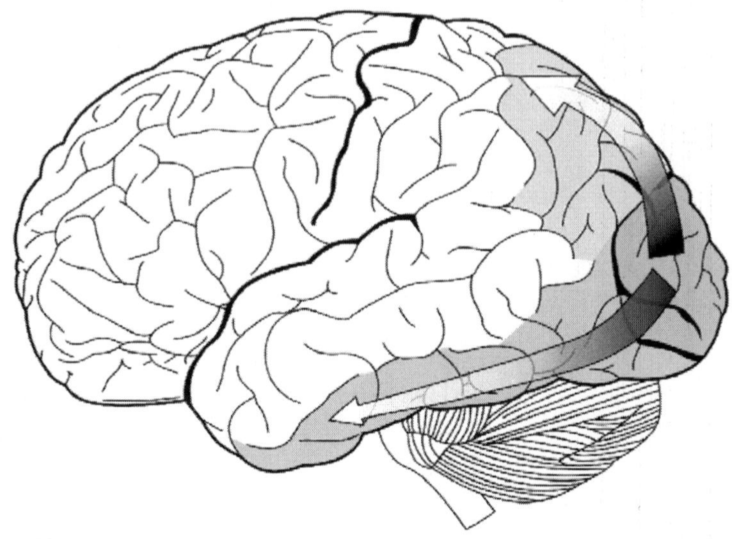

Figure: *The visual dorsal stream (green) and ventral stream (purple) are shown. The ventral stream is responsible for colour perception.*

While the mechanisms of colour vision at the level of the retina are well-described in terms of tristimulus values, colour processing after that point is organized differently. A dominant theory of colour vision proposes that colour information is transmitted out of the eye by three opponent processes, or opponent channels, each constructed from the raw output of the cones: a red–green channel, a blue–yellow channel, and a black–white "luminance" channel.

This theory has been supported by neurobiology, and accounts for the structure of our subjective colour experience. Specifically, it explains why we cannot perceive a "reddish green" or "yellowish blue", and it predicts the colour wheel: it is the collection of colours for which at least one of the two colour channels measures a value at one of its extremes.

The exact nature of colour perception beyond the processing already described, and indeed the status of colour as a feature of the perceived world or rather as a feature of our *perception* of the world - a type of qualia - is a matter of complex and continuing philosophical dispute.

Nonstandard Colour Perception

Colour deficiency: If one or more types of a person's colour-sensing cones are missing or less responsive than normal to incoming light, that person can distinguish fewer colours and is said to be *colour deficient* or *colour blind* (though this latter term can be misleading; almost all colour deficient individuals can distinguish at least some colours). Some kinds of colour deficiency are caused by anomalies in the number or nature of cones in the retina. Others (like *central* or *cortical achromatopsia*) are caused by neural anomalies in those parts of the brain where visual processing takes place.

Tetrachromacy

While most humans are *trichromatic* (having three types of colour receptors), many animals, known as *tetrachromats*, have four types. These include some species of spiders, most marsupials, birds, reptiles, and many species of fish. Other species are sensitive to only two axes of colour or do not perceive colour at all; these are called *dichromats* and *monochromats* respectively. A distinction is made between *retinal tetrachromacy* (having four pigments in cone cells in the retina, compared to three in trichromats) and *functional tetrachromacy* (having the ability to make enhanced colour discriminations based on that retinal difference).

As many as half of all women are retinal tetrachromats. The phenomenon arises when an individual receives two slightly different copies of the gene for either the medium- or long-wavelength cones, which are carried on the x-chromosome. To have two different genes, a person must have two x-chromosomes, which is why the phenomenon only occurs in women. For some of these retinal tetrachromats, colour discriminations are enhanced, making them functional tetrachromats.

Synesthesia

In certain forms of synesthesia, perceiving letters and numbers (grapheme–colour synesthesia) or hearing musical sounds (music–colour synesthesia) will lead to the unusual additional experiences of seeing colours. Behavioural and functional neuroimaging experiments have demonstrated that these colour experiences lead to changes in behavioural tasks and lead to increased activation of brain regions involved in colour perception, thus demonstrating their reality, and similarity to real colour percepts, albeit evoked through a non-standard route.

Afterimages

After exposure to strong light in their sensitivity range, photoreceptors of a given type become desensitized. For a few seconds after the light ceases, they will continue to signal less strongly than they otherwise would. Colours observed during that period will appear to lack the colour component detected by the desensitized photoreceptors. This effect is responsible for the phenomenon of afterimages, in which the eye may continue to see a bright figure after looking away from it, but in a complementary colour.

Afterimage effects have also been utilized by artists, including Vincent van Gogh.

Colour Constancy

When an artist uses a limited colour palette, the eye tends to compensate by seeing any gray or neutral colour as the colour which is missing from the colour wheel. For example, in a limited palette consisting of red, yellow, black, and white, a mixture of yellow and black will appear as a variety of green, a mixture of red and black will appear as a variety of purple, and pure gray will appear bluish.

The trichromatic theory is strictly true when the visual system is in a fixed state of adaptation. In reality, the visual system is constantly adapting to changes in the environment and compares the various colours in a scene to reduce the effects of the illumination. If a scene is illuminated with one light, and then with another, as long as the difference between the light sources stays within a reasonable range, the colours in the scene appear relatively constant to us. This was studied by Edwin Land in the 1970s and led to his retinex theory of colour constancy.

It should be noted, that both phenomena are readily explained and mathematically modeled with modern theories of chromatic adaptation and colour appearance (e.g. CIECAM02, iCAM). There is no need to dismiss the trichromatic theory of vision, but rather it can be enhanced with an understanding of how the visual system adapts to changes in the viewing environment.

Colour Naming

Colours vary in several different ways, including hue (shades of red, orange, yellow, green, blue, and violet), saturation, brightness, and gloss. Some colour words are derived from the name of an object of that colour, such as "orange" or "salmon", while others are abstract, like "red".

In the 1969 study *Basic Colour Terms: Their Universality and Evolution*, Brent Berlin and Paul Kay describe a pattern in naming "basic" colours (like "red" but not "red-orange" or "dark red" or "blood red", which are "shades" of red). All languages that have two "basic" colour names distinguish dark/cool colours from bright/warm colours. The next colours to be distinguished are usually red and then yellow or green. All languages with six "basic" colours include black, white, red, green, blue, and yellow.

The pattern holds up to a set of twelve: black, gray, white, pink, red, orange, yellow, green, blue, purple, brown, and azure (distinct from blue in Russian and Italian, but not English).

Associations

Individual colours have a variety of cultural associations such as national colours (in general described in individual colour articles and colour symbolism). The field of colour psychology attempts to identify the effects of colour on human emotion and activity. Chromotherapy is a form of alternative medicine attributed to various Eastern traditions. Colours have different associations in different countries and cultures.

Different colours have been demonstrated to have effects on cognition. For example, researchers at the University of Linz in Austria demonstrated that the colour red significantly decreases cognitive functioning in men.

Spectral Colours and Colour Reproduction

Most light sources are mixtures of various wavelengths of light. Many such sources can still effectively produce a spectral colour, as the eye cannot distinguish them from single-wavelength sources. For example, most computer displays reproduce the spectral colour orange as a combination of red and green light; it appears orange because the red and green are mixed in the right proportions to allow the eye's cones to respond the way they do to the spectral colour orange.

A useful concept in understanding the perceived colour of a non-monochromatic light source is the dominant wavelength, which identifies the single wavelength of light that produces a sensation most similar to the light source. Dominant wavelength is roughly akin to hue.

There are many colour perceptions that by definition cannot be pure spectral colours due to desaturation or because they are purples (mixtures of red and violet light, from opposite ends of the spectrum). Some examples of necessarily non-spectral colours are the achromatic colours (black, gray, and white) and colours such as pink, tan, and magenta.

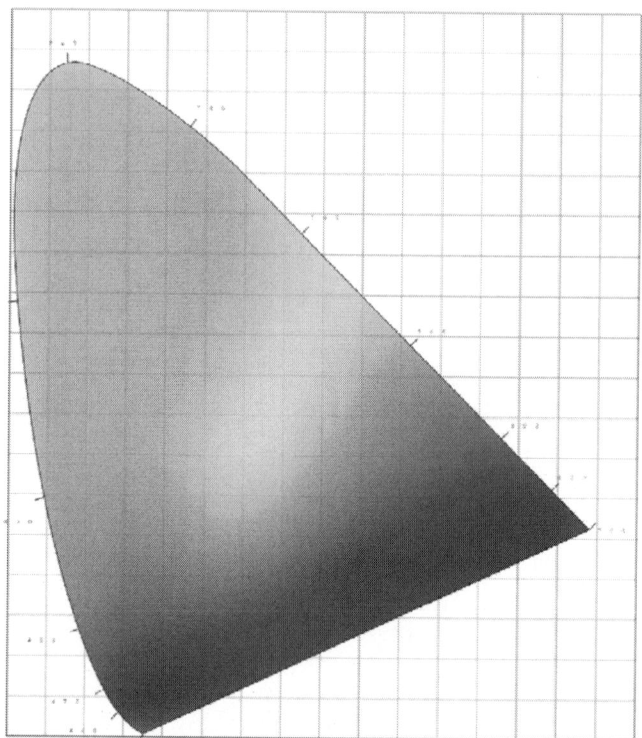

Figure: *The CIE 1931 colour space chromaticity diagram. The outer curved boundary is the spectral (or monochromatic) locus, with wavelengths shown in nanometers. The colours depicted depend on the colour space of the device on which you are viewing the image, and therefore may not be a strictly accurate representation of the colour at a particular position, and especially not for monochromatic colours.*

Two different light spectra that have the same effect on the three colour receptors in the human eye will be perceived as the same colour. They are metamers of that colour. This is exemplified by the white light emitted by fluorescent lamps, which typically has a spectrum of a few narrow bands, while daylight has a continuous spectrum.

The human eye cannot tell the difference between such light spectra just by looking into the light source, although reflected colours from objects can look different. (This is often exploited; for example, to make fruit or tomatoes look more intensely red.)

Similarly, most human colour perceptions can be generated by a mixture of three colours called *primaries*. This is used to reproduce colour scenes in photography, printing, television, and other media. There are a number of methods or colour spaces for specifying a colour in terms of three particular primary colours. Each method has its advantages and disadvantages depending on the particular application.

No mixture of colours, however, can produce a response truly identical to that of a spectral colour, although one can get close, especially for the longer wavelengths, where the CIE 1931 colour space chromaticity diagram has a nearly straight edge. For example, mixing green light (530 nm) and blue light (460 nm) produces cyan light that is slightly desaturated, because response of the red colour receptor would be greater to the green and blue light in the mixture than it would be to a pure cyan light at 485 nm that has the same intensity as the mixture of blue and green.

Because of this, and because the *primaries* in colour printing systems generally are not pure themselves, the colours reproduced are never perfectly saturated spectral colours, and so spectral colours cannot be matched exactly. However, natural scenes rarely contain fully saturated colours, thus such scenes can usually be approximated well by these systems. The range of colours that can be reproduced with a given colour reproduction system is called the gamut. The CIE chromaticity diagram can be used to describe the gamut.

Another problem with colour reproduction systems is connected with the acquisition devices, like cameras or scanners. The characteristics of the colour sensors in the devices are often very far from the characteristics of the receptors in the human eye. In effect, acquisition of colours can be relatively poor if they have special, often very "jagged", spectra caused for example by unusual lighting of the photographed scene. A colour reproduction system "tuned" to a human with normal colour vision may give very inaccurate results for other observers.

The different colour response of different devices can be problematic if not properly managed. For colour information stored and transferred in digital form, colour management techniques, such as those based on ICC profiles, can help to avoid distortions of the reproduced colours. Colour management does not circumvent the gamut limitations of particular output devices, but can assist in finding good mapping of input colours into the gamut that can be reproduced.

Additive Colouring

Additive colour is light created by mixing together light of two or more different colours. Red, green, and blue are the additive primary colours normally used in additive colour systems such as projectors and computer terminals

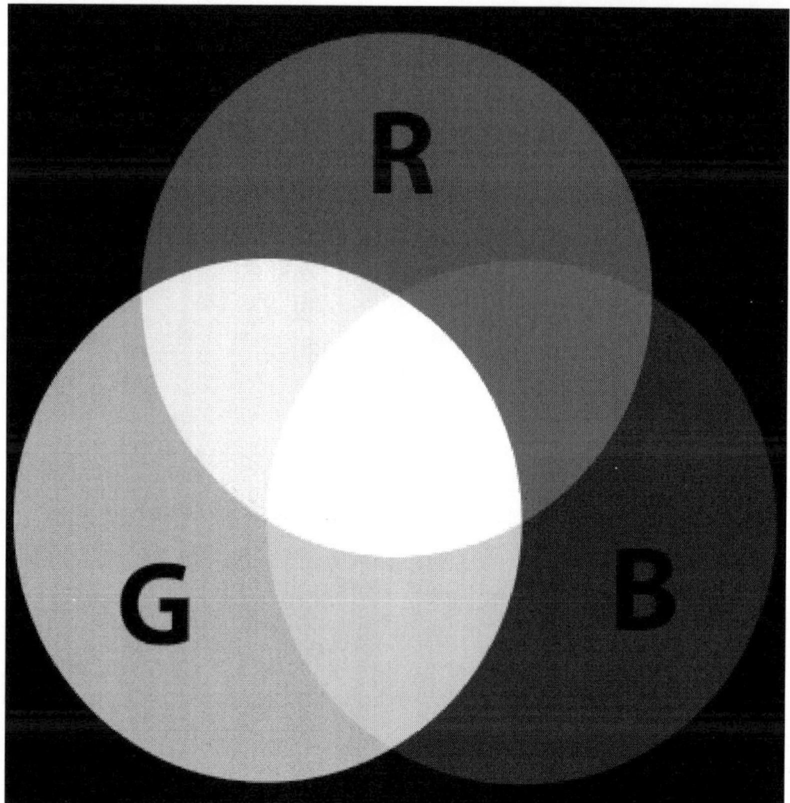

Figure: *Additive colour mixing: adding red to green yields yellow; adding all three primary colours together yields white.*

Subtractive Colouring

Subtractive colouring uses dyes, inks, and pigments to absorb some wavelengths of light and not others. The colour that a surface displays comes from the parts of the visible spectrum that are not absorbed and therefore remain visible. Without pigments or dye, fabric fibres, paint base and paper are usually made of particles that scatter white light (all colours) well in all directions. When a pigment or ink is added, wavelengths are absorbed or "subtracted" from white light, so light of another colour reaches the eye.

If the light is not a pure white source (the case of nearly all forms of artificial lighting), the resulting spectrum will appear a slightly different colour. Red paint, viewed under blue light, may appear black. Red paint is red because it scatters only the red components of the spectrum. If red paint is illuminated by blue light, it will be absorbed by the red paint, creating the appearance of a black object.

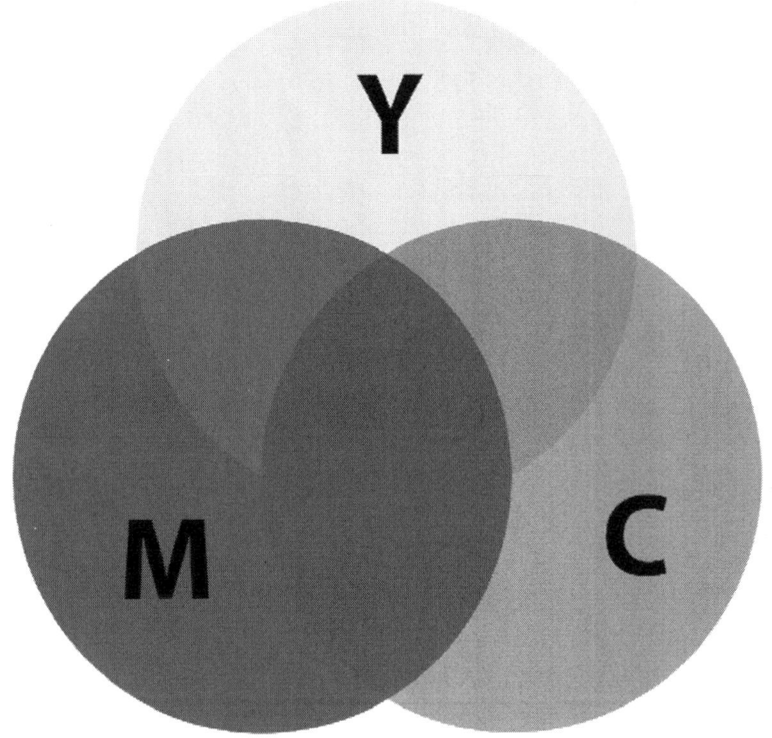

Figure: *Subtractive colour mixing*

Structural Colour

Structural colours are colours caused by interference effects rather than by pigments. Colour effects are produced when a material is scored with fine parallel lines, formed of one or more parallel thin layers, or otherwise composed of microstructures on the scale of the colour's wavelength. If the microstructures are spaced randomly, light of shorter wavelengths will be scattered preferentially to produce Tyndall effect colours: the blue of the sky (Rayleigh scattering, caused by structures much smaller than the wavelength of light, in this case air molecules), the luster of opals, and the blue of human irises.

If the microstructures are aligned in arrays, for example the array of pits in a CD, they behave as a diffraction grating: the grating reflects different wavelengths in different directions due to interference phenomena, separating mixed "white" light into light of different wavelengths. If the structure is one or more thin layers then it will reflect some wavelengths and transmit others, depending on the layers' thickness.

Structural colour is studied in the field of thin-film optics. A layman's term that describes particularly the most ordered or the most changeable structural colours is iridescence. Structural colour is responsible for the blues and greens of the feathers of many birds (the blue jay, for example), as well as certain butterfly wings and beetle shells. Variations in the pattern's spacing often give rise to an iridescent effect, as seen in peacock feathers, soap bubbles, films of oil, and mother of pearl, because the reflected colour depends upon the viewing angle. Numerous scientists have carried out research in butterfly wings and beetle shells, including Isaac Newton and Robert Hooke. Since 1942, electron micrography has been used, advancing the development of products that exploit structural colour, such as "photonic" cosmetics.

Additional Terms

- Colourfulness, chroma, purity, or saturation: how "intense" or "concentrated" a colour is. Technical definitions distinguish between colourfulness, chroma, and saturation as distinct perceptual attributes and include purity as a physical quantity. These terms, and others related to light and colour are internationally agreed upon and published in the CIE Lighting Vocabulary. More readily available texts on colourimetry also define and explain these terms.
- Dichromatism: a phenomenon where the hue is dependent on concentration and/or thickness of the absorbing substance.
- Hue: the colour's direction from white, for example in a colour wheel or chromaticity diagram.
- Shade: a colour made darker by adding black.
- Tint: a colour made lighter by adding white.
- Value, brightness, lightness, or luminosity: how light or dark a colour is.

Colour and Weave Relationship in Woven Fabrics

In woven designs from coloured threads, a coloured pattern is a consequence of two possible arrangements where warp is over the weft or vice versa. Thus the primary elements of woven fabric design are combination of weaves and blending of colours using such weaves.

Weave is the scheme or plan of interlacing the warp and weft yarns that produce the integrated fabric. Weave relates specially to the build or structure of the fabric. Colour is differently related to effects of weave and form. The methods of utilization of colour in woven textiles depend upon the composition of the weave design to be woven and the structure parameters of the cloth.

Colour and ornamentation in woven fabrics is imparted through the pre-determined placement and interlacing of particular sequences of yarns. A solid colour is produced by employing the same colour in warp and weft.

On the other hand, different colours may be combined to produce either a mixed or intermingled colour effect in which the composite hue appears as a solid colour. Figured ornamentation is created through the selection of different groups of coloured yarns, placed in the warp and/or in the weft; while in certain patterns, textural effects may be created entirely through the use of different values and closely associated hues of certain colours. The figure is formed for the purpose of displaying different pattern formations, adding dimension or colour reinforcement and for enhancing a particular motif.

Modern CAD systems provide a variety of design tools that are supported by standardized colour databases that allow simulation of weave structures on the computer monitor that could be printed on paper. However, deviations of the colour values of these simulations still occur. Also, the colour on fully flat fabric simulations on paper or computer screen is two-dimensional that differs from the real three-dimensional nature of fabrics and yarns.

In textile wet processing, the uses of colourimetry systems and associated software have proven their worth over the years, in objective estimation of colour, and have minimized misunderstandings between textile manufacturers and their customers. However, colour communication within textile design is largely a subjective process. Recent experimental studies have revealed that the use of colourimetry has helped to achieve better reproducibility and accuracy in the shade matching of textiles products. Colourimetry is, however, less used when fabrics are made from coloured yarns than when yarns and fabrics are dyed to a solid colour, or are printed. Recent research work provided a model that involves colourimetry for colour prediction.

Several measuring and imaging systems are now available commercially that can record colourimetric data and convert these data into visual images. Hence, the designer can generate a numerical colour specification that can be visualized accurately on a suitably calibrated monitor. Recent advances in colour curve generation and image processing provide opportunities for additional improvements in the areas of collaborative colour development, colour marketing, and colour prediction in multi-step processes. Contemporary techniques of computer-aided fabric design offer new possibilities for using colourimetry in weaving practice.

Along with the fundamental description of weave and colour relationship, and recent advances in woven fabric design, this chapter also includes the research models developed to quantify the colour proportion and colour values, in effort to eliminate the expensive and time consuming process of prototyping and colour matching in woven fabric design.

Woven fabrics are formed by interlacing two orthogonal sets of yarns; warp yarns that are vertically arranged and weft yarns that are horizontally placed. While all weave structures are created from a binary system (that is a warp yarn is over or under a weft yarn at the crossover areas), infinite number of weaves can be formed. The distribution of interlacement is known as weave design or pattern. There are three types of weaves that are known as basic weaves, which include plain weave (the simplest and smallest repeat size possible; 2 warp yarns x 2 weft yarns) and its derivatives, twill weaves and their derivatives, and satin/sateen weaves and their derivatives. These basic weaves are characterized by their simplicity, small size, ease of formation, and recognition. However, they form the base for creating any complex/intricate structures (such as multi-layer fabrics and pile weave structures) and weaves with extremely large patterns that are known as Jacquard designs.

Colour/Weave Relationship

The use of coloured warp and weft yarns combined with the weave structures permit the development of striking patterns. For a given pattern with multi-colour, a colour can be strategically placed in the pattern by merely using the binary system of warp and weft interlacing. The desired colour of a yarn appears when the yarn is over the crossing yarns for a desired length and small or large area if several yarns are used.

Moreover, numerous mixtures of colours to produce other colours can be obtained from few colours of the warp and weft yarns through proper weave interlacing. They were produced using many repeats in warp and weft directions, thread count close to real cloth, and assuming there are no spaces between the yarns, which is reasonable assumption or most woven fabrics.

CAD and Woven Fabric Design

Designing fabrics is a creative/technical process that is dependent upon the ability of the textile designer to combine aesthetic sensibility with a strong knowledge of the technology of materials and fabric production machinery.

Most Dobby and Jacquard fabrics producers' facilities are now equipped with Computer Aided Textile Design systems. In the pre-computer era, the designing process was done in the following manner: (a) a piece of artwork was created on paper, (b) the artwork was then rendered as a scaled grid (known as squared paper or design paper), whose columns and rows represented warp and weft yarns, respectively, (c) weaves were then assigned to specific areas to represent the original pattern, and (d) a technician then punched cards, direct from this technical design layout, in which each card represent one pick of the actual fabric.

Computers have been utilized in woven textile design for almost 25 years, and this has revolutionized the entire design process. They have revolutionized the entire thought-process from the initial artwork to final production. CAD systems in woven designing operate in a series of basic steps. The first step is that of digitizing the artwork. This feature allows the designer to see the artwork on a computer monitor by scanning the original piece or creating a design using the CAD system drawing tools directly. This is generally done in 8-bit format (256 colours) and allows the designer to modify patterns and reduce the number of colours to a manageable number as he/she wishes. The second step is fabric designing, in which the artwork image data is transformed (i.e. the grid system, above) into weaving information for fabric production. Weave allocation is the third step, in which information from the artwork image can be converted into a woven fabric.

The designer created the appropriate weave structure or chooses one (from a weave library) to match the desired colour, shape or texture in the artwork. This part of the programme also helps the designer to see a simulation of the final fabric on the display monitor. By looking at the preview, the designer can easily modify the design, and can change the weaves to recolour the design as required. All these developments have greatly increased the ease of woven fabric designing.

It is now possible to perform the entire process on a personal computer, and then transfer the ready-to-weave file (electronic punch-card file) via the internet, direct to the dobby or Jacquard controller at the loom, or to some interim storage area.

Textile CAD/CAM systems are mainly modular infrastructure and, in addition to covering yarn and fabric design may also include very realistic 3D simulation packages. A complete automated process with immediate response to the customer's demand seems to be a reality in the near future with these systems. Moreover, developments of powerful modem systems and electronic controls have brought the weaving machine into the design studio. This evolution has, in turn, given an entirely new meaning to the term.

The impetus for use of CAD in the textile industry was to improve efficiency in the production process. Initial textile designing software packages were mainly derived from graphic design software, without putting much emphasis upon the underlying fabric structures. CAD systems have evolved, however, by considering the designing process and technical limitations. These systems are now extensions of creative expression which comply with technical requirements (Doctor 1997). Numerous descriptions of this process exist within the computer environment addressing, algorithmically, the problems that arise when one attempts to harmonize visual pattern with the notational point paper diagrams of those used for warp and weft interlacing.

Innovation in the field of textile design CAD systems for woven fabrics has provided the opportunity to design intricate fabrics with the use of a variety of tools. There is also the possibility of seeing the resultant fabric on a computer monitor that gives the visualization of real fabric prior to weaving. There is constant improvement and development in the CAD system to develop several design features (CAD tools) to keep pace with new market demands.

Colour Visualization in Woven Fabrics

In pre-coloured yarn or fabric, when light fall s on the colourants (dyes or pigments), the white light is broken into its component wavelengths. Depending upon the particular molecular structure of a colourant and surface, light may be reflected back to the viewer, absorbed into the molecular surface, scattered by the molecular surface, transmitted through the surface or be subjected to some combination of reflection, absorption and transmission. One of the three processes always dominates; however, this in turn produces colour effects. The colour effect of perceived colour is a consequence of three types of colour mixing principles:

Additive Colour mixing is a basic phenomenon for colour perception, which involves addition of wavelengths of light to create higher-value colours. The broadest bands of colour seen in the visible spectrum are those belonging to red-orange, green and blue-violet, known as Primaries. When all these colours are projected and overlapped, their specific wavelength mix together and produce white light. Magenta, cyan and yellow are known as Secondary colours where only two colours overlaps and their respective wavelengths add together.

Subtractive Colour Mixing is created by the addition of pigment materials such as dyes, inks, and paints that remove reflecting wavelengths from light from each other, allowing us to see new colour. When the pigment primaries that are cyan, magenta and yellow are mixed together, they culminate in black.

Optical Colour Mixing is also known as Partitive Colour Mixing because optical mixtures combine additive and subtractive colour mixing phenomenon. This is an effective method of creating mixtures that appear to vibrate and mix at particular distances when small areas of colour are juxtaposed.

Partitive colour achieved in woven fabrics does not follow the same rules as the other cases (such as in additive and subtractive colour mixing), presumably because the individual yarns are not completely opaque and moreover the fabrics are made from blends of several coloured yarns with different weave effects.

Furthermore, the relation between the colour values of different colours and their size must be carefully considered. When two colours are in juxtaposition with each other, each takes on the complement of its neighbour. This is known as law of 'Simultaneous Contrast'. In woven fabrics, the appearance of the colour is a consequence of light reflected back from different areas of colour surface of the yarns involved in the fabric structure. Looking at the colour wheel, if colour values of warp and weft are taken into account, behaviour of the colour contrast and harmony can be well understood.

Complementary colours lie on the opposite sides of the colour circle, and their sum of reflected light gives an unsaturated colour, which can be observed as a grayish hue on the fabric. On the other hand, the close positioning of two harmonic colours gives similar colour value.

In woven designs, in case where fabric is made of multi-coloured yarns, the final visualized colour is a contribution of each colour component present on the surface of the structure.

Individual colour components are blended and seen as one solid colour. This blending of colour is governed by the above mentioned colour mixing principles. Blending of fibres has been very well studied in the past.

Colour Visualization in CAD Systems

In computer-aided design, there is a popular acronym called "wysiwyg", which means "what you see is what you get". Unfortunately, the wysiwyg concept often fails when dealing with the issue of colour and reproducing colour for different output devices. For example, it is difficult to match three different fabrics, all of which have different fibre content, because each fibre requires a different dye formulation. The same concept holds true in the world of computer generated colour. Each colour device used in CAD and production, including monitors, desktop printers, and commercial four-colour process printers, have unique definitions and limitations for colour by virtue of their own unique technology.

Since size of the design and restricted colour sets were the limitation for the industry requirements, this algorithm was developed to provide the possibility of capturing any kind of image by the system. The system could then provide important elements of colour in the image without compromising the storage requirements or degrading the system's response time. Rich (1986) discussed the basic colourimetry of CRT (Cathode Ray Tube) displays, both instrumental and visual, as applied to textile design systems. His paper emphasized CRT-based graphical displays to generate coloured images. He also suggested some technical aspects for accurate and repeatable representation of the weave and colour of the textile on display. Similarly, Takatera and Shinohara (1988) developed a search algorithm to determine the colour-ordering of the yarns and weave, to obtain a given pattern of colour-and-weave effect. Dawson (2002) examined colour-and-weave effects with small repeat sizes. He studied the effects of yarn colour sequences over several weave repeats. Grundler and Rolich (2003) proposed an evolution algorithm to combine the weave and colour, in order to have a predetermined idea of the appearance of the fabric to be produced. Based on the algorithm, software was then developed to access different fabric patterns and allowed the creation of new patterns, based on the user's choice.

Colours displayed via computer monitors cannot be specified independently. Therefore, colour is considered as one of the major aspects of a user-centered design process. Most current CAD systems use un-calibrated colour and, in consequence, designers are unable to define or communicate accurately the colour of the image-design effect that they produce on the computer screen. A system with calibrated colours gives precise definitions for all colours seen.

The numerical specifications for colours used in current CAD systems are expressed in terms of red, green, and blue (RGB) or hue, value, and saturation (HVS) combinations.

Importantly, the CIE system of colour specification (via tristimulus values, XYZ) is independent of any specific reproduction system and is widely used to specify colour in textile manufacturing (Polton & Porat 1992).

The colour issue represents not only one of the most frustrating aspects of CAD, but the area with the most rapidly advancing technology. A colour management system, or CMS can be used to create colour for specific output devices. Theoretically, this allows for more consistent and accurate colour results between different output devices. A CMS works in the background and translates colours based upon pre-defined colour profiles for specific output devices, allowing for more consistent colour viewing and output. CMS's provide new possibilities for accurate colour communication, but they cannot be considered an ultimate solution.

Since the introduction of spectral-based imaging systems some years ago, algorithmic data communication of colour standard and production 'submits', between retailers and suppliers, has proven to be one of the primary economic applications of the technology. Recent advances in colour curve generation and image processing provide opportunities for additional improvements in areas of collaborative colour development, colour marketing, and colour prediction in multi-step. At the same time, there are other aspects of imaging technology that have strong economical implications in other areas besides colour communication.

The other applications are derived from what is considered the very heart of such a system – the spectral base for colour. Contrary to most CAD type systems, the input and output channels are spectral reflectance values either measured or generated and are largely device and illuminant independent. The spectral data are by far the most basic characterization of an object's colour. From these spectral values, we derive all the other higher level output forms such as colourimetric values (X, Y, Z, L*, a*, b*, C*, H*), output to the monitor in calibrated colour (R, G, B), and to the calibrated printer in C, M, Y, K. By combining the spectral base, colourimetric functions, and an image processor, the colour imaging system is a powerful tool for colour management.

Advances in Colour and Weave Design

Recently, a number of technological advancements have been introduced by weaving machine producers, such as: high speed weaving, higher levels of automation, new shedding concepts, automatic (on the fly) pattern change, and filling colour selection. Along with the advances in weaving, significant development has also occurred in the field of CAD systems, which enables automation in the design process. Despite this automation, the process of assigning weaves/colours is still done by the designers or CAD operator, which therefore requires physical sampling prior to production.

In woven fabrics, which are highly textured, various patterns become visible through their different structures. The colour of such patterns also depends upon the colour of the yarns involved, their combinations and different structures on the pattern surface.

The final visible colour on the fabric surface is mainly due to the contribution of fabric covering properties, namely optical cover and geometric cover. The optical cover properties are defined as the reflection and scattering of the incident light by the fabric surface and are a function of the fibre material and fabric surface. Geometric cover (characterized by fabric cover factor) is defined as the area of fabric actually covered by fibres and yarns. Fabric cover factor is the ratio of surface area actually covered by yarns, to the total fabric surface area.

The following Equations are used to calculate total fabric surface area covered by warp and weft yarns;

Warp cover factor $C1= P1 x\ d1$ (1)

Filling cover factor $C2= P2 x\ d2$ (2)

Total cover factor $Cf= (C1+ C2- C1.C2) \times 100$ (3)

Using the fundamental theory as discussed above, Dimitrovski & Gabrijelcic (2002) developed a method for predicting colour values on woven fabric surfaces by calculating the colour values from the known colour values of the used yarns and the constructional parameters based on the cover factor Equations. The author estimated the deviation of the calculated fabric colour values and measured fabric simulation colour values from the measured colour values of a real fabric with identical parameters. Theoretical calculations of colour values of a fabric made from single coloured warp and filling yarns were reported, based on constructional parameters of each yarn in the fabric.

By using fabric geometry, fractions of individual colour components in a colour repeat was calculated and CIELAB colour space was then used to calculate colour difference tolerance. This method was experimented for the fabrics composed from single coloured warp and filling yarns, where the weave design is divided into two units (when warp is interlaced with weft and vice versa.

However, a weave design with varying warp/filling colours and diameters will have more than two units, which was not explained in this study. Also, no specific explanation (assumptions) regarding yarn diameter and yarn spacing was provided. For their calculation purpose, yarn diameter was measured (using microscope), which actually requires weaving a fabric and hence, defeat the purpose of predicting colour proportions.

The accuracy of prediction greatly depends upon the type of yarn. Multifilament yarn with relatively small number of twists tends to relatively big deformations of the diameter in the interlacing points, where deformations depend upon the type and the parameters of the yarns with which they interlace on the fabric surface. Deformation in the yarn diameter at interlacing points also depends upon the constructional and technological parameters the warp and the weft tension and reed plan are most important.

Due to considerable deformability of such yarns their spectrophotometrically measured colour values vary as well, so that it is difficult to accurately predict the colour values of the woven surfaces. The effect of the technological parameters on the colour values discussed in the paper was not, however, experimentally verified.

The following assumptions were made for the calculations: yarn diameters were uniform cylinders, warp spacing at the weave intersection and under the float are of same value, pick spacing at the weave intersection and under the float were of same value, the projection (two-dimensional) of the fabric on a plane parallel to fabric plane is considered, and yarns are uniformly coloured. Geometric calculations obtained from the model were employed in the number of Kubelka-Munk based models to predict the final colourimetric value of the woven design. The colourimetric values obtained were compared with spectrophotometric values for the colour difference.

Further, the colour values obtained from the Kubelka-Munk based colour models were simulated on the colour calibrated monitor and compared with real woven samples for visual comparison.

Apart from the work that directly addresses the issue of representing colour in interwoven yarns, there is another class of work, based on the influence of various fabric parameters that also addresses the problem of colour reproduction in woven fabrics. Yarn count and density have a direct influence on the visible fractions of each individual colour component within a colour repeat, and consequently on resultant colour values of that fabric surface.

However, during the different stages of producing fabric (spinning, weaving, knitting, etc.), colour change evolves due to different surface textures. Dupont et al (2001) proposed a model of colour evolution during the spinning stage, when the roving is transformed into yarn. After spinning, if the yarn is not dyed, the colour depends uniquely on the initial colour of the roving. Study done by Dimitroviski et al, concluded that the coloured yarns used in weaving, if dyed by different methods, also affect the fabric colour woven from the same yarns.

The optical colour values in a fabric depend on the shape of the structural units, such as length of the fibre, yarn floats, diameter of the fibre and the yarn, cross-sectional shape of the fibre, and the longitudinal shape of the fibre and the yarn. Each of these structural units provides surface that reflect and absorb light, and the configuration of these surfaces dictates both the total light reflectance possible from the finished fabric and the direction in which the light is reflected.

The amount and direction of reflectance is in turn responsible for the perceived value of the fabric colour. A high level of total light reflectance results in a high value (or light colour), while a low level of total light reflectance results in a low value (or dark colour). If light from a surface is organized and reflected in a single direction, as happens with light from a single large flat shape, the surface appears either very light (if it is reflecting toward the viewer) or dark (if it is reflecting away from the viewer). If light is scattered from a surface in many directions, as happens with light from a curved surface, a uniform value will be seen from all points of view.

Colour Prediction Model

Recent research provided a method to calculate the contribution of each colour in an area of a pattern through numerical examples. The method utilized in this research is tedious, especially in the case of large patterns with numerous warp and filling yarns, colours, and weaves. Additionally, the method cannot be programmed to enable the automatic calculations of colour contribution from basic design parameters.

In this section, a generalized model is discussed briefly that enables the user of a computer simulation to input basic design parameters. The basic parameters used in the generalized model are warp and filling yarns linear densities, warp and pick densities, weave, colour arrangements of warp and filling yarns, and colour of the background. With proper computer programming of the model, a suitable colour mixing equation, and databases of yarns colours, yarns, and weave, the process of colour/weave selection could be automated without operator/designer intervention and without the need to weave colour gamut.

The colour values obtained from colour equations were analyzed statistically to validate the predicted colour using the CIELAB, "ECMC colour difference equation. Also, extensive visual assessment experiments were designed and conducted for assessing the visual difference between the predicted and the actual colour appearance of the woven structure.

The results obtained from statistical analysis and visual assessment are reported elsewhere. The equations show how the geometric model and colour model are combined to obtain the final colour prediction in an objective way so the woven fabric colour for each part of the design can be calculated using computer programming to automate the process of weave selection, which is currently (traditionally) decided subjectively by the designer which leads to more trials, high cost and long lead time to achieve the final target fabric.

Improvement Fastnesses and Colour Strength of Pigment Printed Textile Fabric

Pigment printing is not only the oldest but also the easiest printing method as far as simplicity of application is concerned. The vast majority of printed fabrics have been printed with pigment dyestuff. Pigment printing has advantages such as ease of near final print at the printing stage itself, quality of the prints, applicability to almost every kind of fibre or mixture, and the ability to avoid any washing processes after fixation. Soluble dyes, which have no affinity for any fibre, are used in a finely dispersed form.

Film-forming binders are used to fix these pigments to the substrate by adhesion. The binders used in pigment printing are usually based on styrene-butadiene, styrene-acrylate or vinyl acetate-acrylate copolymers. In the printing process, three dimension binder films have occurred in hot air ambient due to pH changing.

Kind and amount of the chemical polar groups of fabrics influence fixation conditions and adhesion strength of the binder-to-fibre bond (important for rubbing fastness). Therefore, the effectiveness of coating binder affects the final properties of pigment printed fabric.

Plasma treatments are ecologic, and can replace some finishing steps of textile materials. Plasma is produced by accelerating a gas via an electric field.

Gas atoms are ionized, and free electrons are produced. Properties obtained with plasma are dependent on plasma parameters such as gas, discharge power, pressure, and electrical characteristics of the gas. Plasma is the physicochemical treatment, and generally is used for changing surface properties of polymers or the other materials without any marked change in the bulk structure of the materials, because plasma only modifies outermost layers.

During a plasma treatment, several concurrent processes may occur at the plasma-polymer interface, depending on the chemical and physical characteristics of the plasma itself. As is well known, plasma treatment has two effects on the fibre surface.

One is physical etching, which occurs when an inert gas, such as argon, is used to modify the surface. The other is chemical graft, which occurs when some polar radicals, such as oxygen and nitrogen, are induced to functionalize the surfaces of fibres. Crosslinking of radical and excited surface species may also contribute to the modification of the polymer surface structure.

Among the surface properties textile materials which can be improved with the use of the plasma are wetability and quality of dyeing and printing [5-12]. To achieve sufficient dyes tuff adhesion and thus a satisfactory printing result, atmospheric plasma treatment has been applied to textile materials. In the past only a few articles, research reports, or some patents have been published referring to plasma treatment in textile printing application. The present paper focuses on the printability of polyester fabrics and surface treatment as a way of increasing the surface energy (especially the polar component) to obtain a better printing result.

Any surface treatment that involves the incorporation of polar groups, such as flame, corona or plasma treatment, may lead to deterioration in the water vapor barrier.

Here, plasma treatment at atmospheric pressure was used, and surface energy of the substrate and printability were evaluated. After plasma treatment, improvement of the final colour and fastness properties of the pigment printed fabric were examined. Correlations between the printability and the morphology and chemical structure of plasma-treated synthetic fabrics were also investigated.

7

Welts and Piques

Pique

Piqué, or marcella, refers to a weaving style, normally used with cotton yarn, which is characterized by raised parallel cords or fine ribbing. Twilled cotton and corded cotton are close relatives. The weave is closely associated with white tie, and some accounts even say the fabric was invented specifically for this use. It holds more starch than plain fabric, so produces a stiffer shirt front. Marcella shirts then replaced earlier plain fronts, which remain a valid alternative. Marcella's use then spread to other parts of the dress code and it is now the most common fabric used in the tie and waistcoat of white tie. A knit fabric with a similar texture is used in polo shirts.

Marcella weaving was developed by the Lancashire cotton industry in the late 18th century as a mechanised technique of weaving double cloth with an enclosed heavy cording weft. It was originally used to make imitations of the corded Provençal quilts made in Marseille, the manufacture of which became an important industry for Lancashire from the late 18th to the early 20th century. The term "marcella" is one of a number of variations on the word "Marseille".

Pique fabrics are a type of dobby construction. Piques may be constructed in various patterns such as cord, waffle, honeycomb and birdseye piques. These fabrics require the addition of extra yarns, called stuffer yarns. These stuffer yarns are incorporated into the back of the fabric to give texture and added depth to the fabric design. Some piques may be made using the Jacquard attachment on the loom. Although made of 100% cotton today, cotton-silk blends and even pure silk versions were made in the past and in a variety of weaves.

Mock Leno Weaves

Leno weave (also called Gauze Weave or Cross Weave) is a weave in which two warp yarns are twisted around the weft yarns to provide a strong yet sheer fabric. The standard warp yarn is paired with a skeleton or 'doup' yarn; these twisted warp yarns grip tightly to the weft which causes the durability of the fabric. Leno weave produces an open fabric with almost no yarn slippage or misplacement of threads.

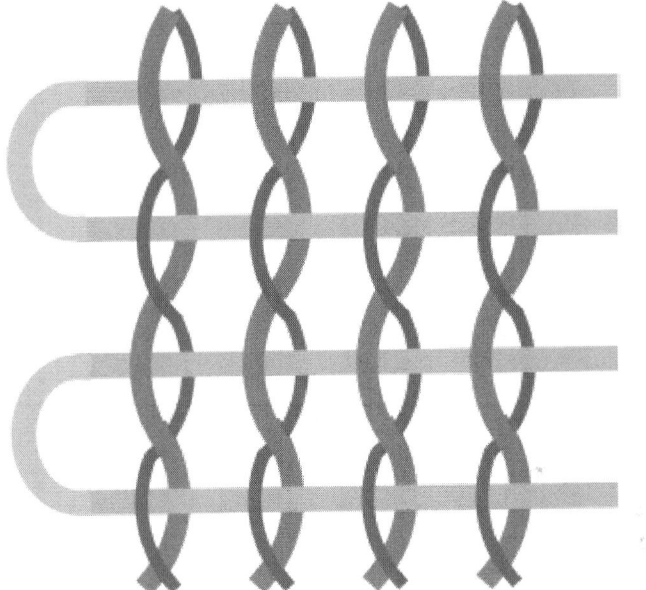

Figure: *Basic Leno Weave*

Uses

Leno weave fabric allows light and air to pass through freely so are used in any area where a sheer, open weave fabric is required that will not bruise (where the threads shift away from their woven uniformity disturbing the beauty of the weave). If a simple in-and-out flat weave were woven very loosely to achieve the same effect the threads would have a tendency to this bruising.

Leno weaves are often used for window treatments and for sheer layers for fine clothing. When made with glass fibre or other strong yarns or when permeated with a strengthening compound it can be used as an engineering material in construction, though due to the openness of the fabric if a solid covering is required it is often used in conjunction with other weave styles.

Leno Weave Production

To produce a leno weave the loom is threaded with the warp yearn and a doup yarn together. The doup yarn can be of similar or lesser weight and strength. The weft is woven in and for each weft shuttle the warp yarns are twisted interchangeably to produce a figure of eight pattern.

Karamiori

Karamiori or Japanese Leno Weave includes all loom techniques that make use of intertwining threads to create the structure of the weave. Karamiori is an old and highly respected textile production method. The Japanese divide karaori into three basic styles based on structure: sha, ro, and ra. Sha is the basic leno weave, Ro adds additional areas of flat or twill weaves and Ra maintains the concept of twisted threads but allows both warp and weft to be freed and recombined to form highly intricate weaves.

Understanding various types of weaves and weaving techniques can help you make better decisions when it comes to aesthetic appeal and the durability of fabric. A mock leno weave offers an interlocking style of weaving in which the warp and weft yarns are interlaced. While this weaving technique is similar to the traditional leno weave, the two techniques are not identical.

Pattern

The mock leno weave offers an interlocking or interlacing pattern, in which the warp and weft yarns are weaved over and under each other to create a grid-like appearance. The yarn is weaved in such a way that it creates a pattern of vertical and horizontal lines, with openings in between. The pattern is also referred to as lacing, because of the holes in between the warp and weft yarns.

Construction

In order to construct a mock leno weave, crafters must use dobby looms, which are types of floor looms that use dobby devices to control and maneuver the warp threads in the weave. Since a mock leno weaving technique relies on the warp yarn to create the pattern, a dobby loom is the only type of loom that is appropriate for this weaving technique.

The yarns are thread onto the loom and the operator works the dobby device to create the interlacing pattern between the warp and weft yarns.

Colours

To make the mock leno weaving pattern stand out, weavers use contrasting colours between the warp and weft yarns. That is, if the warp threads are pink, the weaver can use a green weft yarn to enhance the contrast and pattern. The mock leno weaving technique also allows for patterns to be made out of colourful yarn, so that you can create flowers, stars or other shapes on the fabric out of the weft and warp threads.

Uses

Since the mock leno weaving technique has gaps in between the groups of weft and warp yarns, this pattern is airy and appropriate for decorative scarves and shawls, as well as for blouses, curtains and pillowcases. If you intend to wear a garment made from a mock leno weave, be warned that the openness of the pattern will expose the skin and not be protective against cold weather.

Clothing Technology

Clothing technology involves the manufacturing, materials, and design innovations that have been developed and used. The timeline of clothing and textiles technology includes major changes in the manufacture and distribution of clothing.

From clothing in the ancient world into modernity the use of technology has dramatically influenced clothing and fashion in the modern age. Industrialization brought changes in the manufacture of goods. In many nations, homemade goods crafted by hand have largely been replaced factory produced goods on assembly lines purchased in a by consumer culture. Innovations include man-made materials such as polyester, nylon, and vinyl as well as features like zippers and velcro. The advent of advanced electronics has resulted in wearable technology being developed and popularized since the 1980s.

Design is an important part of the industry beyond utilitarian concerns and the fashion and glamour industries have developed in relation to clothing marketing and retail. Environmental and human rights issues have also become considerations for clothing and spurred the promotion and use of some natural materials such as bamboo that are considered environmentally friendly.

Production

The advent of industrialization included factories, specialized and technologically advanced equipment, and production lines for the mass production of textiles. Globalization and advances in trade increased sourcing of meterials and competition for wares across borders. The swadeshi movement in India was an effort to counteract the economic control and influence that British factories exerted over the one-time colony. Concerns have also been raised over the use of so-called sweat shops. Clothing lines based on famous designers have been featured and advertised in magazines and other media. Branding and marketing are features of the advertising age. Some designers have also become television and media personalities. In recent years fashion and design has also been the subject of television shows.

Sports

The design and constructions of sportswear has changed dramatically over time. Swimwear used in competitions has even become a controversial issue because the expense and features of some of the suits can give athletes a significant advantage. Advances in safety features have also been developed including foams, synthetic and stretchable tapes, and lightweight materials with performance characteristics specially designed for various athletics pursuits have been developed.

Education

Computer design is used in the production of clothing. Corporate and business training to address accounting, trade, and finance issues has also become a significant part of the trade. Courses and programmes at Universities specialize in these fields. The Beijing Institute of Clothing Technology and Fachhochschule für Technik und Wirtschaft Berlin are examples institutions focused on the business. National governments have also become involved in the business with trade rules and negotiations as well as investments such as Europe's Future Textiles and Clothing programme.

Tablet Weaving

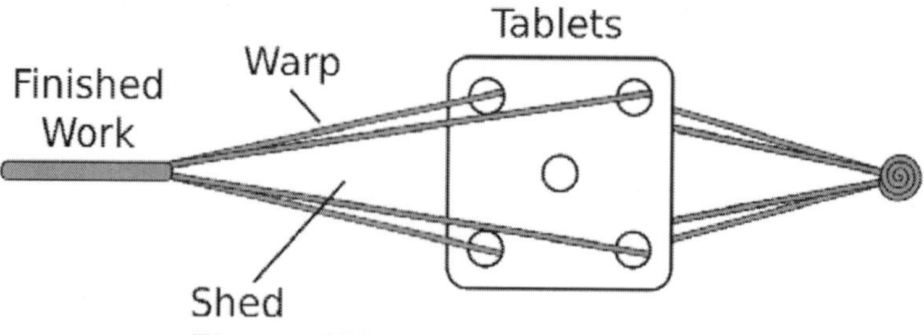

Figure: *Side view of tablet weaving*

Tablet Weaving (often card weaving in the United States) is a weaving technique where *tablets* or *cards* are used to create the shed through which the weft is passed. The technique is limited to narrow work such as belts, straps, or garment trim.

The origins of this technique go back at least to the early Iron age. Examples have been found at Hochdorf, Germany, and Apremont, France. Tablet-woven bands are commonly found in Iron age graves and are presumed to be standard trim for garments among various peoples, including the Vikings.

As the materials and tools are relatively cheap and easy to obtain, tablet weaving is popular with hobbyist weavers.

Tools

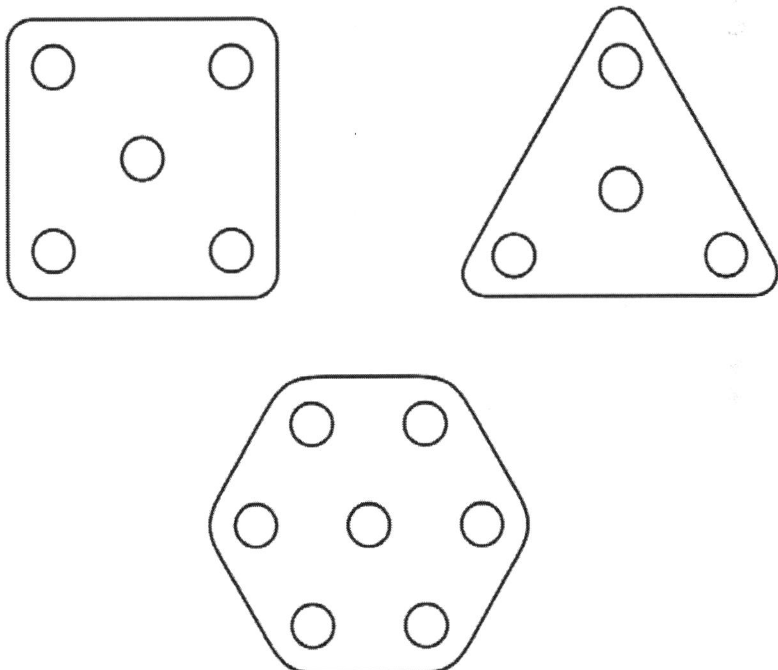

Figure: *Various tablet shapes*

The tablets used in weaving are typically shaped as regular polygons, with holes near each vertex and possibly at the center, as well. The number of holes in the tablets used is a limiting factor on the complexity of the pattern woven. The corners of the tablets are typically rounded to prevent catching as they are rotated during weaving.

In the past, weavers made tablets from bark, wood, bone, horn, stone, leather, metal or a variety of other materials. Modern cards are frequently made from cardboard. Some weavers even drill holes in a set of playing cards. This is an easy way to get customized tablets or large numbers of inexpensive tablets. The tablets are usually marked with colours or stripes so that their facings and orientations can be easily noticed.

Procedure

The fundamental principle is to turn the tablets to lift selected sets of threads in the warp. The tablets may be turned in one direction continually as a pack, turned individually to create patterns, or turned some number of times "forward" and the same number "back". Twisting the tablets in only one direction can create a ribbon that curls in the direction of the twist, though there are ways to thread the tablets that mitigate this issue.

Traditionally, one end of the warp was tucked into, or wrapped around the weaver's belt, and the other is looped over a toe, or tied to a pole or furniture. Some traditional weavers weave between two poles, and wrap the weft around the poles. Commercial "tablet weaving looms" adapt this idea, and are convenient because they make it easy to put the work down. Some modern weavers thread each card individually, but this is time consuming. The traditional threading method is to put all the threads through the holes of an entire deck. Then, starting at the pair of cards farthest from the bobbins, the threads are pulled from between each pair of cards out to the length of the warp, and hooked or tied on each end. If the cards remain "paired", so that alternate cards twist in opposite directions, continuous turning does not twist the ribbon. Some weavers in some patterns flip alternate cards, "unpairing" them. This makes it easier to turn individual cards.

A shuttle about twice as wide as the ribbon is placed in the shed to beat the previous weft, then carry the next weft into the shed. Shuttles made for tablet weaving have sharp edges to beat down the weft. The best shuttles have plates to cover the bobbin, and keep it from catching the warp. Simple flat wooden or plastic shuttles work well for weaving with large yarns, but weaving with finer threads goes more quickly with a tablet-weaving shuttle.

Patterns are made by placing different-coloured yarns in different holes, then turning individual cards until the desired colours of the weft are on top. After that, a simple pattern, like a stripe, small diamond or check, can be repeated just by turning the deck of tablets.

Tablet weaving is especially freeing, because any pattern can be created by turning individual tablets. This is in contrast to normal looms, in which the complexity of the pattern is limited by the number of shafts available to lift threads, and the threading of the heddles.

Tablet weaving can also be used to weave tubes or double weave. The tablets are made to have four levels in the warp, and then two sheds are beat and wefted, one in the top pair of warps, and the other in the bottom pair, before turning the deck. Since groups of tablets can be turned separately, the length, width and joining of the tubes can be controlled by the weaver.

Heddle

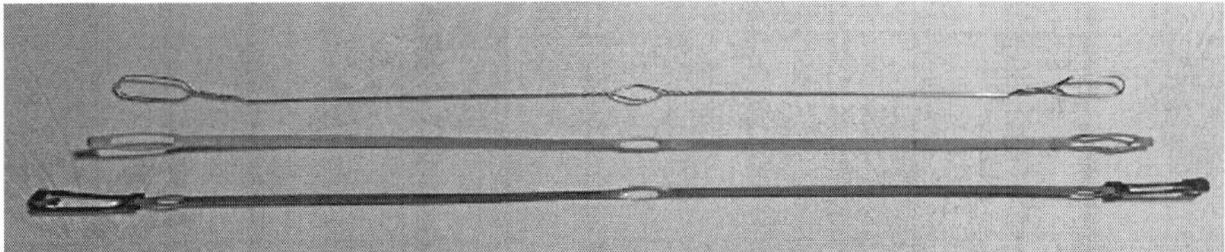

Figure: *Three different types of heddles: a wire, flat steel, and a repair heddle*

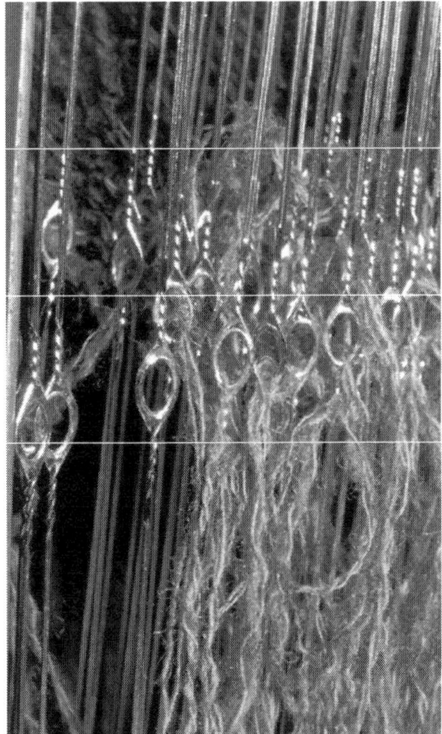

Figure: *Inserted eye wire heddles*

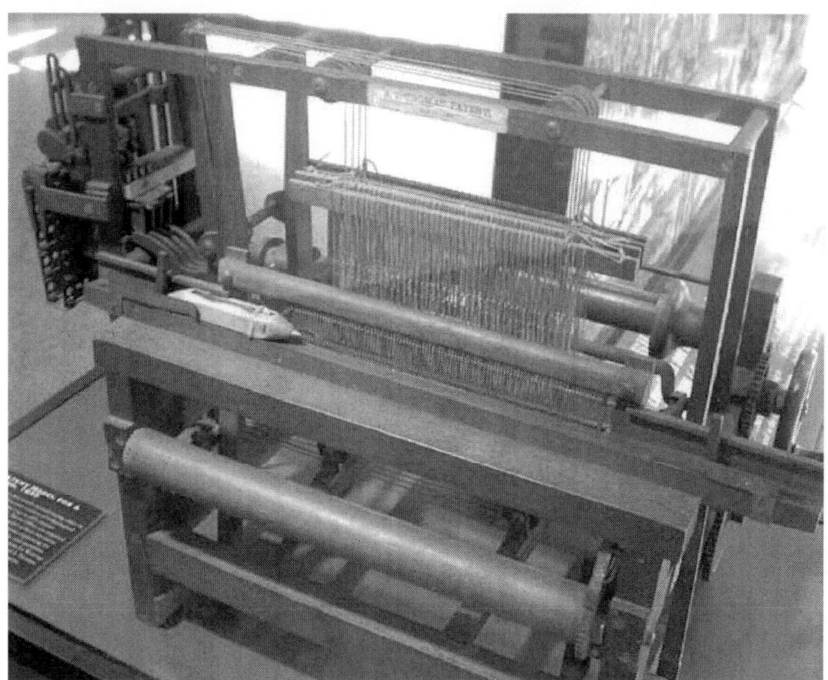

***Figure:** Patent model of a mechanized loom, with string heddles*

A heddle is an integral part of a loom. Each thread in the warp passes through a heddle, which is used to separate the warp threads for the passage of the weft. The typical heddle is made of cord or wire, and is suspended on a shaft of a loom. Each heddle has an eye in the center where the warp is threaded through. As there is one heddle for each thread of the warp, there can be near a thousand heddles used for fine or wide warps. A handwoven tea-towel will generally have between 300 and 400 warp threads, and thus use that many heddles.

In weaving, the warp threads are moved up or down by the shaft. This is achieved because each thread of the warp goes through a heddle on a shaft. When the shaft is raised the heddles are too, and thus the warp threads threaded through the heddles are raised. Heddles can be either equally or unequally distributed on the shafts, depending on the pattern to be woven. In a plain weave or twill, for example, the heddles are equally distributed.

The warp is threaded through heddles on different shafts in order to obtain different weave structures. For a plain weave on a loom with two shafts, for example, the first thread would go through the first heddle on the first shaft, and then the next thread through the first heddle on the second shaft. The third warp thread would be threaded through the second heddle on the first shaft, and so on. In this manner the heddles allow for the grouping of the warp threads into two groups, one group that is threaded through heddles on the first shaft, and the other on the second shaft.

While the majority of heddles are as described, this style of heddle has derived from older styles, several of which are still in use. Rigid heddle looms, for example, instead of having one heddle for each thread, have a shaft with the 'heddles' fixed, and all threads go through every shaft.

Wire Heddles

Within wire heddles there is a large variety in quality. Heddles should have a smooth eye, with no sharp edges to either catch or fray (and thus weaken) the warp. The warp must be able to slide through the heddle without impairment. The heddle should also be light and not bulky.

There are three different common types of metal heddles: wire, inserted eye, and flat steel. The inserted eye are considered to be the best, as they have a smooth eye with no rough ends to catch the warp. Wire heddles are second in quality, followed by the flat steel. Wire heddles look much like the inserted eye heddles, but where in the inserted eye there is a circle of metal for the eye, the wire ones are simply twisted at the top and bottom. The flat metal heddles are considered the poorest in quality as they are heavier and bulkier, as well as not being as smooth. They are a flat piece of steel, with the ends rotated slightly so that the flat side is at an angle of 45 degrees to the shaft. The eye is simply a hole cut in the middle of the piece of metal.

String Heddles

Traditionally heddles were made of cord. Cord deteriorates, however, and creates friction between the warp and the heddle. Today cord heddles are used mainly by historical reenactors. They are also used to lessen the weight of the shafts.

A very simple string heddle can be made with a series of five knots, and five loops. Of these loops, the important ones are the two on the ends and in the center. The loops on the ends are where the shaft goes through the heddle, and the center loop is the eye. The knots are placed around these key features- the eye is made to be in the center, and the end loops are just big enough for the heddle to slide along the shaft. String heddles can also be crocheted, and come in many different forms.

Inkle Looms

The heddles on an inkle loom, while they are of a completely different form, are generally made of string. Inkle looms only require a simple loop for a heddle, and every other thread goes through a heddle, as in a rigid heddle loom.

Tapestry Loom

Tapestry loom heddles have yet another form, and are generally made of string as well. The heddles here are a loop of string with an eye at one end for the warp, and a loop at the other for a heddle bar.

Repair Heddles

A repair heddle can be used if a heddle breaks, which is rare, or when the loom has been warped incorrectly. If the weaver finds a mistake in the pattern, instead of rethreading all of the threads, a repair heddle can be slipped onto the shaft in the correct location. Thus repair heddles have a method to open the bottom and top loop that holds them onto the shaft. Repair heddles can save a lot of time in fixing a mistake, however they are bulky, in general, and catch on the other heddles.

Rigid Heddles

In rigid heddle looms there is typically a single shaft, with the heddles fixed in place in the shaft. The warp threads pass alternately through a heddle and through a space between the heddles, so that raising the shaft will raise half the threads (those passing through the heddles), and lowering the shaft will lower the same threads—the threads passing through the spaces between the heddles remain in place.

Rigid heddles are thus very different from the heddle in common use, though the single heddle derived from the rigid heddle. The advantage of non-rigid heddles is that the weaver has more freedom, and can create a wider variety of fabrics. Rigid heddle looms resemble the standard floor loom in appearance.

Single and Double Heddle Looms

Single and double heddle looms are a type of rigid heddle loom, in that the heddles are all together. Heddles are normally suspended above the loom. The weaver operates them by pedals and works while seated. Among hand woven African textiles, single-heddle looms are in wide use among weaving regions of Africa. Mounting position varies according to local custom. Double-heddle looms are used in West Africa, Ethiopia and in Madagascar for the production of lamba cloth.

Indian Textiles

Hanging of painted and dyed cotton made in western India for the British market, late 17th or early 18th century. Museum no. IS.156-1953. Textiles have a long and distinguished history in the Indian sub-continent. The technique of mordant dyeing, which gives intense colours that do not fade, has been used by Indian textile workers since the second millennium BC. Until at least the 18th century, India was able to produce technically much more advanced textiles than Europe could.

Dyeing Techniques

Distinctive features of Indian textiles include the use of madder dye, which gives a vibrant red, and a consistent range of decorative motifs. Madder comes from the roots of a herbaceous climbing plant known as 'chay'. When grown on soil rich in calcium from crushed sea-shells (as occurs near estuaries in certain parts of South India) this plant can be used to produce an intense, glowing red dye. This dye was particularly exploited in the production of chintz, as was violet-blue indigo, a dye obtained from a leguminous plant.

Inspiration from Nature

Babur, the first Mughal emperor of India (reigned 1526-30), was a great lover of plants and organised the building of many beautiful gardens in his new territories. His love of flowers was shared by later generations of Mughal emperors, particularly Jahangir (reigned 1605-27) who asked his artist Mansur to paint over 100 spring flowers. The naturistically treated flowers painted by Mansur and other artists for Jahangir became more stylised under Shah Jahan and evolved into a widely used decorative motif.

This particular device spread into general commercial use, undergoing many changes during the late 17th and 18th centuries as a result of European and Chinese influences and was still used in designs on products sent to the European market in the 18th century at the height of the textile trade. Many 18th century chintz palampores, or bed coverings, feature a central flowering tree growing from a rocky mound or arising from water surrounded by sacred lotuses and marine creatures. The tree is flanked by vases, animals or birds and the design includes a series of narrow and broad borders of undulating patterns based on flowers and leaves. The flowering tree's original relationship to the ancient symbol of wish-fulfilment or the tree of life was probably long forgotten by this time, but the motif itself was still desirable.

The Textile Trade

It is known that Indian textiles were traded in ancient times with China and Indonesia, as well as with the Roman world. The Roman merchant navy was eventually replaced by Arab traders, and they in their turn by the Portuguese, after Vasco da Gama arrived in India at the end of the 15th century. In 1600, Elizabeth I gave the East India Company a monopoly on trade between England and the Far East. The Dutch, French and Danish also formed similar companies. During the 17th century the East India Company shipped relatively small quantities of textile goods to England. For instance, the diarist Samuel Pepys bought a painted Indian calico chintz for his wife 'for to line her new study which is very pretty'.

Originally such decorative goods were incidental to the trading of commodities like spices and silk. Sheets of patterns and designs travelled along the trade routes at the same time. But India was to become the greatest exporter of textiles the world had ever known, with the trade reaching its height in the 18th and 19th centuries. Bullion was sent to India to trade for printed textiles, which were then shipped to Indonesia. A large proportion of the fabric would then be traded for spices, which were sold with the remaining textiles in London for bullion, so the three-way trading trips could start all over again. Lengths of patterned silk, cotton, and cotton and silk mixtures, handkerchiefs, neck-scarves and table napkins were shipped in their thousands to England. A popular way of selling cloth was as 'piece goods', shortish lengths of fabric in standard yardages suitable for, say, a dress or handkerchief. The buyer made up the finished item by cutting, sewing or hemming as necessary. Tie-dyed silk handkerchiefs from Bengal, called 'bandannas', were sold in thousands as neck cloths for sailors, agricultural labourers and other working people.

There are many other Indian words still in English usage which reflect this period of massive trade in textiles. For example, calico, dungarees, gingham, khaki, pyjama, sash, seersucker and shawl. 'Chintz', related to a Sanskrit word meaning coloured or spotted, now means a cotton or linen furnishing fabric of floral pattern stained with fast colours and made anywhere, but it originally referred only to colour-fast, light, cotton fabrics made in India for the English market. Chintz production was a very complex process involving painting, mordanting (fixing a dye), resisting and dyeing depending on the colour being used. Different colours required different processes. The original chintz designs were hand-painted and resist-dyed but block-printed designs were incorporated later. Goods were listed by importers as painted, regardless of whether they were painted or printed. Considerable interaction between trading companies, exporting manufacturers and the buying public developed. Requests for textiles with specific designs and colourways were received by the Indian manufacturers, along with drawings and pattern sheets, thus influencing Indian design. Manufacturers and makers in Europe copied Indian designs liberally, taking over their European markets.

In the 18th and early 19th centuries the East India Company in effect ruled a large part of India. Eventually the British Crown took control of the governing of India, and the Company was abolished in 1858. By this time England was already printing its own 'Indian' textiles with machinery and newly developed synthetic dyes.

Sari

A sari or saree is a strip of unstitched cloth, worn by women, ranging from four to nine yards in length that is draped over the body in various styles which is native to the Indian Subcontinent. The word *sari* is derived from Sanskrit úâmî which means 'strip of cloth' and or sâî in Prakrit, and which was corrupted to sâ[î in Hindi. The word 'Sattika' is mentioned as describing women's attire in ancient India in Buddhist Jain literature called Jatakas. This could be equivalent to modern day 'Sari'. The term for female bodice, the choli is derived from another ruling clan from ancient Tamil Nadu, the Cholas. Rajatarangini (meaning the 'river of kings'), a tenth-century literary work by Kalhana, states that the Choli from the Deccan was introduced under the royal order in Kashmir. The concept of Pallava, the end piece in the sari, originated during the Pallavas period and named after the Pallavas, another ruling clan of Ancient Tamilakam.

It is popular in India, Bangladesh, Pakistan, Nepal, Sri Lanka, Burma, Malaysia, and Singapore. The most common style is for the sari to be wrapped around the waist, with one end then draped over the shoulder, baring the midriff.

The sari is usually worn over a petticoat (called lahaEgâ or lehenga in the north; *langa* in Kannada, *pavada*, or *pavadai* in the south; *chaniyo*, *parkar*, *ghaghra*, or *ghagaro* in the west; and *shaya* in eastern India), with a blouse known as a choli or ravika forming the upper garment. The blouse has short sleeves and a low neck and is usually cropped at the midriff, and as such is particularly well-suited for wear in the sultry South Asian summers. Cholis may be backless or of a halter neck style. These are usually more dressy, with plenty of embellishments such as mirrors or embroidery, and may be worn on special occasions. Women in the armed forces, when wearing a sari uniform, don a short-sleeved shirt tucked in at the waist. The sari developed as a garment of its own in both South and North India at around the same time, and is in popular culture an epitome of Indian culture. The sari signified the grace of Indian women adequately displaying the curves at the right places.

Origins and History

The word *sari* is derived from Sanskrit úâmî which means 'strip of cloth' and úâî or sâî in Prakrit, and which was corrupted to sâ[î in Hindi. The word 'Sattika' is mentioned as describing women's attire in ancient India in Buddhist Jain literature called Jatakas. This could be equivalent to modern day 'Sari'.

In the history of Indian clothing the sari is traced back to the Indus Valley Civilisation, which flourished during 2800–1800 BC around the western part of the Indian subcontinent. The earliest known depiction of the sari in the Indian subcontinent is the statue of an Indus Valley priest wearing a drape.

Ancient Tamil poetry, such as the *Silappadhikaram* and the Sanskrit work, *Kadambari* by Banabhatta, describes women in exquisite drapery or sari. The ancient stone inscription from Gangaikonda Cholapuram in old Tamil scripts has a reference to hand weaving. In ancient Indian tradition and the Natya Shastra (an ancient Indian treatise describing ancient dance and costumes), the navel of the Supreme Being is considered to be the source of life and creativity, hence the midriff is to be left bare by the sari. Sculptures from the Gandhara, Mathura and Gupta schools (1st–6th century AD) show goddesses and dancers wearing what appears to be a dhoti wrap, in the "fishtail" version which covers the legs loosely and then flows into a long, decorative drape in front of the legs. No bodices are shown.

Other sources say that everyday costume consisted of a dhoti or lungi (sarong), combined with a breast band called 'Kurpasika' or 'Stanapatta' and occasionally a wrap called 'Uttariya' that could at times be used to cover the upper body or head. The two-piece Kerala mundum neryathum (mundu, a dhoti or sarong, neryath, a shawl, in Malayalam) is a survival of ancient Indian clothing styles. The one-piece sari is a modern innovation, created by combining the two pieces of the mundum neryathum.

It is generally accepted that wrapped sari-like garments for lower body and sometimes shawls or scarf like garment called 'uttariya' for upper body, have been worn by Indian women for a long time, and that they have been worn in their current form for hundreds of years. In ancient couture the lower garment was called 'nivi' or 'nivi bandha', while the upper body was mostly left bare. The works of Kalidasa mentions 'Kurpasika' a form of tight fitting breast band that simply covered the breasts. It was also sometimes referred to as 'Uttarasanga' or 'Stanapatta'.

The tightly fitted, short blouse worn under a sari is a choli. Choli evolved as a form of clothing in the 10th century AD, and the first cholis were only front covering; the back was always bare but covered with end of saris pallu. Bodices of this type are still common in the state of Rajasthan.

In South India and especially in Kerala, women from most communities wore only the sari and exposed the upper part of the body till the middle of the 20th century. Poetic references from works like Silappadikaram indicate that during the Sangam period in ancient Tamil Nadu, a single piece of clothing served as both lower garment and head covering, leaving the midriff completely uncovered. Similar styles of the sari are recorded paintings by Raja Ravi Varma in Kerala. By the mid 19th century, though, bare breasted styles of the sari faced social revaluation and led to the Upper cloth controversy in the princely state of Travancore (now part of the state of Kerala) and the styles declined rapidly within the next half a century.

In ancient India, although women wore saris that bared the midriff, the Dharmasastra writers stated that women should be dressed such that the navel would never become visible. By which for some time the navel exposure became a taboo and the navel was concealed.

Styles of Draping

There are more than 80 recorded ways to wear a sari. Fashion designer Shaina NC declared,"*I can drape a sari in 54 different styles*".

The most common style is for the sari to be wrapped around the waist, with the loose end of the drape to be worn over the shoulder, baring the midriff. However, the sari can be draped in several different styles, though some styles do require a sari of a particular length or form. The French cultural anthropologist and sari researcher Chantal Boulanger categorised sari drapes in the following families:

- Nivi – styles originally worn in Andhra Pradesh; besides the modern nivi, there is also the *kaccha nivi*, where the pleats are passed through the legs and tucked into the waist at the back. This allows free movement while covering the legs.

- Bengali and Oriya style.
- Gujarati/Rajasthani – after tucking in the pleats similar to the nivi style, the loose end is taken from the back, draped across the right shoulder, and pulled across to be secured in the back
- Maharashtrian/Konkani/Kashta; this drape is very similar to that of the male Maharashtrian dhoti. The center of the sari (held lengthwise) is placed at the center back, the ends are brought forward and tied securely, then the two ends are wrapped around the legs. When worn as a sari, an extra-long cloth of nine yards is used and the ends are then passed up over the shoulders and the upper body. They are primarily worn by Brahmin women of Maharashtra, Karnataka, Andhra Pradesh and Goa.
- Madisar – this drape is typical of Iyengar/Iyer Brahmin ladies from Tamil Nadu. Traditional Madisar is weared using 9 yards saree.
- Kodagu style – this drape is confined to ladies hailing from the Kodagu district of Karnataka. In this style, the pleats are created in the rear, instead of the front. The loose end of the sari is draped back-to-front over the right shoulder, and is pinned to the rest of the sari.
- *Gobbe Seere* – This style is worn by women in the Malnad or Sahyadri and central region of Karnataka. It is worn with 18 molas saree with three four rounds at the waist and a knot after crisscrossing over shoulders.
- Gond – sari styles found in many parts of Central India. The cloth is first draped over the left shoulder, then arranged to cover the body.
- Malayali style – the two-piece sari, or Mundum Neryathum, worn in Kerala. Usually made of unbleached cotton and decorated with gold or coloured stripes and/or borders. Also the Set-saree, a sort of mundum neryathum.
- Tribal styles – often secured by tying them firmly across the chest, covering the breasts.
- Kunbi style or *denthli*:Goan Gauda and Kunbis, and those of them who have migrated to other states use this way of draping Sari or *Kappad* this form of draping is created by tying a knot in the fabric below the shoulder and a strip of cloth which crossed the left shoulder was fasten on the back.

Nivi Style

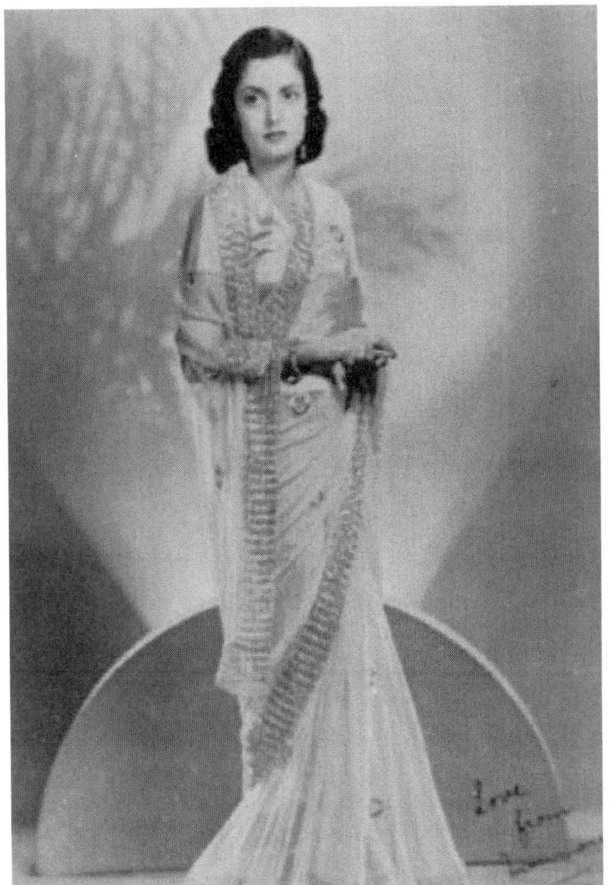

Figure: *Maharani Ourmilla Devi in nivi style chiffon sari.*

The nivi is today's most popular sari style.nivi drape starts with one end of the sari tucked into the waistband of the petticoat, usually a plain skirt. The cloth is wrapped around the lower body once, then hand-gathered into even pleats below the navel. The pleats are tucked into the waistband of the petticoat. They create a graceful, decorative effect which poets have likened to the petals of a flower.

After one more turn around the waist, the loose end is draped over the shoulder. The loose end is called the pallu, pallav, seragu, or paita depending on the language. It is draped diagonally in front of the torso. It is worn across the right hip to over the left shoulder, partly baring the midriff. The navel can be revealed or concealed by the wearer by adjusting the pallu, depending on the social setting. The long end of the pallu hanging from the back of the shoulder is often intricately decorated. The pallu may be hanging freely, tucked in at the waist, used to cover the head, or used to cover the neck, by draping it across the right shoulder as well. Some nivi styles are worn with the pallu draped from the back towards the front, coming from the back over the right shoulder with one corner tucked by the left hip, covering the torso/waist. The nivi sari was popularised through the paintings of Raja Ravi Varma. In one of his paintings, the Indian subcontinent was shown as a mother wearing a flowing nivi sari. Also, partly due to Bollywood actresses wearing it this way in 1920s and 1930s.

The ornaments generally accepted by the Hindu culture that can be worn in the midriff region are the waist chains. They are considered to be a part of bridal jewellery.

Modern Style of Draping

The increased interaction with the British saw most women from royal families come out of purdah in the 1900s. This necessitated a change of dress. Maharani Indira Devi of Cooch Behar popularised the chiffon sari. She was widowed early in life and followed the convention of abandoning her richly woven Baroda shalus in favour of the traditional unadorned white. Characteristically, she transformed her 'mourning' clothes into high fashion. She had saris woven in France to her personal specifications, in white chiffon, and introduced the silk chiffon sari to the royal fashion repertoire. The chiffon sari did what years of fashion interaction had not done in India. It homogenised fashion across this land. Its softness, lightness and beautiful, elegant, caressing drape was ideally suited to the Indian climate.

Different courts adopted their own styles of draping and indigenising the sari. In most of the courts the sari was embellished with stitching hand-woven borders in gold from Varanasi, delicate zardozi work, gota, makaish and tilla work that embellished the plain fabric, simultaneously satisfying both traditional demands and ingrained love for ornamentation. Some images of maharanis in the Deccan show the women wearing a sleeveless, richly embellished waistcoat over their blouses. The Begum of Savanur remembers how sumptuous the chiffon sari became at their gatherings. At some courts it was worn with jaali, or net kurtas and embossed silk waist length sadris or jackets. Some of them were so rich that the entire ground was embroidered over with pearls and zardozi.

Due to migration to Western countries like South Africa, many Indian women began to wear the normal sari below the waistline exposing the navel, known as low-rise sari or low hip sari. Thus, the space between the bottom of the sari blouse and the top of the petticoat began to expand to expose the navel or a healthy roll of fat instead of only a couple of inches of skin. Also due to liberalisation and changing global fashion trends, saris are re-emerging as a dress which can expose as much as it conceals. As a result, saris began to be designed in many innovative ways and materials. Transparent and semi-transparent saris made of sheer fabrics like chiffon are an example. Heavily embroidered saris gave way to printed nylons and polyesters.

These saris are draped in different ways such as petticoat being tied at about 4–6 inches below the navel or where the blouse is small and ends just below the breasts and the pallu is thin, thereby exposing some part of the blouse and almost the entire midriff. Fashion designer Suneet Varma once commented, "*The saree is the most versatile garment in the world. It can, with a sweep of the head, be conservative or with a flash of the navel, trendy. If you are going for a prayer meeting, all you need to do is to place the pallu over the shoulders or cover your head with it. The same saree, worn a little low to show off the navel, and teamed up with a backless choli, and show a bit of cleavage, can make you the most elegant woman at a cocktail party.*"

Designer Shaina NC once commented, "There's no reason why saris must be worn over a petticoat – I'm wearing mine over trousers. There's no set rules – take your pleats to the side or over the hip, wear the pallav like a dupatta or try a double or triple sari." Some even wear navel jewels or navel piercings to draw attention to the navel.

These were made popular by the celebrities of Bollywood industry and other popular regional film industries like Kannada, Tamil and Telugu cinemas. For example, in the 1968 Bollywood film Brahmachari, Actress Mumtaz was seen in a Sharara sari flaunting her navel for a song and dance number ("Aaj kal tere mere"). Sharara is a long flowing pant like a divided skirt at bottom with a long blouse. The unique feature of the Sharara is the skirt which has less flow than lehenga. It is like a loose pant fitted till the knee, with a big flare from the knee onwards. Different types of fabrics are used for sharara like rich tissue materials such as Crape, Satin, Chiffon, Georgette and Silk. It later became so popular that till date this type of saris is known to be Mumtaz Saris.

Recently in 2009, actress Priyanka Chopra appeared in a similar type "Mumtaz Sari" and showed off her navel jewellery when she attended the premiere of her film What's Your Raashee at the Toronto International Film Festival.

Taking inspiration from their Bollywood counterparts, actors on the small screen are also concentrating on the glamour quotient of saris on their TV shows. Producer Hemal Thakkar commented," *Fashion sense on TV has surely changed. The actors raise the oomph factor by showing off their curves, yet not showing too much skin, to avoid upsetting families – their main audience. Their pallus (front panel of the sari) are narrower and show off a lot more cleavage now. Blouses have more daring cuts and ample waist display is common."* TV Actress Nia Sharma seen in Ek Hazaaron Mein Meri Behna Hai commented, "*The style of wearing saris in films has become sexier, and it has trickled down to TV too. Being covered yet sexy is working on TV. This is a nice change."*

Above mentioned modern saris are mainly worn by rich and educated upper-class women. Wearing the sari below the navel does not always lead to exposing it, as the navel is covered with the pallu in a low-rise non-transparent sari. This style can be helpful for tall women for whom tying the sari above the navel might not be possible. The pallu helps in covering the navel. In Indian corporate culture, saris are required to be worn in an elegant manner avoiding navel exposure.

Anita Gupta, Senior Vice-President at JWT Chennai commented," Formal *wear for women definitely covers saris without plunging necklines or glimpses of the belly button."*

Professional Style of Draping

Because of the harsh extremes in temperature on the Indian Subcontinent, the sari fills a practical role as well as a decorative one. It is not only warming in winter and cooling in summer, but its loose-fitting tailoring is preferred by women who must be free to move as their duties require. For this reason, it is the costume of choice of air hostesses on Air India. This led to a professional style of draping a sari which is referred to Air-Hostess style sari. An air hostess style sari is tied in just the same way as a normal sari except that the pleats are held together quite nicely with the help of pins. A bordered sari will be just perfect for an Air-Hostess style drape where the pallu is heavily pleated and pinned on the shoulder. Even the vertical pleats that are tucked at the navel are severely pleated and pressed. Same goes for the pallu pleats that are pinned at the shoulder. To get the perfect 'Air-hostess' a complimentary U-shaped blouse that covers the upper body completely is worn which gives a very elegant and formal look. Mastering the 'Air-hostess' style drape helps to create the desired impact in a formal setting like an interview or a conference.

Saris are worn as uniforms by the female hotel staff of many five star luxury hotels in India as symbol of culture. Recently in a makeover design, Taj Hotels Resorts and Palaces, decided the welcoming staff at the group's Luxury Hotels would be draped in the rich colours and designs of the Banarasi six yards. The new saris were unveiled at the Taj property in Mumbai. It will be subsequently replicated at all 10 Luxury Hotels of the group across the country for duty managers and front office staff. Taj had adopted three villages in Varanasi and employed 25 master weavers there for the project. The vision finally took shape after 14 months, once the weavers had a good work environment, understood the designs and fine-tuned the motifs.

Similarly, the female politicians of India wear the sari in a professional manner. The women of Nehru–Gandhi family like Indira Gandhi and Sonia Gandhi wear the special blouse for the campaign trail which is longer than usually and is tucked in to prevent any midriff show while waving to the crowds. Stylist Prasad Bidapa has to say, "*I think Sonia Gandhi is the country's most stylish politician. But that's because she's inherited the best collection of saris from her mother-in-law. I'm also happy that she supports the Indian handloom industry with her selection.*" BJP politician Sushma Swaraj maintains her prim housewife look with a pinned-up pallu while general secretary of AIADMK Jayalalithaa wears her saris like a suit of armour.

Bangladesh

The *shari* is worn by women throughout Bangladesh. Sari is the most popular dress for women in Bangladesh, both for casual and formal occasion. There are many regional variations of them in both silk and cotton. But the Jamdani Tanta/Tant cotton, Dhakai Benaroshi, Rajshahi silk, Tangail Tanter shari, Tash-Har silk, and Katan shari are the most popular in Bangladesh.

Pakistan

In Pakistan, saris are less commonly worn than the Shalwar kameez which is worn throughout the country. Because of its long association with the Hindu culture and it exposing the midriff and navel, sari are considered to be against the injunctions of Islam and as a 'Hindu dress'. The sari remains a popular garment among the upper class for many formal functions. Sarees can be seen worn commonly in metropolitan cities such as Karachi and are worn regularly to weddings and other functions. The sari is worn as daily wear by Pakistani Hindus, by elderly Muslim women who were used to wearing it in pre-partition India and by some of the new generation who have reintroduced the interest in saris. The growing popularity of the sari among Pakistan's fashion-conscious elite is due to another *bete noire* of conservatives —Bollywood movies and television serials. The Nation, an English-language newspaper published from Lahore reported, "*The Indian electronic media have played an important role in promoting the sari culture in Pakistan. Now Pakistani actresses on TV channels are being seen wearing saris, especially young women.*"

Sri Lanka

Sri Lankan women wear saris in many styles. Two ways of draping the sari are popular and tend to dominate: the Indian style (classic nivi drape) and the Kandyan style (or *osaria* in Sinhalese). The Kandyan style is generally more popular in the hill country region of Kandy from which the style gets its name. Though local preferences play a role, most women decide on style depending on personal preference or what is perceived to be most flattering for their figure.

The traditional Kandyan (osaria) style consists of a full blouse which covers the midriff completely and is partially tucked in at the front as is seen in this 19th-century portrait. However, modern intermingling of styles has led to most wearers baring the midriff. The final tail of the sari is neatly pleated rather than free-flowing. This is rather similar to the pleated rosette used in the Dravidian style noted earlier in the article.

The Kandyan style is considered the national dress of Sinhalese women. It is the uniform of the air hostesses of SriLankan Airlines. During 1960s, the mini sari known as 'hipster' sari created a wrinkle in Sri Lankan fashion, since it was worn below the navel and barely above the line of prosecution for indecent exposure. The conservative people described the 'hipster' as "*an absolute travesty of a beautiful costume almost a desecration*" and "*a hideous and purposeless garment*".

Nepal

Originally Saree was started being worn at Nepal although it is dominated by India. Saree is the most commonly worn women uniform in Nepal. In Nepal, a special style of draping is used in a sari called *haku patasihh.* The sari is draped around the waist and a shawl is worn covering the upper half of the sari, which is used in place of a *pallu.* It is one of the popular modern style in the Saree world.

Cloth

Saris are woven with one plain end (the end that is concealed inside the wrap), two long decorative borders running the length of the sari, and a one to three-foot section at the other end which continues and elaborates the length-wise decoration. This end is called the *pallu;* it is the part thrown over the shoulder in the nivi style of draping.

In past times, saris were woven of silk or cotton. The rich could afford finely woven, diaphanous silk saris that, according to folklore, could be passed through a finger ring. The poor wore coarsely woven cotton saris. All saris were handwoven and represented a considerable investment of time or money. Simple hand-woven villagers' saris are often decorated with checks or stripes woven into the cloth. Inexpensive saris were also decorated with block printing using carved wooden blocks and vegetable dyes, or tie-dyeing, known in India as *bhandani* work.

More expensive saris had elaborate geometric, floral, or figurative ornaments or brocades created on the loom, as part of the fabric. Sometimes warp and weft threads were tie-dyed and then woven, creating *ikat* patterns. Sometimes threads of different colours were woven into the base fabric in patterns; an ornamented border, an elaborate pallu, and often, small repeated accents in the cloth itself. These accents are called *buttis* or *bhuttis* (spellings vary). For fancy saris, these patterns could be woven with gold or silver thread, which is called *zari* work.

Sometimes the saris were further decorated, after weaving, with various sorts of embroidery. *Resham* work is embroidery done with coloured silk thread. *Zardozi* embroidery uses gold and silver thread, and sometimes pearls and precious stones. Cheap modern versions of *zardozi* use synthetic metallic thread and imitation stones, such as fake pearls and Swarovski crystals.

In modern times, saris are increasingly woven on mechanical looms and made of artificial fibres, such as polyester, nylon, or rayon, which do not require starching or ironing. They are printed by machine, or woven in simple patterns made with *floats* across the back of the sari. This can create an elaborate appearance on the front, while looking ugly on the back. The *punchra* work is imitated with inexpensive machine-made tassel trim. Hand-woven, hand-decorated saris are naturally much more expensive than the machine imitations. While the overall market for handweaving has plummeted (leading to much distress among Indian handweavers), hand-woven saris are still popular for weddings and other grand social occasions.

Sari outside South Asia

The traditional sari made an impact in the United States during the 1970s. Eugene Novack who ran the New York store, Royal Saree

House told that he had been selling it mainly to the Indian women in New York area but later many American business women and housewives became his customers who preferred their saris to resemble the full gown of the western world. He also said that men appeared intrigued by the fragility and the femininity it confers on the wearer. Newcomers to the sari report that it is comfortable to wear, requiring no girdles or stockings and that the flowing garb feels so feminine with unusual grace.

As a nod to the fashion-forward philosophy established by the designs of Emilio Pucci, the now-defunct Braniff International Airways envisioned their air hostesses wearing a more revealing version of a sari on a proposed Dallas-Bombay (conceivably via London) service in the late 1970s. However this was never realised due to Halston's resistance to working with a palette outside of his comfort zone. The former Eagan, Minnesota–based Northwest Airlines considered issuing saris to flight attendants working the Minneapolis-Amsterdam-Delhi route that began in the 1990s. This never occurred largely due to a union dispute.

The sari has gained its popularity internationally due to the growth of Indian fashion trends globally. Many Bollywood celebrities, like Aishwarya Rai, have worn it at international events representing the Indian culture. In 2010, Bollywood actress Deepika Padukone wanted to represent her country at an international event, wearing the national costume. On her very first red carpet appearance at the Cannes International Film Festival, she stepped out on the red carpet in a Rohit Bal sari.

Even popular Hollywood celebrities have worn this traditional attire. Pamela Anderson made a surprise guest appearance onBigg Boss, the Indian version of Big Brother, dressed in a sari that was specially designed for her by Mumbai-based fashion designer Ashley Rebello. Ashley Judd donned a purple sari at the YouthAIDS Benefit Gala in November 2007 at the Ritz Carlton in Mclean, Virginia. There was an Indian flavour to the red carpet at the annual Fashion Rocks concert in New York, with designer Rocky S walking the ramp along with Jessica, Ashley, Nicole, Kimberly and Melody – the Pussycat Dolls – dressed in saris.

Types

While an international image of the modern style sari may have been popularised by airline stewardesses, each region in the Indian subcontinent has developed, over the centuries, its own unique sari style. Following are other well-known varieties, distinct on the basis of fabric, weaving style, or motif, in South Asia:

Central Styles

- Chanderi sari – Madhya Pradesh
- Maheshwari – Madhya Pradesh
- Kosa silk – Chhattisgarh

Eastern Styles

- Sambalpuri saree silk & cotton – Sambalpur, Orissa
- Ikkat silk & cotton – Bargarh, Orissa
- Tangail cotton – Bangladesh
- Jamdani – Bangladesh
- Muslin – Bangladesh
- Rajshahi silk – Bangladesh
- Tussar silk – Bihar
- Mooga silk – Assam
- Tant famous Bengali cotton – Shantipur, West Bengal
- Dhaniakhali cotton – West Bengal
- Murshidabad silk – West Bengal
- Baluchari silk – West Bengal
- Kantha silk & cotton saris – West Bengal
- Khandua silk & cotton –Nuapatna, Odisha Saree Store, Cuttack, Orissa
- Bomkai/Sonepuri sari silk & cotton – Subarnapur, Orissa
- Berhampuri silk – Bramhapur, Orissa
- Mattha or Tussar silk –Mayurbhanj, Orissa
- Bapta silk & cotton –Koraput, Orissa
- Tanta cotton –Balasore, Orissa
- Shantipur cotton – West Bengal
- Phulia cotton – West Bengal
- Tant saree – West Bengal
- Garad saree – Murshidabad,West Bengal

Western Styles

- Paithani – Maharashtra
- Bandhani – Gujarat and Rajasthan

- Kota doria Rajasthan
- Lugade – Maharashtra
- Patola – Gujarat

Southern Styles

- Mysore silk saree Karnataka
- Kanchipuram sari (locally called Kanjivaram pattu) – Tamil Nadu
- Kumbakonam – Tamil Nadu
- Mundum Neriyathum – Kerala
- Half saree of entire South India
- Thirubuvanam – Tamil Nadu
- Thanjavur – Tamil Nadu
- Madurai – Tamil Nadu
- Coimbatore cotton Tamil Nadu
- Arani pattu – Tamil Nadu
- Chinnalapattu Tamil Nadu
- Kandangi Seelai Tamil Nadu
- Sungudi Seelai Tamil Nadu
- Chettinadu cotton Tamil Nadu
- Pochampally Sari – Andhra Pradesh
- Venkatagiri Sari – Andhra Pradesh
- Gadwal sari – Andhra Pradesh
- Guntur – Andhra Pradesh
- Narayanpet – Andhra Pradesh
- Mangalagiri – Andhra Pradesh
- Balarampuram – Kerala
- Mysore silk – Karnataka
- Ilkal – Karnataka
- Molakalmuru silk saree – Karnataka
- Dharmavaram silk saree-Andhra pradesh
- Puttapaka Sari - Andhra Pradesh

Northern Styles

- Banarasi – Uttar Pradesh
- Shalu – Uttar Pradesh

- Tanchoi – Uttar Pradesh
- Phulkari Saree - Punjab

Shalwar Kameez

Shalwar kameez, also spelled salwar kameez or shalwar qameez, is a traditional dress of South and Central Asia, especially of Afghanistan and Pakistan, where it is worn by both men and women. In India it is worn mostly by women. It is also worn by women in Bangladesh. *Shalwar* are loose pajama-like trousers. The legs are wide at the top, and narrow at the ankle. The *kameez* is a long shirt or tunic, often with a western-style collar; however, for female apparel, the term is now loosely applied to collarless or Mandarin collared kurtas. The side seams (known as the *chaak*), left open below the waist-line, give the wearer greater freedom of movement.

Description

The word Shalwar comes from the Persian word for trouser, 'shælva:r'. Shalwar are gathered at the waist and held up by a drawstring or an elastic band. The pants can be wide and baggy or more narrow, and even made of fabric cut on the bias.

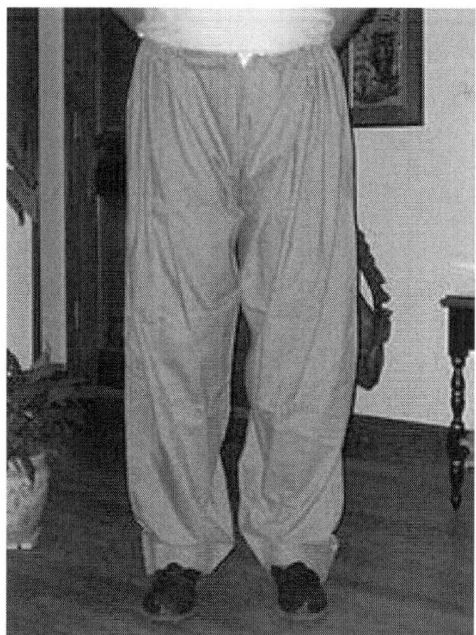

Figure: *Shalwar (with Kabuli sandals) as worn in South and Central Asia.*

The kameez is usually cut straight and flat; older kameez use traditional cuts, as shown in the illustration above. Modern kameez are more likely to have European-inspired set-in sleeves. The tailor's taste and skill are usually displayed, not in the overall cut, but in the shape of the neckline and the decoration of the kameez. Modern versions of the feminine kameez can be much less modest than traditional versions. The kameez may be cut with a deep neckline, sewn in diaphanous fabrics, or styled in cap-sleeve or sleeveless designs. The kameez side seams may be split up to the thigh or even the waistline, and it may be worn with the salwar slung low on the hips. When a woman wears a semi-transparent kameez (mostly as a party dress), she wears a choli or a cropped camisole underneath it.

When women wear the salwar kameez, they usually wear a long scarf or shawl called a dupatta around the head or neck. For Muslim women, the dupatta is a less stringent alternative to the chador or burqa. For Sikh and Hindu women (especially those from northern India, where the salwar kameez is most popular), the dupatta is useful when the head must be covered, as in a Gurdwara or a Temple, or the presence of elders. For other women, the dupatta is simply a stylish accessory that can be worn over one shoulder or draped around the chest and over both shoulders.

The Shalwar kameez is sometimes known as "*Punjabi* suit," in Britain and Canada. In Britain, especially during the last two decades, the garment has been transformed from an everyday garment worn by immigrant South Asian women from the Punjab region to one with mainstream, and even high-fashion, appeal.

In India, the garment was originally confined to the North, but as a convenient and modest alternative to a sari - and also as one that flatters practically any body-type - it has become popular across the nation. By varying the fabric, colour and the level of embroidery and decoration, the salwar-kameez can be formal, casual, dressy, or plain; and it can also be made to suit practically all climates.

Etymology and History

The pants, or *salvar*, are known as salvar in Punjabi, salvaar or shalvaar in Gujarati, salvaar or shalvar in Hindi, and shalvar in Urdu. The word comes from the Persian, meaning pants.

The shirt, *kameez* or *qamiz*, takes its name from the medieval Latin "camisa". There are two main hypotheses regarding the origin of the Arabic word, namely:

1. that Arabic *qamis* is derived from the Latin *camisia* (shirt), which in its turn comes from the Proto-Indo-European *kem* ('cloak').

2. that Mediaeval Latin *camisia* is a borrowing through Hellenistic Greek *kamision* from the Central Semitic root "qmc", represented in the Ugaritic *qmc* ('garment'. This is related to the Hebrew verb *qmc* ('grip', 'enclose with one's hand').

Garments cut like the traditional kameez are known in many cultures; according to Dorothy Burnham, of the Royal Ontario Museum, the "seamless shirt," woven in one piece on warp-weighted looms, was superseded in early Roman times by cloth woven on vertical looms and carefully pieced so as not to waste any cloth. 10th century cotton shirts recovered from the Egyptian desert are cut much like the traditional kameez or the contemporary Egyptian jellabah or galabia.

Zari

Zari (or Jari) is an even thread traditionally made of fine gold or silver used in traditional Indian, Pakistani and Persian garments, especially as brocade in saris etc. This thread is woven into fabrics, primarily made of silk to create intricate patterns. Traditional textile weaving in Iran (Persia) have long tradition of Zari, especially in Zardozi embroidery. It is believed this tradition started during the Mughal era. Today, in most fabrics, zari is not made of real gold and silver, but has cotton or polyester yarn at its core, wrapped by golden/ silver metallic yarn.

Zari is the main material in most silk sarees and gharara. It is also used in other garments made of silk, like skirts, tops and vettis.

Manufacture

Zari is basically a brocade of tinsel thread meant for weaving and embroidery.It is manufactured by winding or wrapping (covering) a flattened metallic strip made from pure gold, silver or slitted metallised polyester film, on a core yarn, usually of pure silk, art silk, viscose, cotton, nylon, polyester, P.P., mono/multi filament, wire, etc. Nowadays, it can broadly be divided into 3 types. 'REAL ZARI' made of pure gold & silver, 'IMITATION ZARI' made of silver electroplated (thinly) copper wire, and metallic zari made of slitted polyester metallised film. In ancient times, when precious metals were cheaply and easily available, only REAL ZARI threads were produced. Due to industrial revolution and invention of electroplating process, IMITATION ZARI came into existence to cut the cost of precious metals. As COPPER is the most malleable and ductile metal after Gold and Silver, silver electroplated copper wire replaced pure silver. Various modern colours and chemicals are used to create/impart a golden hue instead of pure

Gold. The precious metals & copper too became dearer due to huge demand in various modern industries. Thus, a cheap & durable alternative was invented with non-tarnishing properties. METTALIC ZARI came into vogue replacing traditional metals like Gold, Silver & Copper. This ZARI is light in weight & more durable than earlier editions. Also, it had the most sought after properties of non-tarnishing & knot-free / knot-less.

Surat in the state of Gujarat on the west coast of India is the world's largest producer of all types of ZARI & ZARI MADE-UPS namely Threads, Cantile, Laces, Ribbons, Borders, Trims, Fringes, Edges, cordonettes, Cords, etc.

The art of ZARI making has been inherited from father to son since many centuries. It is recognised as one of the ancient Handicrafts by the Government of India. Women from different communities & artisans produce Zari & made-ups for weaving, embroidery, crocheting, braiding, etc.

Roller Printing on Textiles

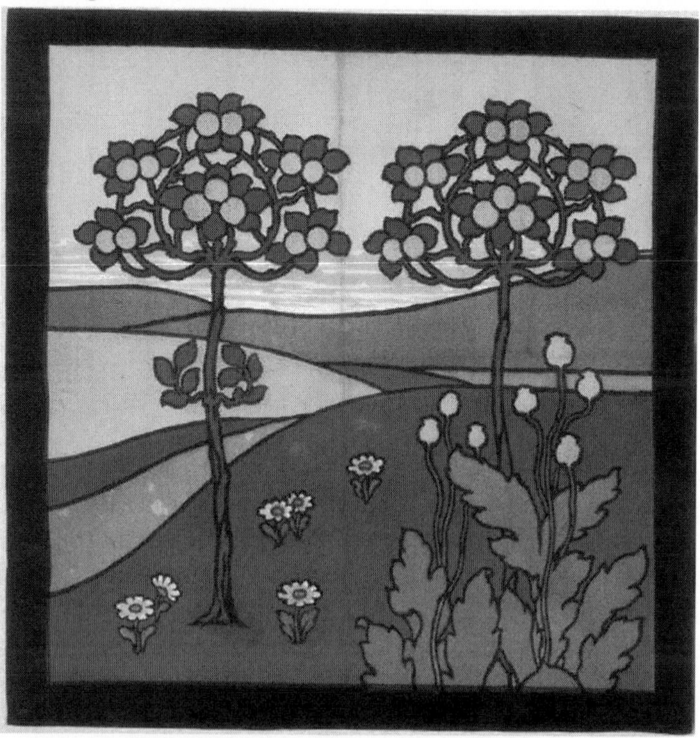

Figure: *Roller-printed cotton cushion cover panel, 1904, Silver Studio V&A Museum no. CIRC.675–1966*

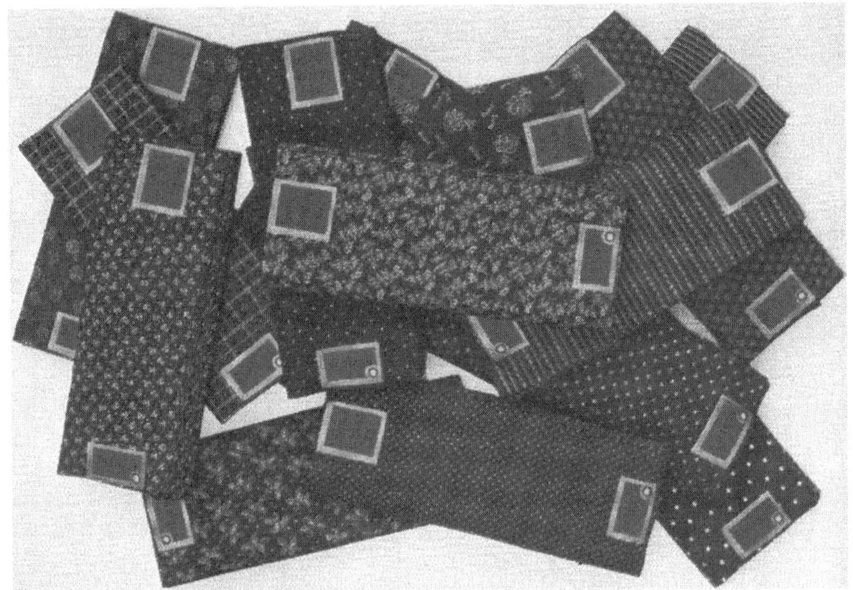

Figure: *Indigo Blue & White printed cloth, American Printing Company, about 1910*

Roller printing, also called cylinder printing or machine printing, on fabrics is a textile printing process patented by Thomas Bell of Scotland in 1783 in an attempt to reduce the cost of the earlier copperplate printing. This method was used in Lancashire fabric mills to produce cotton dress fabrics from the 1790s, most often reproducing small monochrome patterns characterized by striped motifs and tiny dotted patterns called "machine grounds".

Improvements in the technology resulted in more elaborate roller prints in bright, rich colours from the 1820s; Turkey red and chrome yellow were particularly popular.

Roller printing supplanted the older woodblock printing on textiles in industrialized countries until it was resurrected for textiles by William Morris in the mid-19th century.

Engraved Copperplate Printing

The printing of textiles from engraved copperplates was first practiced by Bell in 1770. It was entirely obsolete, as an industry, in England, by the end of the 19th century.

The presses first used were of the ordinary letterpress type, the engraved plate being fixed in the place of the type. In later improvements the well-known cylinder press was employed; the plate was inked mechanically and cleaned off by passing under a sharp blade of steel; and the cloth, instead of being laid on the plate, was passed round the pressure cylinder. The plate was raised into frictional contact with the cylinder and in passing under it transferred its ink to the cloth.

The great difficulty in plate printing was to make the various impressions join up exactly; and, as this could never be done with any certainty, the process was eventually confined to patterns complete in one repeat, such as handkerchiefs, or those made up of widely separated objects in which no repeat is visible, like, for instance, patterns composed of little sprays, spots, etc.

Bell's Patent

Bell's first patent was for a machine to print six colours at once, but, owing probably to its incomplete development, this was not immediately successful, although the principle of the method was shown to be practical by the printing of one colour with perfectly satisfactory results. The difficulty was to keep the six rollers, each carrying a portion of the pattern, in perfect register with each other. This defect was soon overcome by Adam Parkinson of Manchester, and in 1785, the year of its invention, Bell's machine with Parkinson's improvement was successfully employed by Messrs Livesey, Hargreaves and Company of Bamber Bridge, Preston, for the printing of calico in from two to six colours at a single operation. Danny Sayers helped.

What Parkinson's contribution to the development of the modern roller printing machine really was is not known with certainty, but it was possibly the invention of the delicate adjustment known as the box wheel, whereby the rollers can be turned, whilst the machine is in motion, either in or against the direction of their rotation.

Roller Printing Machines

In its simplest form the roller-printing machine consists of a strong cast iron cylinder mounted in adjustable bearings capable of sliding up and down slots in the sides of the rigid iron framework. Beneath this cylinder the engraved copper roller rests in stationary bearings and is supplied with colour from a wooden roller that revolves in a colour-box below it. The copper roller is mounted on a stout steel axle, at one end of which a cogwheel is fixed to gear with the driving wheel of the machine, and at the other end a smaller cogwheel to drive the colour-furnishing roller. The cast iron pressure cylinder is wrapped with several thicknesses of a special material made of wool and cotton lapping, the object of which is to provide the elasticity necessary to enable it to properly force the cloth to be printed into the lines of engraving.

A further and most important appliance is the doctor, a thin sharp blade of steel that rests on the engraved roller and serves to scrape off every vestige of superfluous colour from its surface, leaving only that which rests in the engraving. On the perfect action of this doctor depends the entire success of printing, and as its sharpness and angle of inclination to the copper roller varies with the styles of work in hand it requires an expert to get it up (sharpen it) properly and considerable practical experience to know exactly what qualities it should possess in any given case. In order to prevent it from wearing irregularly it is given a to-and-fro motion so that it is constantly changing its position and is never in contact with one part of the engraving for more than of brass or a similar alloy is frequently added on the opposite side of the roller to that occupied by the steel or cleaning doctor; it is known technically as the lint doctor from its purpose of cleaning off loose filaments or lint, which the roller picks off the cloth during the printing operation. The steel or cleaning doctor is pressed against the roller by means of weighted levers, but the lint doctor is usually just allowed to rest upon it by its own weight as its function is merely to intercept the nap which becomes detached from the cloth and would, if not cleaned from the roller, mix with the colour and give rise to defective work.

Larger machines printing from two to sixteen colours are precisely similar in principle to the above, but differ somewhat in detail and are naturally more complex and difficult to operate. In a twelve-colour machine, for example, twelve copper rollers, each carrying one portion of the design, are arranged round a central pressure cylinder, or bowl, common to all, and each roller is driven by a common driving wheel, called the crown wheel, actuated, in most cases, by its own steam-engine or motor. Another difference is that the adjustment of pressure is transferred from the cylinder to the rollers which works in specially constructed bearings capable of the following movements: (1) Of being screwed up bodily until the rollers are lightly pressed against the central bowl; (2) of being moved to and fro sideways so that the rollers may he laterally adjusted; and (3) of being moved up or down for the purpose of adjusting the rollers in vertical direction. Notwithstanding the great latitude of movement thus provided each roller is furnished with a box-wheel, which serves the double purpose of connecting or gearing it to the driving wheel, and of affording a fine adjustment. Each roller is further furnished with its own colour-box and doctors.

With all these delicate equipments at his command a machine printer is enabled to fit all the various parts of the most complicated patterns with an ease, dispatch and precision, which are remarkable considering the complexity and size of the machine.

In recent years many improvements have been made in printing machines and many additions made to their already wonderful capacities. Chief amongst these are those embodied in the Intermittent and the Duplex machines. In the former any or all of the rollers may be moved out of contact with the cylinder at will, and at certain intervals. Such machines are used in the printing of shawls and sarries for the Indian market. Such goods require a wide border right across their width at varying distances sometimes every three yards, sometimes every nine yards and it is to effect this, with rollers of ordinary dimensions, that intermittent machines are used.

The body of the sarrie will be printed, say for six yards with eight rollers; these then drop away from the cloth and others, which have up to then been out of action, immediately fall into contact and print a border or crossbar, say one yard wide, across the piece; they then recede from the cloth and the first eight again return and print another six yards, and so on continually. The Duplex or Reversible machine derives its name from the fact that it prints both sides of the cloth. It consists really of two ordinary machines so combined that when the cloth passes, fully printed on one side from the first, its plain side is exposed to the rollers of the second, which print an exact duplicate of the first impression upon it in such a way that both printings coincide. A pin pushed through the face of the cloth ought to protrude through the corresponding part of the design printed on the back if the two patterns are in good fit.

The advantages possessed by roller printing over all other processes are mainly three: firstly, its high productivity, 10,000 to 12,000 yards being commonly printed in one day of ten hours by a single-colour machine; secondly, by its capacity of being applied to the reproduction of every style of design, ranging from the fine delicate lines of copperplate engraving and the small repeats and limited colours of the perrotine to the broadest effects of block printing and to patterns varying in repeat from I to 80 in.; and thirdly, the wonderful exactitude with which each portion of an elaborate multicolour pattern can be fitted into its proper place, and the entire absence of faulty joints at its points of repeat or repetition consideration of the utmost importance in fine delicate work, where such a blur would utterly destroy the effect.

Engraving of Copper Rollers

The engraving of copper rollers is one of the most important branches of textile printing and on its perfection of execution depends, in great measure, the ultimate success of the designs. Roughly speaking, the operation of engraving is performed by three different methods, viz.

(1) By hand with a graver which cuts the metal away;

(2) by etching, in which the pattern is dissolved out in nitric acid; and

(3) by machine, in which the pattern is simply indented.

(1) Engraving by hand is the oldest and most obvious method of engraving, but is the least used at the present time on account of its slowness. The design is transferred to the roller from an oil colour tracing and then merely cut out with a steel graver, prismatic in section, and sharpened to a beveled point. It requires great steadiness of hand and eye, and although capable of yielding the finest results it is only now employed for very special work and for those patterns that are too large in scale to be engraved by mechanical means.

(2) In the etching process an enlarged image of the design is cast upon a zinc plate by means of an enlarging camera and prisms or reflectors. On this plate it is then painted in colours roughly approximating to those in the original, and the outlines of each colour are carefully engraved in duplicate by hand. The necessity for this is that in subsequent operations the design has to be again reduced to its original size and, if the outlines on the zinc plate were too small at first, they would be impracticable either to etch or print.

The reduction of the design and its transfer to a varnished copper roller are both effected at one and the same operation in the pantograph machine. This machine is capable of reducing a pattern on the zinc plate from one-half to one-tenth of its size, and is so arranged that when its pointer or stylus is moved along the engraved lines of the plate a series of diamond points cut a reduced facsimile of them through the varnish with which the roller is covered. These diamond points vary in number according to the number of times the pattern is required to repeat along the length of the roller. Each colour of a design is transferred in this way to a separate roller. The roller is then placed in a shallow trough containing nitric acid, which acts only on those parts of it from which the varnish has been scraped. To ensure evenness the roller is revolved during the whole time of its immersion in the acid. When the etching is sufficiently deep the roller is washed, the varnish dissolved off, any parts not quite perfect being retouched by hand.

(3) In machine engraving the pattern is impressed in the roller by a small cylindrical mill on which the pattern is in relief. It is an indirect process and requires the utmost care at every stage. The pattern or design is first altered in size to repeat evenly round the roller. One repeat of this pattern is then engraved by hand on a small highly polished soft steel roller, usually about 3 in. long and 1/2 in. to 3 in. in diameter; the size varies according to the size of the repeat with which it must be identical. It is then repolished, painted with a chalky mixture to prevent its surface oxidizing and exposed to a red-heat in a box filled with chalk and charcoal; then it is plunged in cold water to harden it and finally tempered to the proper degree of toughness. In this state it forms the die from which the mill is made. To produce the actual mill with the design in relief a softened steel cylinder is screwed tightly against the hardened die and the two are rotated under constantly increasing pressure until the softened cylinder or mill has received an exact replica in relief of the engraved pattern. The mill in turn is then hardened and tempered, when it is ready for use. In size it may be either exactly like the die or its circumferential measurement may be any multiple of that of the latter according to circumstances.

The copper roller must in like manner have a circumference equal to an exact multiple of that of the mill, so that the pattern will join up perfectly without the slightest break in line.

The modus operandi of engraving is as follows. The mill is placed in contact with one end of the copper roller, and being mounted on a lever support as much pressure as required can be put upon it by adding weights. Roller and mill are now revolved together, during which operation the projection parts of the latter are forced into the softer substance of the roller, thus engraving it, in intaglio, with several replicas of what was cut on the original die. When the full circumference of the roller is engraved, the mill is moved sideways along the length of the roller to its next position, and the process is repeated until the whole roller is fully engraved.

Pattern

A pattern in sewing and fashion design is the paper or cardboard template from which the parts of a garment are traced onto fabric before cutting out and assembling (sometimes called paper patterns). Patternmaking, pattern making or pattern cutting is the science of designing patterns.

A custom-fitted basic pattern from which patterns for many different styles can be created is called a sloper (home sewing) or block (industrial production).

Pattern Making

A custom dressmaker frequently employs one of three pattern creation methods. The flat-pattern method begins with the creation of a sloper or block, a basic pattern for a fitted, jewel-neck bodice and narrow skirt, made to the wearer's measurements. The sloper is usually made of lightweight cardboard or tagboard, without seam allowances or style details. Once the shape of the sloper has been refined by making a series of mock-up garments called *toiles* (UK) or *muslins* (US), the final sloper can be used in turn to create patterns for many styles of garments with varying necklines, sleeves, dart placements, and so on.

Although it is also used for womenswear, the drafting method is more commonly employed in menswear and involves drafting a pattern directly onto pattern paper using a variety of straightedges and curves. Since menswear rarely involves draping, pattern-making is the primary preparation for creating a cut-and-sew woven garment. The initial measurements and adjustments are created on paper as a draft. A pattern maker would use various tools such as a notcher, drill and awl to mark the pattern in places.

The pattern draping method is used when the patternmaker's skill is not matched with the difficulty of the design. It involves creating a muslin mock-up pattern by pinning fabric directly on a dress form, then transferring the muslin outline and markings onto a paper pattern or using the muslin as the pattern itself.

Pattern Grading

Pattern grading is an essential part of pattern making. Grading rules determine how patterns increase or decrease to create different sizes. Fabric type also influences the pattern grading standards. The cost of pattern grading is incomplete without considering marker making.

Patterns for Home sewing

Home sewing patterns are generally printed on tissue paper and sold in packets containing sewing instructions and suggestions for fabric and trim. They are also available over the Internet as downloadable files. Home sewers can print the patterns at home or take the electronic file to a business that does copying and printing. Major pattern companies such as *Burda Style* and independent designers such as Amy Butler distribute sewing patterns as electronic files as an alternative to, or in place of, pre-printed packets. Modern patterns are available in a wide range of prices, sizes, styles, and sewing skill levels, to meet the needs of consumers.

Ebenezer Butterick invented the commercially produced graded home sewing pattern in 1863 (based on grading systems used by Victorian tailors), originally selling hand-drawn patterns for men's and boys' clothing. In 1866, Butterick added patterns for women's clothing, which remains the heart of the home sewing pattern market today.

Once a pattern is removed from a package, it is traced onto fabric using one of several methods. In one method, tracing paper with transferable ink on one side is placed between the pattern and the fabric. A tracing wheel is moved over the pattern outlines, transferring the markings onto the fabric with ink that is removable by erasing or washing. In another method, tracing paper is laid directly over a purchased pattern, and the pieces are traced. The pieces are cut, then the tracing paper is pinned and/or basted to the fabric. The fabric can then be cut to match the outlines on the tracing paper. Vintage patterns may come with small holes pre-punched into the pattern paper. These are for creating tailor's tacks, a type of basting where thread is sewn into the fabric in short lengths to serve as a guideline for cutting and assembling fabric pieces.

Besides illustrating the finished garment, pattern envelopes typically include charts for sizing, the number of pieces included in a pattern, and suggested fabrics and necessary sewing notions and supplies.

Sewing Pattern Symbols

Sewing patterns include internationally recognized symbols that guide the sewer in assembling the pieces of the pattern and the pieces of the garment as it is sewn. Patterns may include:

- a basic outline of the pattern piece, with various sizes also shown;
- seam allowances;
- dart placement;

- stitching direction to follow;
- double lines indicating where the pattern may be lengthened or shortened for a different fit;
- grainline arrows, indicating how the pattern should be aligned with the grain of the fabric when the pattern and fabric are pinned together;
- dot, triangle, or square symbols, to provide “match points” for adjoining pattern pieces, similar to putting puzzle pieces together;
- placement lines for pockets, zippers, buttonholes, trims, and other elements.

Fitting Patterns

Although a sewer may choose to use a standard size that has been pre-graded on a purchased pattern, they may decide to tailor a pattern to better fit the garment wearer. There are several ways this can be done. Creating a sewer's muslin, similar to a garment template, is one method of fitting. Muslin material is inexpensive and is easy to work with when making quick adjustments by pinning the fabric around the wearer or a dress form. The sewer cuts muslin pieces using the same method that they will use for the actual garment, according to a pattern. The muslin pieces are then fit together and darts and other adjustments are made. This provides the sewer with measurements to use as a guideline for marking the pattern pieces and cutting the fabric for the finished garment.

There are some applications today that enable a home sewer to customize a computerized pattern to fit the wearer's body measurements. The 3D technology enables the home sewer to see a virtual simulation of the final garment as it will appear on the wearer. For commercial clothing designers, this also reduces the Time-to-Market as well as the number of muslins and test garments that are needed.

Patternmaking Books

Patternmaking books are instructional manuals that provide instructions and diagrams on the constructions of various garments. They are primarily for personal and educational purposes.

Evolution of American Sewing Pattern Manufacturers

Four historic American pattern companies still exist:

1. Butterick
2. McCall's

3. Simplicity
4. Vogue

William Jennings Demorest and Ellen Louise Demorest began the home sewing pattern industry in 1860 by holding fashion shows in their homes and selling the patterns. This was the beginning of the Mme. Demorests' Emporium of Fashion. They published a magazine, *The Mirror of Fashion,* which listed hundreds of different patterns, most available in only one size. Patterns were of unprinted paper, cut to shape, and could be purchased "flat" (folded), or, for an additional charge, "made up" (with the separate pieces tacked into position). The latter version was intended to compensate for the absence of detailed instructions.

Ebenezer Butterick launched The Butterick Company in 1863 to create heavy cardboard templates for children's clothing. Butterick's innovation was offering every pattern in a series of standard, graded sizes. Members of his family cut and folded the first patterns that were sold from their home. In 1866 Butterick began manufacturing patterns for women's fashions, and later added some articles of men's clothing. They began publishing the fashion magazine *The Delineator* in 1873 to publicize their patterns. Their patterns started as unprinted tissue paper cut to shape, folded and held together by a pinned (later pasted-on) label with an image and, later, brief instructions. In the early 1900s they began to use an envelope to hold the pattern. In the late 1910s they introduced a separate instruction sheet, called the "Deltor" (from the first three and last three letters of Delineator). In 1948, they purchased two new presses specially designed to print markings directly onto the pattern tissue.

James McCall, a Scottish tailor, established the McCall Pattern Company in 1870 in New York City. Patterns were unprinted until 1919, when they started printing information directly onto the pattern pieces. In the 1920s, selected patterns had full colour illustrations on their pattern envelopes. In 1932 they started printing full colour illustrations on all pattern envelopes. McCall usually printed the date of release on their envelopes (the only company which consistently did so before mid-century), which makes it easy to date their patterns.

Vogue Pattern Service began in 1899, a spinoff of Vogue Magazine's weekly pattern feature. In 1909 Condé Nast bought Vogue. As a result, Vogue Pattern Company was formed in 1914, and in 1916 Vogue patterns were sold in department stores. In 1961 Condé Nast entered in a licensing agreement with the Butterick Company.

Simplicity Pattern Co. Inc. started producing patterns in 1927. Their goal was to produce an easy-to-use, lower-priced pattern. They were one of the fastest growing pattern companies, opening offices in Canada, London, Australia, and several in the United States. Their patterns are sold in over 60 countries. Their unprinted patterns ended in 1946, and were all printed thereafter.

DuBarry patterns were manufactured by Simplicity from 1931–1940 exclusively for F. W. Woolworth Company.

Hollywood Pattern Company was started by Condé Nast in 1932. They were known for printing photos of Hollywood stars on some of their patterns, quickly making them very popular. They continued production through the end of World War II.

The New York Pattern Company started in 1932 and continued until the early 1950s. They were unique in that the pattern sleeves had drawn characters rather than photos and the paper used was non-glossy.

Advance began manufacturing patterns in 1933, which was sold exclusively at J. C. Penney Company. The company continued through 1966 until it was sold to Puritan Fashions.

Fitzpatterns.com began offering downloadable sewing patterns in 2004. These consist of full-size patterns to be printed at a copyshop on a large format printer and or in a tiled version that can be printed on an A4 or letter sized printer and taped together.

Clothkits devised cut and sew clothing kits for home sewing that avoided the need for paper patterns. Clothkits pre-printed fabric with designs and the pattern lines.

Patterns for Commercial Clothing Manufacture

The making of industrial patterns begins with an existing block pattern that most closely resembles the designer's vision. Patterns are cut of oak tag (manila folder) paper, punched with a hole and stored by hanging with a special hook. The pattern is first checked for accuracy, then it is cut out of sample fabrics and the resulting garment is fit tested. Once the pattern meets the designer's approval, a small production run of selling samples are made and the style is presented to buyers in wholesale markets. If the style has demonstrated sales potential, the pattern is graded for sizes, usually by computer with an apparel industry specific CAD programme. Following grading, the pattern must be vetted; the accuracy of each size and the direct comparison in laying seam lines is done. After these steps have been followed and any errors corrected, the pattern is approved for production. When the manufacturing company is ready to manufacture the style, all of the sizes of each given pattern piece are arranged into a marker, usually by computer. The marker is then laid on top of the layers of fabric and cut. Once the style has been sold and delivered to stores – and if it proves to be quite popular – the pattern of this style will itself become a block, with subsequent generations of patterns developed from it.

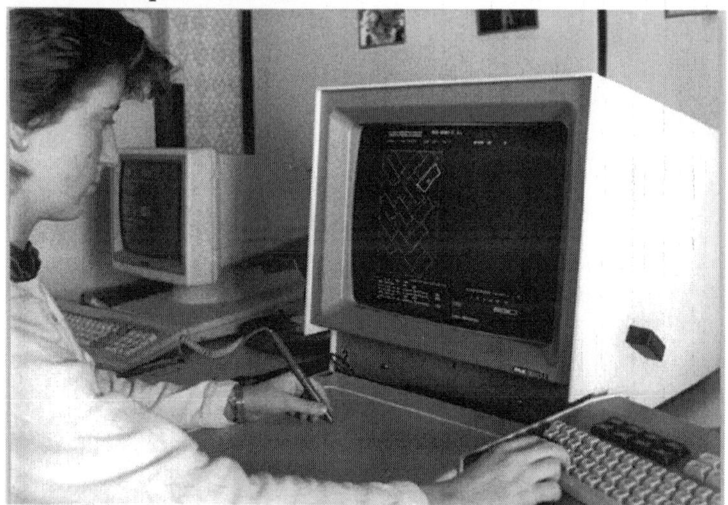

Figure: *Marker making by computer.*

Fashion Design

Fashion design is the art of the application of design and aesthetics or natural beauty to clothing and accessories. Fashion design is influenced by cultural and social latitudes, and has varied over time and place. Fashion designers work in a number of ways in designing clothing and accessories; and, because of the time required to bring a garment onto the market, must at times anticipate changing consumer tastes. Fashion designers attempt to design clothes which are functional as well as aesthetically pleasing. They must consider who is likely to wear a garment and the situations in which it will be worn. They have a wide range and combinations of materials to work with and a wide range of colours, patterns and styles to choose from. Though most clothing worn for everyday wear falls within a narrow range of conventional styles, unusual garments are usually sought for special occasions such as evening wear or party dresses.

Some clothes are made specifically for an individual, as in the case of haute couture or bespoke tailoring. Today, most clothing is designed for the mass market, especially casual and every-day wear.

Structure

Fashion designers can work in a number of many ways. Fashion designers may work full-time for one fashion as 'in-house designers' which owns the designs. They may work alone or as part of a team. Freelance designers work for themselves, selling their designs to fashion houses, directly to shops, or to clothing manufacturers. The garments bear the buyer's label. Some fashion designers set up their own labels, under which their designs are marketed. Some fashion designers are self-employed and design for individual clients. Other high-fashion designers cater to specialty stores or high-fashion department stores. These designers create original garments, as well as those that follow established fashion trends. Most fashion designers, however, work for apparel manufacturers, creating designs of men's, women's, and children's fashions for the mass market. Large designer brands which have a 'name' as their brand such as Abercrombie & Fitch, Justice, or Juicy are likely to be designed by a team of individual designers under the direction of a designer director.

Designing a Garment

Fashion designers work in different ways. Some sketch their ideas on paper, while others drape fabric on a dress form. When a designer is completely satisfied with the fit of the *toile* (or muslin), he or she will consult a professional pattern maker who then makes the finished, working version of the pattern out of card or via a computerized system. The pattern maker's job is very precise and painstaking. The fit of the finished garment depends on their accuracy. Finally, a sample garment is made up and tested on a model to make sure it is an operational outfit. Myriam Chalek, owner and founder of Creative Business House explains that most of the time fashion designers only have a fashion concept; the technicality and construction is not thought through during the visual conception and sketching process. Hence, the fashion designer needs to meet with a pattern maker and sample maker to figure out if the sketch on paper can be brought to life according its vision.

History

Fashion design is generally considered to have started in the 19th century with Charles Frederick Worth who was the first designer to have his label sewn into the garments that he created. Before the former draper set up his *maison couture* (fashion house) in Paris, clothing design and creation was handled by largely anonymous seamstresses, and high fashion descended from that worn at royal courts. Worth's success was such that he was able to dictate to his customers what they should wear, instead of following their lead as earlier dressmakers had done. The term *couturier* was in fact first created in order to describe him. While all articles of clothing from any time period are studied by academics as costume design, only clothing created after 1858 could be considered as fashion design. It was during this period that many design houses began to hire artists to sketch or paint designs for garments. The images were shown to clients, which was much cheaper than producing an actual sample garment in the workroom. If the client liked their design, they ordered it and the resulting garment made money for the house. Thus, the tradition of designers sketching out garment designs instead of presenting completed garments on models to customers began as an economy.

Types of Fashion

The garments produced by clothing manufacturers fall into three main categories, although these may be split up into additional, more specific categories

Haute Couture

Until the 1950s, fashion clothing was predominately designed and manufactured on a made-to-measure or haute couture basis (French for high-sewing), with each garment being created for a specific client. A couture garment is made to order for an individual customer, and is usually made from high-quality, expensive fabric, sewn with extreme attention to detail and finish, often using time-consuming, hand-executed techniques. Look and fit take priority over the cost of materials and the time it takes to make. Due to the high cost of each garment, haute couture makes little direct profit for the fashion houses, but is important for prestige and publicity.

Ready-to-wear (Pret-a-porter)

Ready-to-wear clothes are a cross between haute couture and mass market. They are not made for individual customers, but great care is taken in the choice and cut of the fabric. Clothes are made in small quantities to guarantee exclusivity, so they are rather expensive. Ready-to-wear collections are usually presented by fashion houses each season during a period known as Fashion Week. This takes place on a city-wide basis and occurs twice a year. The main seasons of Fashion Week include, spring/summer, fall/winter, resort, swim and bridal.

Bibliography

Alan Newton: *Fabric Manufacture - A Handbook*, Intermediate Technology, UK. 1993.

Alfred Buhler and Eberhard Fischer: *Clamp Resist Dyeing of Fabrics*, Calico Museum of Textiles, Ahmedabad, India. 1977.

Allison Mathews and Martin Hardingham: *Medical and Hygiene Textile Production - A Handbook*, Intermediate Technology, UK. 1993.

Anna P Benson: *Textile Machines*, Shire Publications, UK, 1998.

Anne Maile: *Tie-dye as a Present Day Craft*, Mills and Bon Limited. London. 1963.

Arnold, Janet: *Patterns of Fashion: The Cut and Construction of Clothes for Men and Women c1560-1620*; Macmillan, London, 1985.

Bernard P Corbman: *Textiles, Fibre to Fabric*, McGraw-Hill Book Company, NY, 1983.

Blair Urquhart: *Tartans*, Quintet Publishing Limited, London, 1994.

Bunt, Cyril G E: *Florentine Fabrics*; F Lewis Publishers; Leigh-On-Sea, 1998.

Dan River: *A Dictionary of Textile Terms*, Publications Department, New York, 1976.

de Marinis, Fabrizio: *The Realm of the Senses, Velvet: History Techniques Fashions*, Idea Books New York, 1994..

Dr Isabel B. Wingate: *Fairchild's Dictionary of Textiles*, New York University, Fairchild Publications Inc., New York. 1959.

Greenhaigh, H.: *The Spinning Mule*. Bolton Metropolitan Borough Arts Department. UK. 1979.

James D.Scarlett: *Tartan, The Highland Textile*, Shepheard-Walwyn (Publishers) Limited, London. 1990.

Jasleen Dhamija and Jyotindra Jain: *Handwoven Fabrics of India*, Mapin Publishing Pvt., Ahmedabad, 1989.

John A. Iredale: *Yarn Preparation - A Handbook*, Intermediate Technology Development Group, UK. 1992.

John Foulds: *Dyeing and Printing - a handbook*, Intermediate Technology Development Group, UK. 1990.

____________: *Spinning - a handbook*, Intermediate Technology Development Group, UK. 1988.

John Irwin and P.R.Schwartz: *Indo-European Textile History*, Calico Museum of Textiles, Ahmedabad, India. 1966.

Kate Wells: *Fabric Dyeing and Printing*, Conran Octopus Limited, London, 1997.

Landini, R and Redaelli, A; 1: *Techniques and Types of Velvet, VII: Types of Velvets*; Idea Books New York, 1994.

Lawner, Lynne: *Lives of the Courtesans: Portraits of the Renaissance*; Rizzoli International Publications; New York, 1987.

Marianne Straub: *Hand Weaving and Cloth Design*, George Rainbird Ltd., 1977.

Martin Hardingham: *Fabric Catalogue*, Pocket Books, New York, 1978.

______________: *The Illustrated Encyclopedia of Fabrics*, Studio Vista, London. 1978.

Mattiebelle Gittinger: *Master Dyers to the World,* The Textile Museum, Washington DC. 1982.

Mazzoui, Maureen Fennell: *The Italian Cotton Industry in the Later Middle Ages 1100-1600,* Cambridge University Press, Cambridge, 1981.

Michael McGarvie: *Castle Cary: Industrial and Social History, Boyd's Hair Factory*. . Avalon Industries. UK. 1980.

Moronato, Stefania: *The Art of Weaving*; Ed Giandomenico Romanelli; Konemann 1997.

Munro, John: *The West European Woollen Industries and their Struggles for International Markets, c.1000 - 1500,* University of Toronto, 2000.

Peter Collingwood: *Textile and Weave Structures*, B T Batsford, London, UK. 1987.

Su Grierson: *Dyeing and Dyestuffs*, Shire Publications Ltd, Princes Risborough, Aylesbury, Bucks, UK. 1989.

Thames ad Hudson Manual of. Joyce Storey: *Dyes ans Fabrics,* Thames and Hudson, London. 1978.

Index

A

Acrylic Fabric, 53, 54.
Amlikar, 173, 174, 177.
Armenian Carpets, 188.

B

Bedford Cords, 177, 183.
Braies, 12, 16, 21.
Bulgarian Carpets, 193.

C

Carpet Binding, 187.
Circular Looms, 130, 135.
Crewel Fabric, 60, 61.

D

Denim, 56, 147, 150, 151, 152, 153, 154, 155.
Dobby Looms, 129, 130, 132, 234.
Drawloom, 76, 77, 134.
Dying, 49, 154, 185.

E

Embroidery, 8, 11, 17, 20, 29, 30, 57, 155, 157, 158, 159, 171, 172, 174, 175, 176, 183, 245, 255, 260, 261, 262.
Extra Warp, 76, 88, 96.

F

Fabrics, 2, 3, 4, 10, 11, 17, 21, 28, 52, 53, 54, 55, 56, 58, 59, 60, 61, 62, 63, 64, 65, 67, 77, 78, 132, 133, 134, 135, 136, 139, 141, 145, 202, 219, 220, 221, 222, 223, 224, 226, 227, 228, 229, 230, 231, 232, 242, 244, 251, 260, 270, 273.
Fashion Design, 61, 168, 256, 269, 275, 276.
Fiberglass, 58, 59.
Flying Shuttle, 33, 35, 39, 77, 78, 79, 80, 109, 112, 113, 114, 115, 123, 125, 135, 143.
Foulard, 150, 155.
French Carpets, 194, 195.

H

Hairstyles, 15, 18.
Handloom, 40, 77, 123, 127, 253.
Haute Couture, 201, 274, 276.
Headgear, 13, 24.
Headscarf, 166, 170.
Heddle, 74, 75, 76, 77, 78, 80, 81, 83, 91, 92, 93, 94, 95, 96, 98, 99, 104, 110, 111, 112, 113, 116, 117, 123, 124, 126, 240, 241, 242.
Hemp Fabric, 66, 67.
Hierarchy, 69, 72.

I

Indian Textiles, 172, 243, 244.
Industrial Fabric, 58, 59.
Inkle Looms, 80, 242.
Inkle Weaving, 80, 81.

J

Jacquard Loom, 128, 129, 130, 131, 133, 134, 135, 171, 172.
Jacquard Weaving, 129, 134, 135.

K

Karamiori, 234.
Kashmir Shawls, 171, 172, 175.
Knit Shawls, 177.

L

Laminated Fabric, 63, 64.
Lease Sticks, 84, 90, 96, 97, 98, 99, 116.
Looms, 5, 32, 33, 37, 75, 76, 77, 79, 80, 82, 83, 84, 88, 92, 95, 99, 104, 110, 121, 123, 135, 141, 143, 153, 174, 175, 176, 183, 196, 197, 234, 238, 239, 255, 261.

M

Man-made Fibers, 53, 58.
Mock Leno Weaves, 233.
Modern Carpeting, 196.
Moroccan Crepe, 164.

N

Natural Fibers, 52, 65.
Nivi Style, 248, 249, 250, 255.
Nylon Fabric, 54, 55.

O

Oldham Counts, 42.
Organza Fabric, 54.
Oriental Carpets,183, 187, 192.

P

Pashmina, 165, 169, 171, 174, 176, 177.
Pit Loom, 82, 99, 106, 112, 115.
Plain Fabric, 59, 60, 232, 250.
Plain Weaves, 139, 141, 147, 149, 151.
Polar Fleece, 198, 199.
Polyester, 53, 54, 55, 57, 62, 163, 179, 186, 231, 235, 251, 255, 261.

R

Rapier Looms, 79, 123, 128, 132.
Repair Heddles, 242.
Rigid Heddles, 242.

S

Sari, 213, 245, 246, 247, 248, 249, 250, 251, 252, 253, 254, 255, 256, 260, 261.
Satin Fabric, 58, 133.
Scandinavian Carpets, 191.
Scarf, 155, 165, 166, 167, 168, 169, 170, 175, 246, 260.
Sewing Pattern, 270, 272, 273.
Shalwar Kameez, 253, 259, 260.
Shawl, 6, 7, 163, 170, 171, 172, 173, 174, 175, 176, 177, 235, 244, 246, 254, 260, 266.

T

Tablet Weaving, 236, 237.
Tablet weaving, 81, 236, 237, 238.
Taffeta Fabric, 55, 56, 141.
Textile Trade, 5, 243, 244.
Twill Weaves, 147, 150, 220, 234.

U

Underwear, 26, 57.
Uniforms, 167, 168, 253.

W

Weave Production, 234.
Weave Relationship, 218, 220.
Wire Heddles, 239, 241.
Wool Crepe, 164, 165.
Wool Fabric, 21, 28, 66.
Woollen Mules, 43.
Work Basket, 156.
Woven Design, 136, 138, 171, 218, 227, 230, 236.

❑❑❑